HORATIO ALGER

Gender and Success
in the Gilded Age

HORATIO ALGER
Gender and Success
in the Gilded Age

Edited by
Charles Orson Cook

BRANDYWINE PRESS • St. James, New York

ISBN   978-1-881089-66-7

1st Printing

Telephone Orders: 1-800-345-1776

TABLE OF CONTENTS

INTRODUCTION

Horatio Alger, Jr. (1832–1899) was among the most prolific and popular of American authors. During the last third of the nineteenth century he wrote more than a hundred novels, most of which were formulaic success stories intended primarily for adolescent male readers. Although none of them has ever been mistaken for great literature, or even for particularly skillful writing, their influence has persisted into the present. Because Alger's stories have resonated with readers in widely different periods, often for highly differing reasons, his luck-and-pluck tales have made his name synonymous with the idea of economic mobility so often identified as the core of the American Dream. In the three decades after his death, his books actually sold more copies in inexpensive reprints than they had in his own lifetime. And in our era the United States Postal Service in 1984 issued an Alger commemorative stamp. The famous Horatio Alger Awards are still given to upwardly-bound politicians like Richard Nixon and to celebrities like Oprah Winfrey. There is even a Horatio Alger Society with its own internet web site and annual convention.

Alger joins a long and sometimes distinguished tradition of Americans who have written extensively about the nature and meaning of individual accomplishment and success. Certainly he is in some ways a literary descendant of Benjamin Franklin and the direct intellectual ancestor of Booker T. Washington and Dale Carnegie.[1] What stands out most about Alger and his work is not so much the volume of his writing or the way in which he articulated his credo, but rather the willingness of Americans of all ages and stations to embrace his optimistic message about the fruits of diligence, thrift, and honesty. The political scientist Carol Nackenoff has recently argued that Alger's fiction was a moral allegory for an American republic caught between the virtues of the past and the uncertainties of the future.[2] Like his renowned and more intellectual contemporary Henry Adams, Alger was among traditional moralists whose cultural guardianship was under assault in the Gilded Age while they attempted to guide well-meaning citizens into the future. Alger's immense popularity shaped the public consciousness in ways that more cerebral writers could only dream of.

Alger's biographer Gary Scharnhorst points out that very little is known about his early life.[3] He was born in 1832 in Chelsea, Massachusetts, the eldest child of a Unitarian minister. Despite numerous stories and anecdotes about a repressive and domineering father, few sources throw any light on his pre-adolescent life. We also know that at fourteen Horatio was sent to boarding school at nearby Gates Academy and that two years later he was at Harvard, where he finished near the top of his class of eighty or so graduates in 1851. He was chosen to be the student poet laureate, or Class Odist as it was called, an early suggestion that it was to a life of letters that he most aspired. A few essays and stories (one of which made it into the pages of the prestigious *North American Review*) followed graduation, but none of his early writing hinted at his future popular success. He tried teaching in New England boarding schools for several years while he continued to publish stories and even a little doggerel, but his efforts failed to generate a reliable income. The clergy became Alger's default career, a choice that some biographers, with little hard evidence, would claim was dictated by the will of an overbearing father. It is more likely that Alger—not yet thirty and faced with the harsh truth that he could not support himself adequately with his pen—was guided as much by economic necessity as by parental pressure. Whatever his true motivation may have been, the choice was disastrous. After taking a degree at Harvard Divinity School, he secured a position at a small Unitarian congregation in Brewster, Massachusetts, in 1864. His new parishioners were admiring at first, but within months rumors circulated about his relationship with some adolescent males in the congregation. One boy openly accused Alger of sexual molestation, a charge he never challenged, and others threatened to do the same. The church voted overwhelmingly not to renew his contract, and some in the congregation contemplated civil and criminal proceedings. The incident ended his career in the ministry and came perilously close to condemning him to a long prison term.

Alan Trachtenberg of Yale University, to cite one example from recent scholarship, has emphasized the Brewster episode, arguing that Alger never escaped his sexual fascination with boys. Most of Alger's stories, Professor Trachtenberg points out, feature mature men who shepherd young charges to success, and Alger in real life spent an enormous amount of time gathering material for his books on the mean streets of late nineteenth-century New York City. Trachtenberg notes Alger's committed activity in the Newsboys Society, a philanthropic organization dedicated to helping street urchins.

In writing about Ragged Dick and his ilk, Alger was capitalizing on a popular literary style.[4] Charles Dickens, among others, had not only popularized the genre in Victorian England, but also raised it to the level of an art form. Alger was no Dickens, but he shared the reform-minded Englishman's concern about the debilitating effects of urbanization on family life. Many readers, moreover, will no doubt find a goodly number of Dickensian themes and literary conceits throughout Alger's work. To emphasize Alger's sexuality is to obscure the seriousness of his reformist career. The didactic moralism of his stories—including heavy-handed warnings about the harmful effects of alcohol and the equally obvious praise of education, especially that of the Sunday School—can be seen as legitimate efforts to save a generation of wayward youth.

Alger's quick and desperate departure from the pulpit in Brewster forced him to return to writing popular fiction for financial support. He soon moved to New York City, where he was closer to the emerging world of writing and publishing. After a modest reception for an early piece of serialized fiction in a boys' magazine, he quickly turned to producing the longer pieces for which he is now famous. He often dreamed of writing more serious stories for adult audiences and eventually published a few, but the bulk of his professional life was dedicated to younger readers in a market where he could at least achieve some economic success. At one level, Alger's professional career is actually a case study in how perilous and unpredictable the life of an author can be. In an era in which popular literature often brushed shoulders with high culture and competition for public and critical approval was sometimes capricious, he carved out a small but livable niche for himself. It was a life in which far more talented writers than he struggled mightily to stay afloat. During the next three decades until his death in 1899, Alger wrote over a hundred books in a remarkable effort to achieve literary recognition. While he longed to write more substantial stuff, his adolescent fiction kept him financially solvent.

A curiosity about Alger's career, the meaning of which is still debated, is that he was just as widely read and perhaps as popular in the Progressive Era of the early twentieth century as in his own lifetime. Stock characters, predictable plots, and painfully contrived dialogue frame stories in which an orphaned boy on the streets of New York makes good. By serious literary standards, especially of more recent times, they are little better than period melodramas. That Alger used this authorial device—sometimes with the same characters—scores of times will puzzle many present-day readers. But the stories are not historically worthless. They are revealing primary documents precisely because they were popular rather than great. Alger's novels tell us a good deal about his values, about his social vision, and about his fears. But because he was always sensitive to popular tastes, they may also reveal even more about what he thought his readers wanted to hear and about their anxieties and aspirations in the rapidly industrializing and urbanizing society of the Gilded Age.

Ragged Dick, published in 1868, is the most famous and the prototypical Alger story. Its several hundred thousand copies sold make the novel also his most popular, both in his lifetime and later. One of the revelations in *Ragged Dick* is that Alger's poor boy does not find great wealth. In neither this novel nor others in which he is a character does the hero Richard Hunter achieve wealth. What he does achieve, as the literary critic John Cawelti pointed out more than a generation ago, is respectability. From a street bootblack, Dick becomes an office clerk, not a full-blown capitalist or industrial magnate.[5] But in so doing, he experiences a kind of moral uplift and social transformation that Alger and presumably his public thought more desirable than money. In this way Alger seems to be reassuring his readers about the desirability of old-fashioned virtues like honesty and hard work in a swiftly changing and threatening world. In a little known work of adult fiction, for example, Alger writes about a wealthy and aristocratic New York debutante who flees conspicuous consumption and takes on the life of schoolteacher in provincial New Hampshire, where she finds success in teaching and marriage.[6]

Yet *Ragged Dick* is not nostalgic. The overwhelming majority of Alger's novels are set in the city, not in the countryside, and his hero is seldom a bucolic innocent who has wandered into an alien urban world. Dick Hunter himself is a child of the city, and, although he learns much from hinterland visitors, he is their and our primary guide both to the pitfalls and to the opportunities of city life. It is precisely Ragged Dick's street savvy and worldly-wise knowledge of the city that preserves morality against a host of urban and industrial marauders. Many of Alger's knightly protagonists merge traditional values with modern industrial life, providing an ethical model for coping with the harsh realities of the late nineteenth century. More than anything else, Dick is a good boy, naughty at times, reckless at others, but essentially decent and always honest. This goodness generates his good fortune, which surfaces in several scenes, a circumstance described by one modern scholar as "moral luck," and a theme that runs through a great many Alger books. As in almost all of Alger's fiction, good fortune appears in the guise of a paternalistic adult male benefactor who recognizes the main character's redeeming qualities and rewards the lad with a job and legitimacy. In Dick's world, all ends respectably, if not affluently.[7] As Alger wrote on the last page of the novel, "he is Ragged Dick no longer. He has taken a step upward, and is determined to mount still higher." Alger had annointed him "Richard Hunter, Esq., a young gentleman on the way to fame and fortune."

Tattered Tom (1871) is an interesting variation on the *Ragged Dick* model, so noteworthy that it is printed first in this volume even though *Ragged Dick* chronologically precedes it. Superficially, it is one more Alger story of an orphan temporarily out of luck in an urban setting. Like Dick Hunter, Tom struggles with the forces of urban and industrial evil—including a panoply of street thugs and wretched tenement dwellers. But unlike Dick Hunter, Tom is a girl. Alger occasionally wrote about women, sometimes at length, but *Tattered Tom* is a rare example of a success novel with a female protagonist. With generous doses of Victorian melodrama featuring some near-misses and mistaken identities, Tom struggles with the dangers of urban life. She survives by taking on the mannerisms of a boy and a tough one at that. Like Ragged Dick, Tom gets lucky, especially when she meets a kindly and childless sea captain who finds a good, albeit temporary, home for her. Tom's story is more luck than pluck, but there is little doubt that she deserves it. Tom learns the value of money and, with paternalistic guidance, makes a prudent investment in gold bullion.

This is a success story all right, but not quite the one Alger writes for his boys. The vehicle of strive and succeed is at work, but with an altogether different outcome defines success as Victorian domesticity: Tom (now Jane) becomes a dutiful daughter, a true woman in a new life of grace and charm. There are hints of Tom's metamorphosis scattered along the way, most especially the dramatic changes in her clothing as she turns into a respectable young woman. These, of course, are echoed in *Ragged Dick* when an important installment in Richard Hunter's make-over occurs as he is presented with a new suit of clothes. There are the predictable lessons about frugality, thrift, and even good grammar and etiquette. For Alger, at least, an important part of success was looking and acting the part of a respectable citizen. But in the end, Tom/Jane cannot enjoy the same success as Richard Hunter. As long as she is dressed as a male and conducts herself like a male, she is indistinguishable from Ragged Dick or any of a plethora of Alger heroes. But once she takes on the persona of a young woman, complete with respectable dress and polite manners, her life takes her along the feminine and domestic path of her mother. As Alger puts it, Tom "was very different now from the young Arab fifteen months since. She was now a young lady in manners, and her handsome dress set off a face which had always been attractive." In a way, indeed, Tom does not have to make her own way; she only has to survive some Dickensian hard times and to be reunited with her mother. Alger could not fathom, let alone describe, female success in conventional male terms.[8]

Much of the style of *Tattered Tom* is recognizably Alger. The quaint street slang, which Alger apparently studied with great care among the newsboys of New York, is here and so are the cunning street smarts of the protagonist who resorts to sleight-of-hand and trickery only for survival. An interesting and not altogether unique twist on the plot is the exploitive housekeeper, Granny, who despite her comforting name holds our heroine in a state of virtual slavery for a time. But in the end, Granny's evil spell is broken by fortuitous circumstances and stronger familial ties that emerge in the form of a long-lost aristocratic mother who presides over Tom's final transformation into womanhood. And Granny, hopelessly addicted to tobacco and alcohol, comes to a fitting and fiery end; in Alger's stories the vile and villainous seldom go unpunished. It is a reassuring finish to an unsettling story. Men and women are restored to their proper roles, children are rescued, and the family survives, even in a hostile world.

Readers both casual and scholarly have several critical interpretations of Horatio Alger from which to choose. The best known is Alger the defender of free market self-interest and unrestrained capitalism. As an apologist for great wealth and its aspirants, this Alger was probably at his most popular in the 1920s when frequent abridged editions of his books cast him as an apostle of free enterprise and laissez-faire economics and the chief exponent of the myth of rising from poverty to wealth. Juxtaposed, there is the darker Alger whose work is an excursion into prurience that turns virtually all of his stories into disturbing journeys into the mind of a Victorian deviant. Seen in this way, characters like Dick Hunter and Henry Fosdick in *Ragged Dick* are the objects of their creator's carnal desire rather than examples for a moral analysis of the Gilded Age. And then there is Alger the struggling writer whose summary expulsion from the clergy flung him into the highly competitive world of mass-market fiction. This side of him probably reflects what he thought his readership—much of it affluent, and both adult and adolescent—wanted to hear. Finally, there is the Alger whose fiction is a metaphor for the redefinition of a society undergoing enormous stress and change. This would-be allegorist struggles with some weighty issues of public morality and has some especially timely things to say about the limits of capitalist materialism. In this view, he is not the tireless advocate of the profit motive, the nouveau riche, and self-interest, but a moral teacher advising us to treat raw materialism and pecuniary ambition with suspicion. This is civic-mindedness of the highest order and a kind of fictional blueprint for reform and good citizenship in an acquisitive age.

Perhaps the most compelling reality about Alger's influence is its persistence. Others of his era wrote in the same genre as he, and some even had a following for a time. But he informs, instructs, and even outrages us long after the plots of his books have faded from memory. To be sure, our time is simply not his, and our values are not likely to be shared by his characters. Yet we continue to re-interpret him at every opportunity and from widely different perspectives. Each new round of critical analysis reveals as much about us in our time as it does about him in his. If ever there was evidence that pulp fiction—more than highbrow culture and landmark literature—is closer to telling us who we are and to reminding us of how we perceive ourselves, both now and in the past, it is the writing of Horatio Alger.[9]

Charles Orson Cook
St. John's School
Houston, Texas

Notes

1. Jeffrey Louis Decker, *Made in America: Self-Styled Success from Horatio Alger to Oprah Winfrey* (Minneapolis: University of Minnesota Press, 1994) puts much of the success literature of this century in historical perspective. For another account that also covers the nineteenth century, see Irvin G. Wylie, *The Self-Made Man in America: The Myth of Rags to Riches* (New Brunswick: Rutgers University Press, 1954). Wylie and others show that Alger was not alone in his efforts to market success stories to juveniles and that the competition for young readers was intense.

2. Carol Nackenoff, *The Fictional Republic: Horatio Alger and Political Discourse* (New York: Oxford University Press, 1994).

3. Gary Scharnhorst with Jack Bales, *The Lost Life of Horatio Alger, Jr.* (Bloomington: Indiana University Press, 1985).

4. Alan Trachtenberg, "Introduction," contained in Horatio Alger, Jr.,

Ragged Dick, or Life in New York with the Boot Blacks (New York: Penguin, 1990). Perhaps the most extreme version of this sexual interpretation is John Tebbel's summary of Alger's life contained in John Garraty and Jerome Stern-stein, eds., *Encyclopedia of American Biography*, Second Edition (New York: Harper Collins, 1996), 28–29. Tebbel's summary is based mostly on his earlier undocumented study, *From Rags to Riches: Horatio Alger and the American Dream* (New York: Macmillan, 1963). Scharnhorst has been critical of some of Tebbel's conclusions and of his sources. Scharnhorst's version of these events, by contrast, is measured and well-documented: *The Lost Life of Horatio Alger, Jr.*, 66–67; 72–74. For a more laudatory view of Alger, see Ralph Gardner's *Horatio Alger; or, The American Hero Era* (Mendota, Illinois: Wayside Press, 1964).

5. John G. Cawelti, *Apostles of the Self-Made Man* (Chicago: University of Chicago Press, 1965). See also Jeffrey Louis Decker, *Made in America*, 1–3, for an interesting discussion of this topic.

6. *The New Schoolma'am, Or a Summer in North Sparta* (Boston: Loring and Company, 1877).

7. Not all of Alger's most popular books were urban in setting. He wrote, for example, a series of juvenile biographies of great Americans that have no particular urban bias, and he even made trips to California in the 1870s and 1880s to gather material for a series of books with western themes. A "Campaign Series" and the "Rod and Gun" books used similar settings. Although Alger spent a good deal of time on these projects, none of them has drawn much scholarly attention. For a more complete account of his literary production, see Scharnhorst, *The Lost Life*.

8. Jeffrey Decker has an interesting discussion of the insidious ways in which gender and race helped inform the definition of self-made success in American society at the turn of the century and beyond. See especially his *Made in America*, 15–52. Alger also wrote stories about boys who were reunited with their long-lost respectable and usually affluent parents. An Alger enthusiast might want to compare *Tattered Tom* with one of its author's early works, *Helen Ford*, which has an interesting twist on the typical Alger plot. In *From Rags to Riches*, 168–184, Tebbel has a lengthy summary of this book.

9. In *The Lost Life of Horatio Alger*, 149–156, Bales has a useful review of Alger's historical impact.

ACKNOWLEDGMENTS

I am much indebted to St. John's School whose generous resources made this volume possible. St. John's provided two professional development grants and some excellent computer hardware and software that were essential to the completion of the project. I am especially grateful to Diana Heideman, a student assistant, who frequently came to my rescue with her technical skills. I owe even more gratitude to Sarah Potvin whose keen eye and editorial diligence helped identify and eliminate many errors in the final manuscript. The book would have been difficult to finish without her help. Finally, my thanks to my wife, Elsie, whose grammar skills are exceeded only by her patience.

Charles Orson Cook

TATTERED TOM

OR

The Adventures of

a Street Arab

PREFACE

. . . Some surprise may be felt at the discovery that [Tattered] Tom is a girl; but I beg to assure my readers that she is not one of the conventional kind. Though not without her good points, she will be found to differ very widely in tastes and manners from the young ladies of twelve usually to be met in society. I venture to hope that she will become a favorite in spite of her numerous faults, and that no less interest will be felt in her fortunes than in those of the heroes of earlier volumes.

[Horatio Alger]
New York, April, 1871.

CHAPTER I
INTRODUCES TATTERED TOM

MR. FREDERIC PELHAM, a young gentleman very daintily dressed, with exquisitely fitting kids [fine gloves] and highly polished boots, stood at the corner of Broadway and Chambers Streets, surveying with some dismay the dirty crossing, and speculating as to his chances of getting over without marring the polish of his boots.

He started at length, and had taken two steps, when a dirty hand was thrust out, and he was saluted by the request, "Gi' me a penny, sir?"

"Out of my way, you bundle of rags!" he answered.

"You're another!" was the prompt reply.

Frederic Pelham stared at the creature who had dared to imply that he—a leader of fashion—was a bundle of rags.

The street-sweeper was apparently about twelve years of age. It was not quite easy to determine whether it was a boy or girl. The head was surmounted by a boy's cap, the hair was cut short, it wore a boy's jacket, but underneath was a girl's dress. Jacket and dress were both in a state of extreme raggedness. The child's face was very dark and, as might be expected, dirty; but it was redeemed by a pair of brilliant black eyes, which were fixed upon the young exquisite in an expression half-humorous, half-defiant, as the owner promptly retorted, "You're another!"

"Clear out, you little nuisance!" said the dandy, stopping short from necessity, for the little sweep had planted herself directly in his path; and to step out on either side would have soiled his boots irretrievably.

"Gi' me a penny, then?"

"I'll hand you to the police, you little wretch!"

"I ain't done nothin'. Gi' me a penny?"

Mr. Pelham, provoked, raised his cane threateningly.

But Tom (for, in spite of her being a girl, this was the name by which she was universally known; indeed she scarcely knew any other) was wary. She dodged the blow, and by an adroit sweep of her broom managed to scatter some mud on Mr. Pelham's boots.

"You little brat, you've muddied my boots!" he exclaimed, with vexation.

"Then why did you go for to strike me?" said Tom, defiantly. He did not stop to answer, but hurried across the street. His pace was accelerated by an approaching vehicle, and the instinct of self-preservation, more powerful than even the dictates of fashion, compelled him to make a detour through the mud, greatly to the injury of his no longer immaculate boots. But there was a remedy for the disaster on the other side. "Shine your boots, sir?" asked a boot-black, who had stationed himself at the other side of the crossing.

Frederic Pelham looked at his boots. Their former glory had departed. Their virgin gloss had been dimmed by plebeian mud. He grudged the boot-black's fee for he was thoroughly mean, though he had plenty of money at his command. But it was impossible to walk up Broadway in such boots. Suppose he should meet any of his fashionable friends, especially if ladies, his fashionable reputation would be endangered.

"Go ahead, boy!" he said. "Do your best."

"All right, sir."

"It's the second time I've had my boots blacked this morning. If it hadn't been for that dirty sweep I should have got across safely."

The boy laughed—to himself. He knew Tom well enough, and he had been an interested spectator of her encounter with his present customer, having an eye to business. But he didn't think it prudent to make known his thoughts.

The boots were at length polished, and Mr. Pelham saw with satisfaction that no signs of the street mire remained.

"How much do you want, boy?" he asked.

"Ten cents."

"I thought five cents was the price."

"Can't afford to work on no such terms."

Mr. Pelham might have disputed the fee, but he saw an acquaintance approaching, and did not care to be caught chaffering with a boot-black. He therefore reluctantly drew out a dime, and handed it to the boy, who at once deposited it in the pocket of a ragged vest.

He stood on the sidewalk on the lookout for another customer, when Tom marched across the street, broom in hand.

"I say, Joe, how much did he give you?"

"Ten cents."

"How much yer goin' to give me?"

"Nothin'!"

"You wouldn't have got him if I hadn't muddied his boots."

"Did you do it a-purpose?"

Tom nodded.

"What for?"

"He called me names. That's one reason. Besides, I wanted to give you a job."

Joe seemed struck by this view, and, being alive to his own interest, did not disregard the application.

"Here's a penny," he said.

"Gi' me two."

He hesitated a moment, then diving once more into his pocket, brought up another penny, which Tom transferred with satisfaction to the pocket of her dress.

"Shall I do it ag'in?" she asked.

"Yes," said Joe. "I say, Tom, you're a smart un."

"I'd ought to be. Granny makes me smart whenever she gets a chance."

Tom returned to the other end of the crossing, and began to sweep diligently. Her labors did not extend far from the curbstone, as the stream of vehicles now rapidly passing would have made it dangerous. However, it was all one to Tom where she swept. The cleanness of the crossing was to her a matter of comparative indifference. Indeed, considering her own disregard of neatness, it could hardly have been expected that she should feel very solicitous on that point. Like some of her elders who were engaged in municipal labors, she regarded street-sweeping as a "job," out of which she was to make money, and her interest began and ended with the money she earned.

There were not so many to cross Broadway at this point as lower down, and only a few of these seemed impressed by a sense of the pecuniary value of Tom's services.

"Gi' me a penny, sir," she said to a stout gentleman.

He tossed a coin into the mud.

Tom darted upon it, and fished it up, wiping her fingers afterwards upon her dress.

"Ain't you afraid of soiling your dress?" asked the philanthropist, smiling.

"What's the odds?" said Tom, coolly.

"You're a philosopher," said the stout gentleman.

"Don't you go to callin' me names!" said Tom, "'cause if you do I'll muddy up your boots."

"So you don't want to be called a philosopher?" said the gentleman.

"No, I don't," said Tom, eying him suspiciously.

"Then I must make amends."

He took a dime from his pocket, and handed it to the astonished Tom.

"Is this for me?" she asked.

"Yes."

Tom's eyes glistened; for ten cents was a nugget when compared with her usual penny receipts. She stood in a brown study till her patron was half across the street, then, seized with a sudden idea, she darted after him, and tugged at his coat-tail.

"What's wanted?" he asked, turning round in some surprise.

"I say," said Tom, "you may call me that name ag'in for five cents more."

The ludicrous character of the proposal struck him, and he laughed with amusement.

"Well," he said, "that's a good offer. What's your name?"

"Tom."

"Which are you,—a boy or a girl?"

"I'm a girl, but I wish I was a boy."

"What for?"

"Cause boys are stronger than girls, and can fight better."

"Do you ever fight?"

"Sometimes."

"Whom do you fight with?"

"Sometimes I fight with the boys, and sometimes with granny."

"What makes you fight with your granny?"

"She gets drunk and fires things at my head; then I pitch into her."

The cool, matter-of-fact manner in which Tom spoke seemed to amuse her questioner.

"I was right," he said; "you're a philosopher,—a practical philosopher."

"That's more'n you said before," said Tom; "I want ten cents for that."

The ten cents were produced. Tom pocketed them in a business-like manner, and went back to her employment. She wondered, slightly, whether a philosopher was something very bad; but, as there was no means of determining, sensibly dismissed the inquiry, and kept on with her work.

CHAPTER II

TOM GETS A SQUARE MEAL

ABOUT twelve o'clock Tom began to feel the pangs of hunger. The exercise which she had taken, together with the fresh air, had stimulated her appetite. It was about the time when she was expected to go home, and accordingly she thrust her hand into her pocket, and proceeded to count the money she had received. "Forty-two cents!" she said, at last, in a tone of satisfaction. "I don't generally get more'n twenty. I wish that man would come round and call me names every day."

Tom knew that she was expected to go home and carry the result of her morning's work to her granny; but the unusual amount suggested to her another idea. Her mid-day meal was usually of the plainest and scantiest,—a crust of dry bread, or a cold sausage on days of plenty,—and Tom sometimes did long for something better. But generally it would have been dangerous to appropriate a sufficient sum from her receipts, as the deficit would have been discovered, and quick retribution would have followed from her incensed granny, who was a vicious old woman with a pretty vigorous arm. Now, however, she could appropriate twenty cents without danger of discovery.

"I can get a square meal for twenty cents," Tom reflected, "and I'll do it."

But she must go home first, as delay would be dangerous, and have disagreeable consequences.

She prepared for the visit by dividing her morning's receipts into two parcels. The two ten-cent scrips she hid away in the lining of her tattered jacket. The pennies, including one five-cent scrip, she put in the pocket of her dress. This last was intended for her granny. She then started homewards, dragging her broom after her.

She walked to Centre Street, turned after a while into Leonard, and went on, turning once or twice, until she came to one of the most wretched tenement houses to be found in that not very choice locality. She passed through an archway leading into an inner court, on which fronted a rear house more shabby, if possible, than the front dwelling. The court was redolent of odors far from savory; children pallid, dirty, and unhealthy-looking, were playing about, filling the air with shrill cries, mingled with profanity; clothes were hanging from some of the windows; miserable and besotted faces were seen at others.

Tom looked up to a window in the fourth story. She could descry a woman, with a pipe in her mouth.

"Granny's home," she said to herself.

She went up three flights, and, turning at the top, went to the door and opened it.

It was a wretched room, containing two chairs and a table, nothing more. On one of the chairs was seated a large woman, of about sixty, with a clay pipe in her mouth. The room was redolent of the vilest tobacco-smoke.

This was granny.

If granny had ever been beautiful, there were no traces of that dangerous gift in the mottled and wrinkled face, with bleared eyes, which turned towards the door as Tom entered.

"Why didn't you come afore, Tom?" she demanded.

"I'm on time," said Tom. "Clock ain't but just struck."

"How much have you got?"

Tom pulled out her stock of pennies and placed them in the woman's outstretched palm.

"There's twenty-two," she said.

"Umph!" said granny. "Where's the rest?"

"That's all."

"Come here."

Tom advanced, not reluctantly, for she felt sure that granny would not think of searching her jacket, especially as she had brought home as much as usual.

The old woman thrust her hand into the child's pocket, and turned it inside-out with her claw-like fingers, but not another penny was to be found.

"Umph!" she grunted, apparently satisfied with her scrutiny.

"Didn't I tell you so?" said Tom.

Granny rose from her chair, and going to a shelf took down a piece of bread, which had become dry and hard.

"There's your dinner," said she.

"Gi' me a penny to buy an apple," said Tom, rather by way of keeping up appearances than because she wanted one. Visions of a more satisfactory repast filled her imagination.

"You don't want no apple. Bread's enough," said granny.

Tom was not much disappointed. She knew pretty well beforehand how her application would fare. Frequently she made sure of success by buying the apple and eating it before handing the proceeds of her morning's work to the old woman. Today she had other views, which she was in a hurry to carry out.

She took the bread, and ate a mouthful. Then she slipped it into her pocket, and said, "I'll eat it as I go along, granny."

To this the old woman made no objection, and Tom went out.

In the court-yard below she took out her crust, and handed it to a hungry-looking boy of ten, the unlucky offspring of drunken parents, who oftentimes was unable to command even such fare as Tom obtained.

"Here, Tim," she said, "eat that; I ain't hungry."

It was one of Tim's frequent fast days, and even the hard crust was acceptable to him. He took it readily, and began to eat it ravenously. Tom looked on with benevolent interest, feeling the satisfaction of having done a charitable act. The satisfaction might have been heightened by the thought that she was going to get something better herself.

"So you're hungry, Tim," she said.

"I'm always hungry," said Tim.

"Did you have any breakfast?"

"Only an apple I picked up in the street."

"He's worse off than me," thought Tom; but she had no time to reflect on the superior privileges of her own position, for she was beginning to feel hungry herself.

There was a cheap restaurant near by, only a few blocks away. Tom knew it well, for she had often paused before the door and inhaled enviously the appetizing odor of the dishes which were there vended to patrons not over-fastidious, at prices accommodated to scantily lined pocket-books. Tom had never entered, but had been compelled to remain outside, wishing that a more propitious fortune had placed it in her power to dine there every day. Now, however, first thrusting her fingers into the lining of her jacket to make sure that the money was there, she boldly entered the restaurant and took a seat at one of the tables.

The room was not large, there being only eight tables, each of which might accommodate four persons. The floor was sanded, the tables were some of them bare, others covered with old newspapers, which had become greasy, and were rather worse than no table-cloth at all. The guests of whom perhaps a dozen were seated at the table, were undoubtedly plebeian. Men in shirt-sleeves, rough-bearded sailors and long-shore men, composed the company, with one ragged boot-black, who had his blacking-box on the seat beside him.

It was an acquaintance of Tom, and she went and sat beside him.

"Do you get dinner here, Jim?" she asked.

"Yes, Tom; what brings you here?"

"I'm hungry."

"Don't you live along of your granny?"

"Yes; but I thought I'd come here to-day. What have you got?"

"Roast beef."

"Is it good?"

"Bully!"

"I'll have some, then. How much is it?"

"Ten cents."

Ten cents was the standard price in this economical restaurant for a plate of meat of whatever kind. Perhaps, considering the quality and amount given, it could not be regarded as very cheap; still the sum was small, and came within Tom's means.

A plate of beef was brought and placed before Tom. Her eyes dilated with pleasure as they rested on the delicious morsel. There was a potato besides, and a triangular slice of bread, with an infinitesimal dab of butter,—all for ten cents. But Tom's ambition soared higher.

"Bring me a cup o' coffee" she said to the waiter.

It was brought,—a very dark, muddy, suspicious looking beverage,—a base libel upon the fragrant berry whose name it took; but such a thought did not disturb Tom. She never doubted that it was what it purported to be. She stirred it vigorously with the spoon, and sipped it as if it had been nectar.

"Ain't it prime just?" she exclaimed, smacking her lips.

Then ensued a vigorous onslaught upon the roast beef. It was the first meat Tom had tasted for weeks, with the exception of occasional cold sausage; and she was in the seventh heaven of delight as she hurriedly ate it. When she had finished, the plate was literally and entirely empty. Tom did not believe in leaving anything behind. She was almost tempted to "lick the platter clean," but observed that none of the other guests did so, and refrained.

"Bring me a piece of apple pie," said Tom, determined for once to have what she denominated a "good square meal." The price of the pie being five cents, this would just exhaust her funds. Payment was demanded when the pie was brought, the prudent waiter having some fears that his customer was eating beyond her means.

Tom paid the money, and, vigorously attacking the pie, had almost finished it, when, chancing to lift her eyes to the window, she saw a sight that made her blood curdle.

Looking through the pane with a stony glare that meant mischief was her granny, whom she had supposed safe at home.

CHAPTER III

CAUGHT IN THE ACT

IT was Tom's ill luck that brought granny upon the scene, contrary to every reasonable expectation. After smoking out her pipe, she made up her mind to try another smoke, when she found that her stock of tobacco was exhausted. Being constitutionally lazy, it was some minutes before she made up her mind to go out and lay in a fresh supply. Finally she decided, and made her way downstairs to the court, and thence to the street.

Tim saw her, and volunteered the information,

"Tom gave me some bread."

"When?" demanded granny.

"When she come out just now."

"What did she do that for?"

"She said she wasn't hungry."

The old woman was puzzled. Tom's appetite was usually quite equal to the supply of food which she got. Could Tom have secreted some money to buy apples? This was hardly likely, since she had carefully searched her. Besides, Tom had returned the usual amount. Still, granny's suspicions were awakened, and she determined to question Tom when she returned at the close of the afternoon.

The tobacco shop where granny obtained her tobacco was two doors beyond the restaurant where Tom was then enjoying her cheap dinner with a zest which the guests at Delmonico's do not often bring to the discussion of their more aristocratic viands. It was only a chance that led granny, as she passed, to look in; but that glance took in all who were seated at the tables, including Tom.

Had granny received an invitation to preside at a meeting in the Cooper Institute, she would hardly have been more surprised than at the sight of Tom, perfidiously enjoying a meal out of money from which she had doubtless been defrauded.

"The owdacious young reprobate!" muttered the old woman, glaring fiercely at her unconscious victim.

But Tom just then happened to look up, as we have seen. Her heart gave a sudden thump, and she said to herself, "I'm in for a lickin', that's so. Granny's mad as blazes."

The old woman did not long leave her in doubt as to the state of her feelings.

She strode into the eating-house, and, advancing to the table, seized Tom by the arm.

"What are you here for?" she growled, in a hoarse voice.

"To get some dinner," said Tom.

By this time she had recovered from her temporary panic. She had courage and pluck, and was toughened by the hard life she had led into a stoical endurance of the evils from which she could not escape.

"What business had you to come?"

"I was hungry."

"Didn't I give you a piece of bread?"

"I didn't like it."

"What did you buy?"

"A plate of beef, a cup o' coffee, and some pie. Better buy some, granny. They're bully."

"You're a reg'lar bad un. You'll fetch up on the gallus," said granny, provoked at Tom's coolness.

So saying, she seized Tom by the shoulder roughly. But by this time the keeper of the restaurant thought fit to interfere.

"We can't have any disturbance here, ma'am," he said. "You must leave the room."

"She had no right to get dinner here," said granny. "I won't let her pay for it."

"She has paid for it already."

"Is that so?" demanded the old woman, disappointed.

Tom nodded, glad to have outwitted her guardian.

"It was my money. You stole it."

"No it wa'n't. A gentleman give it to me for callin' me names."

"Come out of here!" said granny, jerking Tom from her chair. "Don't you let her have no more to eat here," she added, turning to the keeper of the restaurant.

"She can eat here whenever she's got money to pay for it."

Rather disgusted at her failure to impress the keeper of the restaurant with her views in the matter, granny emerged into the street with Tom in her clutches.

She gave her a vigorous shaking up on the sidewalk.

"How do you like that?" she demanded.

"I wish I was as big as you!" said Tom, indignantly.

"Well, what if you was?" demanded the old woman, pausing in her punishment, and glaring at Tom.

"I'd make your nose bleed," said Tom, doubling up her fist.

"You would, would you?" said granny, fiercely. "Then it's lucky you ain't;" and she gave her another shake.

"Where are you going to take me?" asked Tom.

"Home. I'll lock you up for a week, and give you nothin' to eat but bread once a day."

"All right!" said Tom. "If I'm locked up at home, I can't bring you any money."

This consideration had not at first suggested itself to the vindictive old woman. It would cut off all her revenue to punish Tom as she proposed; and this would be far from convenient. But anger was more powerful just then than policy; and she determined at all events to convey Tom home, and give her a flogging, before sending her out into the street to resume her labors.

She strode along, dragging Tom by the arm; and not another word was spoken till they reached the rear tenement house.

"What's the matter with the child?" asked Mrs. Murphy, who had just come down into the court after one of her own children.

"She stole my money," said granny; "and was eatin' a mighty fine dinner out of it."

"It was my money, Mrs. Murphy," said Tom. "I gave granny twenty-two cents when I came home."

"I hope you won't go to hurt the child," said kindhearted Mrs. Murphy.

"I'll be much obliged to you, Mrs. Murphy, if you'll mind your own business," said granny, loftily. "When I want your advice, mum, I'll come and ask it; begging your pardon, mum."

"She's a tough craythur [creature]," said Mrs. Murphy to herself. "She beats that poor child too bad entirely."

Granny drew Tom into the room with no gentle hand.

"Now you're goin' to catch it," said she, grimly.

Tom was of the same opinion, and meant to defend herself as well as she knew how. She had all her wits about her, and had already planned out her campaign.

On the chair was a stout stick which granny was accustomed to use on such occasions as the present. When wielded by a vigorous arm, it was capable of inflicting considerable pain, as Tom very well knew. That stick she determined to have.

Accordingly when granny temporarily released her hold of her, as she entered the room, Tom sprang for the chair, seized the stick, and sent it flying out of the window.

"What did you do that for?" said granny, fiercely.

"I don't want to be licked," said Tom, briefly.

"You're going to be, then."

"Not with the stick."

"We'll see."

Granny poked her head out of the window, and saw Tim down in the court. "Bring up that stick," she said; "that's a good boy."

Tim picked up the stick, and was about to obey the old woman's request, when he heard another voice—Tom's—from the other window.

"Don't you do it, Tim. Granny wants to lick me."

That was enough. Tim didn't like the old woman,—no one in the building did,—and he did like Tom, who, in spite of being a tough customer, was good-natured and obliging, unless her temper was aroused by the old woman's oppression. So Tim dropped the stick.

"Bring it right up," said granny, angrily.

"Are you goin' to lick Tom?"

"None of your business! Bring it up, or I'll lick you too."

"No, you don't!" answered Tim. "You must come for it yourself if you want it."

Granny began to find that she must do her own errands. It was an undertaking to go down three flights of stairs to the court and return again, especially for one so indolent as herself; but there seemed to be no other way. She inwardly resolved to wreak additional vengeance upon Tom, and so get what satisfaction she could in this way. Muttering imprecations which I do not care to repeat, she started downstairs, determined to try the stick first upon Tim. But when she reached the court Tim had disappeared. He had divined her benevolent intentions, and thought it would be altogether wiser for him to be out of the way.

Granny picked up the stick, and, after a sharp glance around the court, commenced the ascent. She did not stop to rest, being spurred on by the anticipated pleasure of flogging Tom. So, in a briefer space of time than could have been expected, she once more arrived at her own door.

But Tom had not been idle.

No sooner was the door closed than Tom turned the key in the lock, making herself a voluntary prisoner, but having in the key the means of deliverance.

Granny tried the door, and, to her inexpressible wrath, discovered Tom's new audacity.

"Open the door, you trollop!" she screamed.
"You'll lick me," said Tom.
"I'll give you the wust lickin' you ever had."
"Then I shan't let you in," said Tom, defiantly.

CHAPTER IV

THE SIEGE

"OPEN the door," screamed granny, beside herself with rage, "or I'll kill you."
"You can't get at me," said Tom, triumphantly.
The old woman grasped the knob of the door and shook it vigorously. But the lock resisted her efforts. Tom's spirit was up, and she rather enjoyed it.
"Shake away, granny," she called through the key-hole.
"If I could only get at you!" muttered granny.
"I won't let you in till you promise not to touch me."
"I'll skin you alive."
"Then you can't come in."
The old woman began alternately to pound and kick upon the door. Tom sat down coolly upon a chair, her dark eyes flashing exultingly. She knew her power, and meant to keep it. She had not reflected how it was to end. She supposed that in the end she would get a "lickin'," as she had often done before. But in the mean while she would have the pleasure of defying and keeping the old woman at bay for an indefinite time. So she sat in placid enjoyment in her stronghold until she heard something that suggested a speedy raising of the siege.
"I'm goin' for a hatchet," said granny, through the key-hole.
"If you break the door, you'll have to pay for it."
"Never you mind!" said the old woman. "I know what I'm about."
She heard the retreating steps of granny, and, knowing only too well her terrible temper, made up her mind that she was in earnest. If so, the door must soon succumb. A hatchet would soon accomplish what neither kicks nor pounding had been able to effect.
"What shall I do?" thought Tom.
She was afraid of something more than a lickin' now. In her rage at having been so long baffled, the old woman might attack her with the hatchet. She knew very well that on previous occasions she had flung at her head anything she could lay hold of. Tom, brave and stout-hearted as she was, shrunk from this new danger, and set herself to devise a way of escape. She looked out of the window; but she was on the fourth floor, and it was a long distance to the court below. If it had been on the second floor she would have swung off.
There was another thing she could do. Granny had gone down below to borrow a hatchet. She might unlock the door, and run out upon the landing; but there was no place for hiding herself, and no way of getting downstairs without running the risk of rushing into granny's clutches. In her perplexity her eyes fell upon a long coil of rope in one corner. It was a desperate expedient, but she resolved to swing out of the window, high as it was. She man-

aged to fasten one end securely, and let the other drop from the window. As it hung, it fell short of reaching the ground by at least ten feet. But Tom was strong and active, and never hesitated a moment on this account. She was incited to extra speed, for she already heard the old woman ascending the stairs, probably provided with a hatchet.

Tom got on the window-sill, and, grasping the rope, let herself down rapidly hand over hand, till she reached the end of the rope. Then she dropped. It was rather hard to her feet, and she fell over. But she quickly recovered herself.

Tim, the recipient of her dinner, was in the court, and surveyed her descent with eyes and mouth wide open.

"Where'd you come from, Tom?" he asked.

"Can't you see?" said Tom.

"Why didn't you come downstairs?"

"Cause granny's there waitin' to lick me. I must be goin' before she finds out where I am. Don't you tell of me, Tim."

"No, I won't," said Tim; and he was sure to keep his promise.

Tom sped through the arched passage to the street, and did not rest till she had got a mile away from the home which had so few attractions for her.

Beyond the chance of immediate danger, the young Arab conjured up the vision of granny's disappointment when she should break open the door, and find her gone; and she sat down on the curbstone and laughed heartily.

"What are you laughing at?" asked a boy, looking curiously at the strange figure before him.

"Oh it's too rich!" said Tom, pausing a little, and then breaking out anew.

"What's too rich?"

"I've run away from granny. She wanted to lick me, and now she can't."

"You've been cutting up, I suppose."

"No, it's granny that's been cuttin' up. She's at it all the time."

"But you'll catch it when you do go home, you know."

"Maybe I won't go home."

It was not a street-boy that addressed her; but a boy with a comfortable home, who had a place in a store near by. He did not know, practically, what sort of a thing it was to wander about the streets, friendless and homeless; but it struck him vaguely that it must be decidedly uncomfortable. There was something in this strange creature—half boy in appearance—that excited his interest and curiosity, and he continued the conversation.

"What sort of a woman is your granny, as you call her?" he asked.

"She's an awful old woman," was the answer.

"I shouldn't think you would like to speak so of your grandmother."

"I don't believe she is my grandmother. I only call her so."

"What's your name?"

"Tom."

"Tom!" repeated the boy, in surprise. "Ain't you a girl?"

"Yes; I expect so."

"It's hard to tell from your clothes, you know;" and he scanned Tom's queer figure attentively.

Tom was sitting on a low step with her knees nearly on a level with her chin, and her hands clasped around them. She had on her cap of the morning, and her jacket, which, by the way, had been given to granny when on a begging expedition, and appropriated to Tom's use, without special reference to her sex. Tom didn't care much. It made little difference to her whether she was in the fashion or not; and if the street boys chaffed her, she was abundantly able to give them back as good as they sent.

"What's the matter with my clothes?" said Tom

"You've got on a boy's cap and jacket."

"I like it well enough. As long as it keeps a feller warm I don't mind."

"Do you call yourself a feller?"

"Yes."

"Then you're a queer feller."

"Don't you call me names, 'cause I won't stand it;" and Tom raised a pair of sharp, black eyes.

"I won't call you names, at least not any bad ones. Have you had any dinner?"

"Yes," said Tom, smacking her lips, as she recalled her delicious repast, "I had a square meal."

"What do you call a square meal?"

"Roast beef, cup o' coffee, and pie."

The boy was rather surprised, for such a dinner seemed beyond Tom's probable resources.

"Your granny don't treat you so badly, after all. That's just the kind of dinner I had."

"Granny didn't give it to me. I bought it. That's what she wants to lick me for. All she give me was a piece of hard bread."

"Where did you get the money? Was it hers?"

"That's what she says. But if a feller works all the mornin' for some money, hasn't she got a right to keep some of it?"

"I should think so."

"So should I," said Tom, decidedly.

"Have you got any money?"

"No, I spent it all for dinner."

"Then here's some."

The boy drew from his vest-pocket twenty-five cents, and offered it to Tom.

The young Arab felt no delicacy in accepting the pecuniary aid thus tendered.

"Thank you," said she. "You can call me names if you want to."

"What should I want to call you names for?" asked the boy, puzzled.

"There was a gent called me names this mornin', and give me twenty cents for doin' it."

"What did he call you?"

"I dunno; but it must have been something awful bad, it was so long."

"You're a strange girl, Tom,"

"Am I? Well, I reckon I am. What's your name?"

"John Goodwin."

"John Goodwin?" repeated Tom, by way of fixing it in her memory.

"Yes; haven't you got any other name than Tom?"

"I dunno. I think granny called me Jane once. But it's a good while ago. Everybody calls me Tom, now."

"Well, Tom, I must be getting back to the store. Good-by. I hope you'll get along."

"All right!" said Tom. "I'm goin' into business with that money you give me."

CHAPTER V

TOM GAINS A VICTORY

GRANNY mounted the stairs two at a time; so eager was she to force a surrender on the part of the rebellious Tom. She was a little out of breath when she reached the fourth landing, and paused an instant to recover it. Tom was at that moment half-way down the rope; but this she did not suspect. Recovering her breath, she strode to the door. Before making an assault with the hatchet, she decided to summon Tom to a surrender.

"Tom!" she called out.

Of course there was no answer.

"Why don't you answer?" demanded granny, provoked.

She listened for a reply, but Tom remained obstinately silent, as she interpreted it.

"If you don't speak, it'll be the wuss for ye," growled granny.

Again no answer.

"I'll find a way to make you speak. Come and open the door, or I'll break it down. I've got a hatchet."

But the old woman had the conversation all to herself.

Quite beside herself now with anger, she no longer hesitated; but with all her force dealt a blow which buried the hatchet deep in the door.

"Jest wait till I get in!" she muttered. "Will ye open it now?"

But there was no response.

While she was still battering at the door one of the neighbors came up from below.

"What are you doin' Mrs. Walsh?" for such was granny's name.

"I'm tryin' to get in."

"Why don't you open the door?"

"Tom's locked it. She won't let me in," said granny, finishing the sentence with a string of profane words which had best be omitted.

"You'll have a good bill to pay to the landlord, Mrs. Walsh."

"I don't care," said granny. "I'm goin' to get at that trollop, and beat her within an inch of her life."

Another vigorous blow broke the lock, and the door flew open.

Granny rushed in, after the manner of a devouring lion ready to pounce upon her prey. But she stopped short in dismay. Tom was not visible!

Thinking she might be in the closet, the old woman flung open the door: but again she was balked.

"What has 'come of the child?" she exclaimed, in bewilderment.

"She got out of the window," said the neighbor, who had caught sight of the rope dangling from the open casement.

Granny hastened to the window, and the truth flashed upon her. Her prey had escaped her!

It was a deep disappointment to the vindictive old woman, whose hand itched to exercise itself in punishing Tom.

"She's a bold un," said the neighbor, with some admiration of Tom's pluck. Granny answered with a strain of invective, which gave partial vent to the rage and disappointment she felt.

"If I could only get at her!" she muttered between her teeth; "I'd give her half-a-dozen lickin's in one. She'd wish she hadn't done it."

Not a doubt entered granny's mind that Tom would return. It never occurred to her that her young servant had become tired of her bondage, and had already made up her mind to break her chains. She knew Tom pretty well, but not wholly. She did not realize that the days of her rule were at an end; and that by her tyranny she had driven from her the girl whose earnings she had found so convenient.

If there had been much chance of meeting Tom outside, granny would have gone out into the streets and hunted for her. But to search for her among the numerous streets, lanes, and alleys in the lower part of the city would have been like trying to find a needle in a haystack. Then, even if she found her, she could not very well whip her in the street. Tom would probably come home at night as usual, bringing money, and she could defer the punishment till then.

Fatigued with her exercise and excitement, the old woman threw herself down on her rude pallet, first drawing the contents of a jug which stood in the closet, and was soon in a drunken sleep. Leaving her thus, we go back to Tom.

She had made up her mind not to go back to sweeping the streets; partly, indeed, because she no longer had her broom with her. Moreover, she thought that she would in that case be more likely to fall into the clutches of the enemy she so much dreaded. With the capital for which she was indebted to her new boy acquaintance she decided to lay in a supply of evening papers, and try to dispose of them. It was not a new trade to her; for there was scarcely one of the street trades in which the young Arab had not more or less experience.

She bought ten copies of the "Express," and selected the corner of two streets for the disposal of her stock in trade.

"Here's the 'Express,'—latest news from the seat of war!" cried Tom; catching the cry from a boy engaged in the same business up on Broadway.

"What's the news?" asked one of two young men who were passing.

"The news is that you're drafted," said Tom, promptly. "Buy the paper, and you'll find out all about it."

It was in the midst of the draft excitement in New York; and as it so happened that the young man had actually been drafted, his companion laughed.

"You must buy a paper for that, Jack," he said.

"I believe I will," said the first, laughing. "Here's ten cents. Never mind about the change."

"Thank you," said Tom. "Come round tomorrow, and I'll sell you another."

"You'll have me drafted again, I am afraid. Perhaps you will go as my substitute?"

"I would if I was old enough," said Tom.

"You're a girl,—ain't you? Girls can't fight."

"Try me and see," said Tom. "I can fight any boy of my size." The two young men passed on, laughing.

Tom soon had an opportunity to test her prowess. The corner where she had stationed herself was usually occupied by a boy somewhat larger than Tom, who considered that it belonged to him by right. He came up rather late, having a chance to carry a carpet-bag for a guest at French's Hotel to the Hudson River station. Tom had disposed of half her papers when he came blustering up:—

"Clear out of here!" he said, imperiously.

"Who was you speakin' to?" asked Tom, coolly.

"To you. Just clear out!"

"What for?" asked Tom.

"You've got my stand."

"Have I?" said Tom, not offering to move.

"Yes, you have."

"Then I'm goin' to keep it. 'Ere's the 'Express,'—latest news from the seat of war."

"Look here!" said the newsboy, menacingly, "if you don't clear out, I'll make you."

"Will you?" said Tom, independently, taking his measure, and deciding that she could fight him. "I ain't afraid of you!"

Her rival advanced, and gave her a push which nearly thrust her from the sidewalk into the street. But he was rather astonished the next moment at receiving a blow in the face from Tom's fist.

"If you want to fight, come on!" said Tom, dropping her papers and squaring off.

He was not slow in accepting the defiance, being provoked by the unexpected blow, and aimed a blow at Tom's nose. But Tom, who had some rudimental ideas of boxing, while her opponent knew nothing of it, fended off the blow, and succeeded in getting in another.

"Ho! ho!" laughed another boy, who had just come up; "you're licked by a gal." Bob, for this was the newsboy's name, felt all the disgrace of the situation. His face reddened, and he pitched in promiscuously, delivering blow after blow wildly. This gave a decided advantage to Tom, who inflicted considerably more damage than she received.

The fight would have gone on longer if a gentleman had not come up, and spoken authoritatively. "What is all this fighting about? Are you not ashamed to fight with a girl?"

"No, I ain't," said Bob, sullenly. "She took my place, and wouldn't give it up."

"Is that true?" turning to Tom.

"I've got as much right to it as he," said Tom. "I'll give it to him if I am a gal."

"Don't you know it is wrong to fight?" asked the gentleman, this time addressing Tom.

"No, I don't," said Tom. "Wouldn't you fight if a feller pitched into you?"

This was rather an embarrassing question, but the gentleman said, "It would be better to go away than to get into a fight."

"He hit me."

"It is bad enough for boys to fight, but it is worse for girls."

"Don't see it," said Tom.

Had Tom been in a higher social position, it might have been suggested to her that to fight was not lady-like; but there was such an incongruity between Tom's appearance and anything lady-like, that such an appeal would have been out of place. The fact is, Tom claimed no immunity or privilege on the score of sex, but regarded herself, to all intents and purposes, as a boy, and strongly wished that she were one.

The gentleman looked at her, rather puzzled, and walked away, satisfied with having stopped the fight.

Bob did not seem inclined to renew hostilities, but crossed the street, and took his stand there. Tom, by right of conquest, held her place until she had sold out her whole stock of papers.

CHAPTER VI

AN UNFASHIONABLE HOTEL

TOM found at the end of the afternoon that her capital had increased from twenty-five to fifty cents.

"Granny won't get none of this," she soliloquized, complacently. "It's all mine."

Sitting on a doorstep she counted over the money with an entirely different feeling from what she had experienced when it was to be transferred to granny. Now it was all her own, and, though but fifty cents, it made her feel rich.

"What shall I do with it?" thought Tom.

She had a square meal in the middle of the day; but several hours had passed since then, and she felt hungry again. Tom did not see any necessity for remaining hungry, with fifty cents in her possession. She made her way, therefore, to another eating-house, where the prices were the same with those at the one before mentioned, and partook of another square meal, leaving out the pie. This reduced her capital to thirty cents. She felt that she ought to save this, to start in business upon in the morning. As a street-sweeper she required no capital except her broom; but though Tom was not troubled with pride, she preferred to sell papers, or take up some other street vocation. Besides, she knew that as a street-sweeper on Broadway, she would be more likely to be discovered by the old woman whom she was now anxious to avoid.

After eating supper Tom went out into the streets, not knowing exactly how to spend her time. Usually, she had gone down into the court, or the street, and played with the children of her own and neighboring tenement houses. But now she did not care to venture back into the old locality.

So she strolled about the streets aimlessly, until she felt sleepy, and began to consider whereabouts to bestow herself for the night. She might have gone to the "Girls' Lodging House," if she had known of such an institution; but she had never heard of it. Chance brought her to a basement, on which was the sign,—

"LODGINGS—FIVE CENTS."

This attracted Tom's attention. If it had not been a cold night, she would have been willing to sleep out, which would have been cheaper; but it was a damp and chilly evening, and her dress was thin.

"Five cents won't bust me!" thought Tom. "I'll go in."

She went down some steps, and opened a door into a room very low-studded, and very dirty.

A stout woman, in a dirty calico loose-gown, was sitting in a chair, with a fat, unhealthy-looking baby in her lap.

"What you want, little gal?" she asked.

"Where's your lodgin'?" asked Tom.

"In back," answered the woman, pointing to an inner room, partially revealed through a half-open door. It was dark, having no windows, and dirtier, if possible, than the front room. The floor was covered with straw, for beds and bedsteads were looked upon as unnecessary luxuries in this economical lodging-house.

"Is that the place?" asked Tom.

"Yes. Do you want to stop here to-night?"

Tom had not been accustomed to first-class hotels, still the accommodations at granny's were rather better than this. However, the young Arab did not mind. She had no doubt she could sleep comfortably on the straw, and intimated her intention of stopping.

"Where's your money?" asked the woman.

The invariable rule in this establishment was payment in advance, and, perhaps, considering the character of the customers, it was the safest rule that could be adopted.

Tom took out her money, and counted out five cents into the woman's palm. She then put back the remainder in her pocket. If she had been less sleepy, she might have noticed the woman's covetous glance, and been led to doubt the safety of her small fortune. But Tom was sleepy, and her main idea was to go to bed as soon as possible.

"Lay down anywhere," said the landlady, dropping the five cents into her pocket.

Tom's preparation for bed did not take long. No undressing was required, for it was the custom here to sleep with the day's clothes on. Tom stowed herself away in a corner, and in five minutes was asleep.

It was but little after eight o'clock, and she was, at present, the only lodger.

No sooner did her deep, regular breathing indicate slumber, than the landlady began to indulge in various suspicious movements. She first put down her baby, and then taking a lantern,—the only light which could safely be carried into the lodging-room, on account of the straw upon the floor,—crept quietly into the inner room.

"She's fast asleep," she muttered.

She approached Tom with cautious step. She need not have been afraid to awaken her. Tom was a good sleeper, and not likely to wake up, unless roughly awakened, until morning.

Tom was lying on her side, with her face resting on one hand.

The woman stooped down, and began to look for the pocket in which she kept her money; but it was in that part of her dress upon which she was lying. This embarrassed the woman somewhat, but an idea occurred to her. She took up a straw, and, bending over, gently tickled Tom's ear. Tom shook her head, as a cat would under similar circumstances, and on its being repeated turned over, muttering, "Don't, granny!"

This was what her dishonest landlady wanted. She thrust her hand into Tom's pocket, and drew out the poor girl's entire worldly treasure. Tom, unconscious of the robbery, slept on; and the woman went back to the front room to wait for more lodgers. They began to come in about ten, and by twelve the room was full. It was a motley collection, and would have been a curious, though sad study, to any humane observer. They were most of them in the last stages of ill-fortune yet among them was more than one who had once filled a respectable position in society. Here was a man of thirty-five, who ten years before had filled a good place, with a fair salary, in a city bank. But in an evil hour he helped himself to some of the funds of the bank. He lost his situation, and, though he escaped imprisonment, found his prospects blasted. So he had gone down hill, until at length he found himself reduced to such a lodging-house as this, fortunate if he could command the small sum needful to keep him from a night in the streets.

Next him was stretched a man who was deserving still more pity, since his misfortunes sprang rather from a want of judgment than from his own fault. He was a scholar, with a fair knowledge of Latin and Greek, and some ability as a writer. He was an Englishman who had come to the city in the hope of making his acquisitions available, but had met with very poor encouragement. He found that both among teachers and writers the demand exceeded the supply, at least for those of moderate qualifications; and, having no influential friends, had sought for employment almost in vain. His small stock of money dwindled, his suit became shabby, until he found himself, to his deep mortification and disgust, compelled to resort to such lodging-houses as this, where he was obliged to herd with the lowest and most abandoned class.

Next to him lay a mechanic, once in profitable employment. But drink had been his ruin; and now he was a vagabond, spending the little money he earned, at rum-shops, except what was absolutely necessary for food.

There is no need of cataloguing the remainder of Meg Morely's lodgers. Her low rates generally secured her a room-full, and a dozen, sometimes more, were usually packed away on the floor. On the whole she found it a paying business, though her charges were low. Sixty cents a day was quite a respectable addition to her income, and she had occupied the same place for two years already. Tom's experience will show that she had other, and not quite so lawful, ways of swelling her receipts, but she was cautious not to put them in practice, unless she considered it prudent, as in the present instance.

It was seven o'clock when Tom awoke. She looked around her in bewilderment, thinking at first she must be in granny's room. But a glance at the prostrate forms around her brought back the events of the day before, and gave her a realizing sense of her present situation.

"I've had a good sleep," said Tom to herself, stretching, by way of relief from her constrained position. "I guess it's time to get up."

She rubbed her eyes, and shook back her hair, and then rising, went into the front room. Her landlady was already up and getting breakfast.

"What time is it?" asked Tom.

"It's just gone seven," said Meg, looking sharply at Tom to see if she had discovered the loss of her money. "How did you sleep?"

"Tip-top."

"Come ag'in."

"All right!" said Tom. "Maybe I will."

She climbed up the basement stairs to the street above, and began to think of what the day had in store for her. Her prospects were not brilliant certainly; but Tom on the whole felt in good spirits. She had thrown off the yoke of slavery. She was her own mistress now, and granny's power was broken. Tom felt that she could get along somehow. She had confidence in herself, and was sure something would turn up for her.

"Now, what'll I do first?" thought Tom.

With twenty-five cents in her pocket, and a good appetite, breakfast naturally suggested itself.

She dove her hand into her pocket, but the face of the little Arab almost instantly expressed deep dismay.

Her money was gone!

CHAPTER VII

TOM MAKES A FRIEND

TWENTY-FIVE cents is not a large sum, but it was Tom's entire fortune. It was all she had, not only to buy breakfast with, but also to start in business. She had an excellent appetite, but now there was no hope of satisfying it until she could earn some more money. Tom hurried back to the lodging, and entered, looking excited.

"Well, what's wanted?" asked Meg, who knew well enough without asking.

"I've lost some money."

"Suppose you did," said the woman, defiantly, "you don't mean to say I took it."

"No," said Tom, "but I had it when I laid down."

"Where was it?"

"In my pocket."

"Might have tumbled out among the straw," suggested Meg.

This struck Tom as not improbable, and she went back into the bedroom, and, getting down on her hands and knees, commenced poking about for it. But even if it had been there, any of my readers who has ever lost money in this way knows that it is very difficult to find under such circumstances.

Tom persevered in her search until her next-door neighbor growled out that he wished she would clear out. At length she was obliged to give it up.

"Have you found it?" asked Meg.

"No," said Tom, soberly.

"How much was it?"

"Twenty-five cents."

"That ain't much."

"Its enough to bust me. I don't believe it's in the straw."

"What do you believe?" demanded Meg, whose guilty conscience made her scent an accusation.

"I think some of them took it while I was asleep," said Tom, indicating the other lodgers by a jerk of her finger.

"Likely they did," said Meg, glad to have suspicion diverted elsewhere.

"I wish I knew," said Tom.

"What'ud you do?"

"I'd get it back again," said Tom, her black eyes snapping with resolution.

"No, you wouldn't. You're nothin' but a baby. You couldn't do nothin'!"

"Couldn't I?" returned Tom. "I'd let 'em know whether I was a baby."

"Well, you go along now," said Meg. "Your money's gone, and you can't get it back. Next time give it to me to keep, and it'll be safe."

Being penniless, Tom was in considerable uncertainty when she would again be mistress of so large a sum. At present she felt in no particular dread of being robbed. She left the lodgings, realizing that the money was indeed gone beyond hope of recovery.

There is some comfort in beginning the day with a good breakfast. It warms one up, and inspires hope and confidence. As a general rule people are good-natured and cheerful after a hearty breakfast. For ten cents Tom might have got a cup of coffee, or what passed for such, and a plate of tea-biscuit. With the other fifteen she could have bought a few morning papers, and easily earned enough to pay for a square meal in the middle of the day. Now she must go to work without capital, and on an empty stomach, which was rather discouraging. She would have fared better than this at granny's, though not much, her breakfast there usually consisting of a piece of stale bread, with perhaps a fragment of cold sausage. Coffee, granny never indulged in, believing whiskey to be more healthful. Occasionally, in moments of extreme good nature, she had given Tom a sip of whiskey; but the young Arab had never got to like it, fortunately for herself, though she had accepted it as a variation of her usual beverage, cold water.

In considering what she should do for the day, Tom decided to go to some of the railway stations or steamboat landings, and try to get a chance to carry a carpet-bag. "Baggage-smashing" required no capital, and this was available in her present circumstances.

Tom made her way to the pier where the steamers of the Fall River line arrive. Ordinarily it would have been too late, but it had been a windy night, the sound was rough, and the steamer was late, so that Tom arrived just in the nick of time.

Tom took her place among the hackmen, and the men and boys who, like her, were bent on turning an honest penny by carrying baggage.

"Clear out of the way here, little gal!" said a stout, overgrown boy. "Smash your baggage, sir?"

"Clear out yourself!" said Tom, boldly. "I've got as much right here as you."

Her little, sharp eyes darted this way and that in search of a possible customer. The boy who had been rude to her got a job, and this gave Tom a better chance. She offered her services to a lady, who stared at her with curiosity and returned no answer. Tom began to think she should not get a job. There seemed a popular sentiment in favor of employing boys, and Tom, like others of her sex, found herself shut out from an employment for which she considered herself fitted. But, at length, she saw approaching a big, burly six-footer, with a good-natured face. There was something about him which inspired Tom with confidence, and, pressing forward, she said, "Carry your bag, sir?"

He stopped short and looked down at the queer figure of our heroine. Then, glancing at his carpetbag, which was of unusual size and weight, the idea of his walking through the streets with Tom bending beneath the weight of his baggage, struck him in so ludicrous a manner that he burst into a hearty laugh.

"What's up?" demanded Tom, suspiciously. "Who are you laughin' at?"

"So you want to carry my carpet-bag?" he asked, laughing again.

"Yes," said Tom.

"Why, I could put you in it," said the tall man, his eyes twinkling with amusement.

"No, you couldn't," said Tom.

"Do you think you could carry it?"

"Let me try."

He set it down, and Tom lifted it from the ground; but it was obviously too much for her strength.

"You see you can't do it. Have you found anything to do this morning?"

"No," said Tom.

"Business isn't good, hey?"

"No," said Tom, "but I wouldn't mind so much if I hadn't had my money stole. I'm bust!"

"How's that? Did the bank break or have you been speculating?"

"Oh, you're gasin'! I ain't got nothing to do with banks. Somebody stole two shillin's I had, so I've had no breakfast."

"Come, that's bad. I guess I must give you a job, after all. You can't carry my bag, but you can carry this."

He had under his arm something wrapped in a paper, making a small bundle. He handed it to Tom, and she trudged along with it after him.

"You couldn't guess what that is, I suppose?" said her companion, sociably.

"No," said Tom; "it feels soft."

"It's a large wax doll, for my little niece," said her patron. "You haven't got any dolls, I suppose?"

"I had one once," said Tom. "It was made of rags. But granny threw it into the fire."

"I suppose you were sorry."

"I was then; but I'm too old for dolls now."

"How old are you?"

"I ain't sure. Somewheres about twelve."

"You live with your granny, then?"

"No, I don't,—not now."

"Why not?"

"She wanted to lick me, so I ran away."

"Then where do you live now?"

"Nowhere."

"You have no home?"

"I don't want no home. I can take care of myself," said Tom, briskly.

"I see you are an independent, young woman. Now, if you were a boy, I'd give you a chance on board my ship."

"Have you got a ship?" asked Tom, becoming interested.

"Yes, I am a sea-captain, and go on long voyages. If you wasn't a girl, I'd take you along with me as cabin-boy."

"I wish you would," said Tom, eagerly.

"But you are a girl, you know? You couldn't climb a mast."

"Try me," said Tom. "I'm strong. I fit with a boy yesterday, and licked him."

Captain Barnes laughed, but shook his head.

"I see you're spunky, if you are a girl," he said. "But I never heard of a girl being cabin-boy, and I don't think it would do."

"I'd put on a boy's clothes," suggested Tom.

"You've begun to do it already," said the captain, glancing at the cap and jacket. "I didn't know at first but you were a boy. What makes you wear a cap?"

"Granny gave it to me. I like it better than a bonnet."

They had by this time reached Broadway.

"You may steer across the Park to French's Hotel," said the sailor. "It's too late to get breakfast at my sister's."

"All right," said Tom.

They crossed the Park, and the street beyond, and reached the door of the brick hotel on the corner of Frankfort Street.

"I'll go down into the restaurant first," said Captain Barnes. "I feel like laying in a cargo before navigating any farther."

"Here's your bundle," said Tom.

He took it, and handed Tom twenty-five cents, which she received with gratification, not having expected so much for carrying so small a bundle.

"Stay a moment," said the sailor, as she was about to go away. "You haven't had any breakfast, I think you said."

"No."

"Then you shall come in, and breakfast with me."

This invitation astonished Tom not a little. It was the first invitation she had ever received to breakfast with a gentleman. French's restaurant being higher priced than those which her class were in the habit of patronizing, she entered with some hesitation not feeling quite sure how her entrance would be regarded by the waiters. She was not generally wanting in self-possession, but as she descended the stairs and entered the room, she felt awkward and out of her element.

CHAPTER VIII

AT FRENCH'S HOTEL

"CLEAR out of here!" said a waiter, arresting Tom's progress, and pointing to the steps by which she had descended from the sidewalk.

If Tom had been alone, she would have felt bound to obey the summons; but being under the protection of Captain Barnes, who, she reflected, looked a good deal stronger than the waiter, she stood her ground.

"Did you hear what I said?" demanded the waiter angrily, about to take Tom by the shoulder.

"Avast there!" put in the captain, who thought it time to interfere; "is that the way you treat your customers?"

"She ain't no customer."

"She is going to take breakfast here, my friend, and I should like to know what you have got to say about it."

The waiter seemed taken aback by this unexpected championship, of one whom he had supposed to be an unprotected street girl.

"I didn't know she was with you," he stammered.

"Well, you know it now. Come, child, you can sit down here."

Tom enjoyed her triumph over the waiter, and showed it in a characteristic manner, by putting her thumb to her nose.

Captain Barnes sat down on one side of a table at one of the windows, and motioned Tom to sit opposite.

"I don't think you told me your name," he said.

"Tom."

"Then, Tom, let me suggest that you take off your cap. It's usual in the best society."

"I never was there," said Tom; but she removed her cap. This revealed a mop of hair, tangled it is true, but of a beautiful brown shade. Her black eyes sparkled from beneath, giving a bright, keen look to her face, browned by exposure to all weathers. I regret to say that the face was by no means clean. If it had been, and the whole expression had not been so wild and untamed, Tom would certainly have been considered pretty. As it was, probably no one would have wasted a second glance upon the little street girl.

"What will you have, sir, you and the young lady?" asked the waiter, emphasizing the last word, with a grin at Tom.

"What will you have, Tom?" asked the captain.

"Beefsteak, cup o' coffee, and bread-and-butter," said Tom, glibly.

Her knowledge of dishes was limited; but she had tried these and liked them, and this guided her in the selection.

"Very good," said Captain Barnes; "the same for me, with fried potatoes and an omelet."

Tom stared at this munificent order. She fixed her black eyes meditatively upon her entertainer, and wondered whether he always indulged in such a superlatively square meal.

"What are you thinking about, Tom?" questioned the captain.

"You must be awful rich," said Tom.

Captain Barnes laughed.

"What makes you think so?"

"It'll cost you a lot for breakfast."

"But you know I don't always have company to breakfast."

"Do you call me company?"

"Of course I do."

"I shouldn't think you'd want to have me eat with you."

"Why not?"

"You're a gentleman."

"And you're a young lady. Didn't you hear the waiter call you so?"

"He was chaffin'."

"You may be a lady some time."

"Taint likely," said Tom.

"Why not?"

"I haven't got no good clothes to wear, nor don't know nothin'."

"Can you read?"

"A little, but I don't like to. It's too hard work."

"Makes your head ache, eh?"

"Yes," said Tom, seriously.

Captain Barnes looked attentively at the odd little creature opposite him. He wondered what would be her fate. She was quick, sharp, pretty, but withal an untamed Arab of the streets. The chances seemed very much against her in the warfare of life. Society seemed leagued against her, and she was likely to be at war with it.

"I'll make an effort to save her," he thought. But of this he did not speak to Tom at present, more especially as the waiter was seen advancing with the breakfast ordered.

He deposited the various dishes, some before Tom, and the remainder before the captain.

Tom was not used to restaurants of the better class, and did not see the necessity of an empty plate in addition to the dish which contained the meat. Such ceremony was not in vogue at the ten-cent restaurants which she had hitherto patronized. She fixed her eyes eagerly upon the beefsteak, which emitted a very savory odor.

"Pass your plate, Tom, and I will give you some meat."

Tom passed her plate, nothing loath, and the captain transferred to it a liberal supply of meat.

Tom waited for no ceremony, but, seizing her knife, attacked the meat vigorously.

"How is it?" asked her companion, amused.

"Bully!" said Tom, too busy to raise her eyes from her plate.

"Let me help you to a little of the omelet."

Tom extended her plate, and a portion of the omelet was placed upon it.

Tom raised a little to her lips, cautiously, for it was a new dish to her, and she did not know whether she would like it. It seemed to be satisfactory, however, none being left upon her plate when she had finished eating.

Not much conversation went on during the meal. Tom's entire energies were given to disposing of the squarest meal in which she had ever indulged, and the captain's attention was divided between his breakfast and the young waif upon whom he was bestowing perfect bliss.

At length Tom's efforts relaxed. She laid down her knife and fork, and heaved a sigh of exquisite enjoyment.

"Well," said the captain, "would you like some more?"

"No," said Tom, "I'm full."

"Did you enjoy your breakfast?"

"Didn't I, just?" and Tom's tone spoke volumes.

"I'm glad of that. I think it's very good myself."

"You're a brick!" said Tom, in a tone of grateful acknowledgment.

"Thank you," said Captain Barnes, his eyes twinkling a little; "I try to be."

"I wonder what granny would say if she knowed where I was," soliloquized Tom, aloud.

"She'd be glad you had enjoyed your breakfast."

"No, she wouldn't. She'd be mad."

"You don't give your grandmother a very good character. Doesn't she like you?"

"No; she hates me, and I hate her. She takes all my money, and then licks me."

"That's unpleasant, to be sure. Then you don't want to go back to her?"

"Not for Joe!" said Tom, shaking her head very decidedly.

"Then you expect to take care of yourself? Do you think you can?"

Tom nodded confidently.

"What are you going to do this morning, for instance?"

"Buy some papers with the money you give me."

"What a self-reliant spirit the little chit has!" thought Captain Barnes. "I've known plenty of young men, who had less faith in their ability to cope with the world, and gain a livelihood, than she. Yet she has next to no clothes, and her entire capital consists of twenty-five cents. There is a lesson for the timid and despondent in her philosophy."

Tom had no idea of what was passing in the mind of her companion. If she had been able to read his thoughts, it is not likely she would have understood them. Her own thoughts had become practical. She had had a good breakfast, —thanks to the kindness of her new friend,—but for dinner she must depend upon herself. She felt that it was quite time to enter upon the business of the day.

She put on her cap and rose to her feet.

"I'm goin'," she said, abruptly.

"Where are you going?"

"To buy some papers. Thank you for my breakfast."

It was probably the first time Tom ever thanked anybody for anything. I am not quite sure whether anybody before this had given her any cause for gratitude. Certainly, not granny, who had bestowed far less than she had received from the child, upon whom she had not been ashamed to be a selfish dependent. There was something, possibly, in her present companionship with a kind-hearted gentleman something, perhaps, in her present more respectable surroundings, which had taught Tom this first lesson in good manners. She was almost surprised herself at the expression of gratitude to which she had given utterance.

"Stop a minute, Tom!" said the captain.

Tom had got half way to the door, but she stopped short on being called back.

"You haven't asked me whether I have got through with you."

Tom looked surprised. She knew of no further service in which she could make herself useful to her companion.

"Haven't you got through with me?" she asked,

"Not quite. I'm not going to stop here, you know,—I am going to my sister's."

"Where does she live?"

"In Sixteenth Street."

"Do you want me to carry your carpet-bag?" asked Tom.

"Well, no; I think you couldn't manage that. But you can carry the bundle."

"All right!" said Tom.

It was all one to her whether she sold papers, or carried bundles. The main thing was to earn the small amount of money necessary to defray her daily expenses. Of the two she would rather go up to Sixteenth Street; for as she had seldom found occasion to go up town, the expedition promised a little novelty.

Captain Barnes paid his bill, and left the restaurant, with Tom at his heels.

CHAPTER IX

MRS. MERTON

"WE'LL go across Broadway, and take the Sixth Avenue cars, Tom," said the captain.

"Are we goin' to ride?" asked Tom, surprised.

"Yes, you don't catch me lugging this heavy carpet-bag up to Sixteenth Street."

Tom was rather surprised at this. She did not understand why her services were required to carry the bundle if they were going to ride. However, she very sensibly remained silent, not feeling called upon to comment on her employer's arrangements.

At this time in the day there was no difficulty in obtaining a seat in the cars. Tom, however, was not disposed to sit down quietly.

"I'll stand outside," she said.

"Very well," said Captain Barnes, and he drew out a copy of a morning paper which he had purchased on leaving the hotel.

Tom took her position beside the driver. She rather enjoyed the ride, for, though she had lived in the city for years, she had seldom been on the car as a passenger, though she had frequently stolen a ride on the steps of a Broadway omnibus.

"Well, Johnny, are you going up town to look after your family?" asked the driver, good-naturedly.

"I'd have to look a long time before I found 'em," said Tom.

"Haven't you got any relations, then?"

"There's an old woman that calls herself my granny."

"Does she live up on Fifth Avenue?"

"Yes," said Tom; "next door to you."

"You've got me there," said the driver, laughing. "Give my respects to your granny, and tell her she's got a smart grand-daughter."

"I will, when I see her."

"Don't you live with her?"

"Not now. She ain't my style."

Here the conductor tapped Tom on the shoulder.

"*He* pays for me," said Tom, pointing back at Captain Barnes.

"I suppose he's your grandfather," said the driver, jocosely.

"I wish he was. He's a trump. He gave me a stunnin' breakfast."

"So you like him better than your granny?"

"You can bet on that."

Captain Barnes, sitting near the door, heard a part of this conversation, and it amused him.

"I wonder," he thought, "whether my sister will be willing to assume charge of this wild little girl? There's enough in her to make a very smart woman, if she is placed under the right influences and properly trained. But I suspect that will require not a little patience and tact.

"Well, we shall see."

After a while the car reached Sixteenth Street, and the captain left it, with Tom following him.

They turned down Sixteenth Street from the avenue, and finally stopped before a fair-looking brick house. Captain Barnes went up the steps, and rang the bell.

"Is Mrs. Merton at home?" he asked.

"Yes," said the servant, looking hard at Tom.

"Then I'll come in. Tell her her brother wishes to see her. Come in, Tom."

Tom followed the captain, the servant continuing to eye her suspiciously. They entered the parlor, where Captain Barnes took a seat on the sofa, motioning Tom to sit beside him. Tom obeyed, surveying the sofa with some curiosity. The families in the tenement house with whom she had been on visiting terms did not in general possess sofas. She had sometimes seen them in furniture stores, but this was the first time she had sat upon one.

"What are you thinking of, Tom?" asked the captain, desiring to draw her out.

"Does your sister live here?"

"Yes."

"She's rich, isn't she?"

"No, she makes a living by keeping boarders. Perhaps you'd like to board with her."

Tom laughed.

"She don't take the likes of me," she said.

"Suppose you were rich enough, wouldn't you like to board here?"

"I don't know," said Tom, looking round. "It's dark."

"All the rooms are not dark. Besides, you'd get three square meals every day."

"I'd like that," said Tom, seriously.

Their further conversation was interrupted by the entrance of the captain's sister, Mrs. Merton. She was rather a stout woman, but there was an expression of care on her face, which was not surprising, for it is no light thing to keep a New York boarding-house.

"When did you arrive in the city, Albert?" she asked, giving him her hand cordially.

"Only just arrived, Martha. How does the world use you?"

"I can't complain, though it's a wearing thing looking after a household like this. Have you had any breakfast?"

"I took some down town."

Just then Mrs. Merton's eye fell for the first time upon Tom. She started in surprise, and looked doubtfully at her brother.

"Who is this?" she asked. "Did she come with you?"

"It's a young friend of mine. She met me at the wharf, and wanted to carry my carpet-bag."

"You didn't let her do it?"

"Bless you, no. It's big enough to pack her away in. But I employed her to carry a bundle. Didn't I, Tom?"

"What did you call her?" asked his sister.

"Tom. That's her name, so she says."

"What made you bring her here?" asked Mrs. Merton, who evidently regarded her brother's conduct as very queer.

"I'll tell you, but not before her. Tom, you can go out into the entry, and shut the door behind you. I'll call you in a few minutes."

Tom went out, and Captain Barnes returned to the subject.

"She's got no relations except an intemperate old grandmother," he said. "I've taken a fancy to her, and want to help her along. Can't you find a place for her in your kitchen?"

"I take a girl from the street!" ejaculated Mrs. Merton. "Albert, you must be crazy."

"Not at all. I am sure you can find something for her to do,—cleaning knives, running of errands, going to market, or something of that kind."

"This is a very strange proposal."

"Why is it? At present she lives in the street, being driven from the only home she had, by the ill-treatment of a vicious grandmother. You can see what chance she has of growing up respectably."

"But there are plenty such. I don't see that it's our business to look after them."

"I don't know why it is, but I've taken a fancy to this little girl."

"She looks perfectly wild."

"I won't deny that she is rather uncivilized, but there's a good deal in her. She's as smart as a steel trap."

"Smart enough to steal, probably."

"Perhaps so, under temptation. I want to remove the temptation."

"This is a very strange freak on your part, Albert."

"I don't know about that. You know I have no child of my own, and am well off, so far as this world's goods are concerned. I have long thought I should like to train up a child in whom I could take an interest, and who would be a comfort to me when I am older."

"You can find plenty of attractive children without going into the street for them."

"I don't want a tame child. She wouldn't interest me. This girl has spirit. I'll tell you what I want you to do, Martha. I'm going off on a year's voyage. Take her into your house, make her as useful as you can, civilize her, and I will allow you a fair price for her board."

"Do you want her to go to school?"

"After a while. At present she needs to be civilized. She is a young street Arab with very elementary ideas as to the way in which people live. She needs an apprenticeship in some house like this. My little niece must be about her age."

"Mary? How can I trust her to the companionship of such a girl?"

"Tom isn't bad. She is only untrained. She will learn more than she will teach at first. Afterwards Mary may learn something of her."

"I am sure I don't know what to say," said Mrs. Merton, irresolutely.

Here the captain named the terms he was willing to pay for Tom's board. This was a consideration to Mrs. Merton, who found that she had to calculate pretty closely to make keeping boarders pay.

"I'll try her," she said.

"Thank you, Martha. You can let her go into the kitchen at first, till she is fit to be promoted."

"She must have some clothes. She had on a boy's jacket."

"Yes, and cap. In fact she is more of a boy than a girl at present."

"I am not sure but some of Mary's old dresses may fit her. Mary must be a little larger than she is."

"That reminds me. I brought a doll for Fanny. She has not grown too large for dolls yet."

"No, she is just the age to enjoy them. She will be delighted."

"I think we may call in Tom now, and inform her of our intention."

"She must have another name. It won't do to call a girl Tom."

"She said her name used to be Jenny, but she has been nicknamed Tom."

The door was opened, and Captain Barnes called in Tom.

"Come in, Tom," he said.

"All right!" said Tom. "I'm on hand!"

"We've been talking about you, Tom," pursued the captain.

"What have you been sayin'?" asked Tom, suspiciously.

"I've been telling my sister that you had no home, and were obliged to earn your own living in the streets."

"I don't care much," said Tom. "I'd rather do that than live with granny, and get licked."

"But wouldn't you like better to have a nice home, where you would have plenty to eat, and a good bed to sleep in?"

"Maybe I would."

"I've been asking my sister to let you stay here with her. Would you like that?"

Tom regarded Mrs. Merton attentively. The face was careworn, but very different from granny's. On the whole, it inspired her with some degree of confidence.

"If she wouldn't lick me very often," she said.

"How about that, Martha?" he asked.

"I think I can promise that," said Mrs. Merton, amused in spite of herself.

"Of course you will have to work. My sister will find something for you to do."

"I aint afraid of work," said Tom, "if I only get enough to eat, and aint licked."

"You see, Tom, I feel an interest in you."

"You're a brick!" said Tom, gratefully.

"Little girl," said Mrs. Merton, shocked, "you mustn't use such language in addressing my brother."

"Never mind, Martha; she means it as a compliment."

"A compliment to call you a brick!"

"Certainly. But now about clothes. Can't you rig her out with something that will make her presentable?"

"She needs a good washing first," said Mrs. Merton, surveying Tom's dirty face and hands with disfavor.

"A very good suggestion. You won't mind being washed, I suppose, Tom?"
"I'd just as lives," said Tom.
In fact she was quite indifferent on the subject. She was used to being dirty, but if she could oblige her new protector by washing, she was quite willing.
"I've got to go out for an hour or two," said Captain Barnes, "but I will leave my carpet-bag here, and come back to lunch."
"Of course, Albert. When do you sail?"
"In three days at farthest."
"Of course you will remain here up to the day of sailing."
"Yes, if you can find a spare corner to stow me in."
"It would be odd if I couldn't find room for my only brother."
"So be it, then. You may expect me."
He rose and taking his hat left the house. Tom and Mrs. Merton were now alone.

CHAPTER X
TOM DROPS HER TATTERS

"NOW, what is your name, little girl?" asked Mrs. Merton, surveying Tom doubtfully, half sorry that she had undertaken the care of her.
"Tom."
"That's a boy's name."
"Everybody calls me Tom,—sometimes Tattered Tom."
"There's some reason about the first name," thought Mrs. Merton, as her glance rested on the ragged skirt and well-ventilated jacket of her brother's protégée.
"As you arc a girl, it is not proper that you should have a boy's name. What is your real name?"
"I think it's Jenny. Granny used to call me so long ago, but I like Tom best."
"Then I shall call you Jenny. Now, Jenny, the first thing to do, is to wash yourself clean. Follow me."
Mrs. Merton went up the front stairs, and Tom followed, using her eyes to good advantage as she advanced.
The landlady led the way into a bath-room. She set the water to running, and bade Tom undress.
"Am I to get into the tub?" asked Tom.
"Yes, certainly. While you are undressing, I will try and find some clothes that will fit you."
Though she did not at first fancy the idea of bathing, Tom grew to like it, and submitted with a good grace. Mrs. Merton took care that it should be thorough. After it, she dressed Tom in some clothes, still very good, which had been laid aside by her daughter Mary. Then she combed Tom's tangled locks, and was astonished by the improvement it made in the appearance of the little waif.
I have already said that Tom had elements of beauty, but it took sharp eyes to detect them under the rags and dirt which had so effectually disguised her. She had very brilliant dark eyes, and a clear olive complexion, with cheeks that had a tinge of red instead of the pallor usually to be found in those children who have the misfortune to be reared in a tenement house. In her new

clothes she looked positively handsome, as Mrs. Merton thought, though she did not see fit to say so to Tom herself.

When her toilet was concluded she turned Tom to the glass, and said, "There, Jenny, do you know who that is?"

Tom stared in open-eyed wonder at the image which she saw. She could hardly believe the testimony of her eyes.

"Is that me?" she asked.

"I believe so," said Mrs. Merton, smiling.

"It don't look like me a bit," continued Tom.

"It doesn't look like 'Tattered Tom,' certainly. Don't you like it better?"

"I dunno," said Tom, doubtfully. "It looks too much like a girl."

"But you are a girl, you know."

"I wish I wasn't."

"Why?"

"Boys have more fun; besides, they are stronger, and can fight better."

"But you don't want to fight?" said Mrs. Merton, scandalized.

"I licked a boy yesterday," said Tom, proudly.

"Why did you do that?"

"He sassed me, and I licked him. He was bigger'n I was, too!"

"I can't allow you to fight in future, Jenny," said Mrs. Merton. "It isn't at all proper for girls, or indeed for boys, to fight; but it is worse for girls."

"Why is it?" asked Tom.

"Because girls should be gentle and lady-like."

"If you was a girl, and a boy should slap you in the face, what would you do?" asked Tom, fixing her bright eyes upon her mentor.

"I should forgive him, and hope he would become a better boy."

"I wouldn't," said Tom. "I'd give him Hail Columby."

"You've got some very wrong ideas, Jenny," said Mrs. Merton. "I fear that your grandmother has not brought you up properly."

"She did not bring me up at all. I brought myself up. As for granny, she didn't care as long as I brought her money to buy whiskey."

Mrs. Merton shook her head. It was very evident to her that Tom had been under very bad influences.

"I hope you will see the error of your ways after a while, Jenny. My brother takes an interest in you, and for his sake I hope you will try to improve."

"If he wants me to, I will," said Tom, decidedly.

Arab as she was, she had been impressed by the kindness of Captain Barnes, and felt that she should like to please him. Still, there was a fascination in the wild independence of her street life which was likely for some time to interfere with her enjoyment of the usages of a more civilized state. There was little prospect of her taming down into an average girl all at once. The change must come slowly.

"My brother will be very much pleased if he finds that you have improved when he returns from his voyage."

"When is he goin' to sea?"

"In two or three days."

"I asked him to take me with him," said Tom "but he wouldn't."

"You would only be in the way on a ship, Jenny."

"No, I shouldn't. I could be a cabin-boy."

"But you are not a boy."

"I could climb the masts as well as a boy. If there was only a pole here, I'd show you."

"What a child you are!"

"Did you ever read about the female pirate captain?" asked Tom.

"No."

"Jim Morgan told me all about it. He'd read it in some book. It was a bully story."

"Such stories are not fit to read."

"I'd like to be a pirate captain," said Tom, thoughtfully.

"You mustn't talk so, Jenny," said Mrs. Merton, shocked.

"But I would, though, and carry two pistols and a dagger in my belt, and then if anybody sassed me I'd give 'em all they wanted."

"My brother wouldn't like to hear you talk so, Jenny. I'm sure I don't know what has got into you to say such dreadful things."

"Then I won't," said Tom. "I wonder what granny would say if she saw me in these fixin's. She wouldn't know me."

"When my brother comes, you shall go down and open the door for him, and see if he knows you."

"That will be bully."

"Now I must be thinking what I can find for you to do. You will be willing to help me?"

"Yes," said Tom, promptly.

"Do you know how to make beds?"

"I can learn," said Tom.

"Didn't your grandmother ever teach you?" asked Mrs. Merton, who, though for a long time a resident of New York, had a very imperfect knowledge of how the poorest classes lived.

"Granny never made her bed," said Tom. "She just gave it a shake, and tumbled into it."

"Bless me, how shiftless she must be!" ejaculated Mrs. Merton, in surprise.

"Oh, granny don't mind!" said Tom, carelessly.

"Did you ever sweep?"

"Lots of times. That's the way I got money to carry to granny."

"Were you paid for sweeping, then?" asked Mrs. Merton.

"Yes, people that came along would give me money. If they wouldn't I'd muddy their boots."

"What do you mean, child? Where did you sweep?"

"Corner of Broadway and Chambers' Streets."

"Oh, you swept the crossing, then."

"In course I did. If you'll give me a broom, I'll go out and sweep front of your house; but I guess there ain't so many people come along here as in Broadway."

"I don't want you to do that," said Mrs. Merton, hastily. "I want you to sweep the rooms in the house. Sarah, the chambermaid, will show you how, and also teach you to make beds."

"All right," said Tom. "Bring her on, and I'll help her."

"We will defer that till to-morrow. Now you may come down to the kitchen with me, and I'll see if I can find anything for you to do there."

Tom felt ready for any enterprise, and started to follow Mrs. Merton downstairs, but rather startled the good lady by making a rapid descent astride the banisters.

"Don't you do that again, Jenny," she said reprovingly.

"Why not?" asked Tom. "It's jolly fun."

CHAPTER XI

THE MISTAKES OF A MORNING

ON the way to the kitchen they met Sarah, the chambermaid, going upstairs to make the beds.

"Sarah," said Mrs. Merton, "here is a little girl who is going to stay with me, and help about the house. You may take her upstairs, and show her how to help you make the beds."

If Tom had been in her street costume, Sarah would have preferred to dispense with her assistance, but she looked quite civilized and respectable now, and she accepted the offer. Tom accompanied her upstairs to the second floor. The first chamber was that of Mr. Craven,—a gentleman in business down town. It was of course vacant, therefore.

Tom looked about her curiously.

"Now," said Sarah, "do you know anything about making beds?"

"No," said Tom.

"Then stand on one side, and I will tell you what to do."

Tom followed directions pretty well, but, as the task was about finished, an impish freak seized her, and she caught the pillow and threw it at Sarah's head, disarranging that young lady's hair, and knocking out a comb.

"What's that for?" demanded Sarah, angrily.

Tom sat down and laughed boisterously.

"It's bully fun!" she said. "Throw it at me."

"I'll give you a shaking, you young imp," said Sarah. "You've broke my comb."

She picked up the comb, and dashed round the bed after Tom, who, seeing no other way for escape, sprang upon the bed, where she remained standing.

"Come down from there," demanded Sarah.

"Let me alone, then!"

"I'll tell the missis, just as sure as you live!"

"What'll she do? Will she lick me?"

"You'll see."

This would not have checked Tom, but it occurred to her, all at once, that her freak would be reported to the captain, and might displease him.

"I'll stop," said she. "I was only in fun."

By this time Sarah had ascertained that the comb was not broken, after all, and this made her more inclined to overlook Tom's offence.

"Now behave decent!" she said.

She gave Tom further directions about the proper way of doing chamberwork, which Tom followed quite closely, being resolved apparently to turn over a new leaf. But her reformation was not thorough. She caught sight of Mr. Craven's shaving materials, which he had carelessly left on the bureau, and before Sarah anticipated her intention, she had seized the brush and spread the lather over her cheeks.

"What are you doing, you little torment?" asked Sarah.

"I'm goin' to shave," said Tom. "It must feel funny."

"Put that razor down!" said Sarah, approaching.

Tom brandished the razor playfully, in a manner that considerably startled the chamber-maid, who stopped short in alarm.

"I'll go and tell the missis how you cut up," said she, going to the door.

This was unnecessary, however, for at this moment Mrs. Merton, desirous of learning how Tom was getting along, opened the door. She started back in dismay at the spectacle which greeted her view, and, in a tone unusually decided for so mild a woman, said, "Jenny, put down that razor instantly, and wipe the soap from your cheeks. Not so," she added hastily, seeing that Tom was about to wipe it off upon her skirt. "Here, take the towel. Now, what do you mean by such conduct?"

"Wouldn't *he* like it?" asked Tom, somewhat abashed.

"Do you mean my brother?"

"Yes, the sailor man."

"No, he would be very angry."

"Then I won't do so again;" and Tom seemed quite decided in her repentance.

"What possessed you to touch those things, Jenny?"

"That isn't all she did, mum," said Sarah. "She threw the pillow at me, and almost druv the comb into my head. She's the craziest creetur' I ever sot eyes on."

"Did you do that?" asked Mrs. Merton.

"Yes," said Tom. "I told her she might pitch it at me. It's bully fun."

"I can't allow such goings-on," said Mrs. Merton. "If you do so again, I must send you back to your grandmother."

"You don't know where she lives," said Tom.

"At any rate I won't keep you here."

Tom thought of the three square meals which she would receive daily, and decided to remain. . . .

CHAPTER XII

THE VANQUISHED BULLY

NOTWITHSTANDING Tom's mistake, she was still intrusted [sic] with the duty of answering the bell. At length, to her satisfaction, she opened the door to her friend of the morning.

He looked at her in surprise.

"What, is this Tom?" he asked.

"Yes," she said, enjoying his surprise. "Didn't you know me?"

"Hardly. Why, you look like a young lady!"

"Do I?" said Tom, hardly knowing whether or not to feel pleased at the compliment, for she fancied she should prefer to be a boy.

"Yes, you are much improved. And how have you been getting on this morning?"

"I've been cutting up," said Tom, shaking her head.

"Not bad I hope."

"I'll tell you what I did;" and Tom, in her own way gave an account of the events related in the previous chapter.

The captain laughed heartily.

"You ain't mad?" questioned Tom.

"Did you think I would be?"

"She said so," said Tom.

"Who is she?"

"Your sister."

The captain recovered his gravity. He saw that his merriment might encourage Tom in her pranks, and so increase the difficulties his sister was likely to find with her.

"No, I am not angry," he said, "but I want you very much to improve. You will have a good home here, and I want you to do as well as you can, so that when I get home from my voyage I may find you very much improved. Do you think I shall?"

Tom listened attentively.

"What do you want me to do?" she asked.

"To learn, as fast as you can, both about work and study. I shall leave directions to have you sent to school. Will you like that?"

"I don't know," said Tom. "I'm afraid I'll be bad, and get licked."

"Then try not to be bad. But you want to know something when you grow up,—don't you?"

"Yes."

"Then you will have to go to school and study. Can you read?"

"Not enough to hurt me," said Tom.

"Then, if you find yourself behind the rest, you must work all the harder. Will you promise me to do it?"

Tom nodded.

"And will you try to behave well?"

"Yes," said Tom. "I'll do it for you. I wouldn't do it for granny."

"Then do it for me."

Here Mrs. Merton appeared on the scene, and Tom was directed to go downstairs to assist the cook.

"Well, what do you think of her, Martha?"

"She's a regular trial. I'll tell you what she did this morning."

"I know all."

"Did she tell you?" asked his sister, in surprise.

"Yes, she voluntarily told me that she had been 'cutting up;' and, on my questioning her, confessed how. However, it was partly the result of ignorance."

"I wish I hadn't undertaken the charge of her."

"Don't be discouraged, Martha. There's some good in her, and she's as smart as a steel trap. She's promised me to turn over a new leaf, and do as well as she can."

"Do you rely upon that?"

"I do. She's got will and resolution, and I believe she means what she says."

"I hope it'll prove so," said Mrs. Merton, doubtfully.

"I find she knows very little. I should like to have her sent to school as soon as possible. She can assist you when at home, and I will take care that you lose nothing by it."

To this Mrs. Merton was brought to agree, but could not help expressing her surprise at the interest which her brother took in that child. She was a good woman, but it was not strange if the thought should come to her that she had two daughters of her own, having a better claim upon their uncle's money than this wild girl whom he had picked up in the streets. But Captain Barnes showed that he had not forgotten his nieces, as two handsome dress-patterns, sent in from Stewart's during the afternoon, sufficiently evinced.

Tom had not yet met Mrs. Merton's daughters, both being absent at school. They returned home about three o'clock. Mary, a girl of about Tom's age, had rather pretty, but insipid, features, and was vain of what she regarded as her beauty. Fanny, who was eight, was more attractive.

"Children, can't you speak to your uncle?" said Mrs. Merton; for the captain declared himself tired, and did not go out after lunch.

"How do you do, uncle?" said Mary, advancing and offering her hand.

"Why, Mary, you have become quite a young lady," said her uncle.

Mary simpered and looked pleased.

"And Fanny too. Martha, where is that doll I brought for her?"

The doll was handed to the delighted child.

"I suppose you are too old for dolls, Mary," said the captain to his eldest niece.

"I should think so, Uncle Albert," answered Mary, bridling.

"Then it's lucky I didn't bring you one. But I've brought you a playmate."

Mary looked surprised.

Tom was passing through the hall at the moment, and her guardian called her.

"Come in, Tom."

Mary Merton stared at the new-comer, and her quick eyes detected that the dress in which she appeared was one of her own.

"Why, she's got on my dress," she said.

"She is about your size, Mary, so I gave her your dress."

"Didn't she have any clothes of her own?"

"Were you unwilling to let her have that dress?" asked her uncle.

Mary pouted, and Captain Barnes said, "Martha, I will put money in your hands to supply Jenny with a suitable wardrobe. I had intended to give Mary new articles for all which had been appropriated to Tom's use; but I have changed my mind."

"She can have them," said Mary, regretting her selfishness, from an equally selfish motive.

"I won't trouble you," said her uncle, rather coldly.

Tom had listened attentively to this conversation, turning her bright eyes from one to the other.

"Come here, Tom, and shake hands with these two little girls."

"I'll shake hands with her," said Tom, indicating Fanny.

"And won't you shake hands with Mary?"

"I don't want to."

"Why not?"

"I don't like her."

"Shake hands with her, for my sake."

Tom instantly extended her hand, but now it was Mary who held back. Her mother would have forced her to give her hand, but Captain Barnes said, "It don't matter. Leave them to become friends in their own time."

Two days afterwards the captain sailed. Tom renewed her promise to be a good girl, and he went away hopeful that she would keep it.

"I shall have somebody to come home to, Jenny," he said. "Will you be glad to see me, back?"

"Yes, I will," she said; and there was a heartiness in her tone which showed that she meant what she said.

The next day Tom went to school. She was provided with two or three books such as she would need, and accompanied Fanny; for, though several years older, she was not as proficient as the latter.

In the next street there was a boy, whose pleasure it was to bully children smaller than himself. He had more than once annoyed Fanny, and when the latter saw him a little in advance, she said, nervously, "Let us cross the street, Jenny."

"Why?" asked Tom.

"There's George Griffiths just ahead."

"What if he is?"

"He's an awful bad boy. Sometimes he pulls away my books, and runs away with them. He likes to plague us."

"He'd better not try it," said Tom.

"What would you do?" asked Fanny, in surprise.

"You'll see. I won't cross the street. I'm goin' right ahead."

Fanny caught her companion's arm, and advanced, trembling, hoping that George Griffiths might not see them. But he had already espied them, and, feeling in a bullying mood, winked to a companion and said, "You'll see how I'll frighten these girls."

He advanced to meet them, and took off his hat with mock politeness.

"How do you do this morning, young ladies?" he said.

"Go away, you bad boy!" said little Fanny, in a flutter.

"I'll pay you for that," he said, and tried to snatch one of her books, but was considerably startled at receiving a blow on the side of the head from her companion.

"Just let her alone," said Tom.

"What have you got to say about it?" he demanded insolently.

"You'll see."

Hereupon he turned his attention to Tom, and tried to snatch her books, but was rather astounded when his intended victim struck him a sounding blow in the face with her fist.

"Take my books, Fanny," she said, and, dropping them on the sidewalk, squared off scientifically.

"Come on, if you want to!" said Tom, her eyes sparkling with excitement at the prospect of a fight.

"I don't want to fight with a girl," he said, considerably astonished at vigorous resistance where he had expected timid submission.

"You're afraid!" said Tom, triumphantly.

"No, I'm not," said George, backing out all the while; "I don't want to hurt you."

"You can't do it," said Tom; "I can lick you any day."

"How could you do it?" asked Fanny, as the dreaded bully slunk away. "How brave you are, Jenny! I'm awful afraid of him."

"You needn't be," said Tom, taking her books. "I've licked boys bigger'n him. I can lick him, and he knows it."

She was right. The story got about, and George Griffiths was so laughed at, for being vanquished by a girl, that he was very careful in future whom he attempted to bully.

CHAPTER XIII

GRANNY IS COMPELLED TO EARN HER OWN LIVING

LEAVING Tom in her new home, we return to Mrs. Walsh, which was the proper designation of the old woman whom she called granny. Though Tom had escaped from her clutches, granny had no idea that she intended to stay away permanently. She did not consider that all the advantages of the connection between them had been on her side, and that Tom had only had the privilege of supporting them both. If she had not carried matters so far our heroine would have been satisfied to remain; but now she had fairly broken away, and would never come back unless brought by force.

When six o'clock came granny began to wonder why Tom did not come back. She usually returned earlier, with whatever money she had managed to obtain.

"She's afraid of a lickin'," thought granny. "She'll get a wuss one if she stays away."

An hour passed, and granny became hungry; but unfortunately she was penniless, and had nothing in the room except a crust of hard bread which she intended for Tom's supper. Hunger compelled her to eat this herself, though it was not much to her taste. Every moment's additional delay irritated her the more with the rebellious Tom.

"I wish I had her here," soliloquized granny, spitefully.

When it was half-past seven granny resolved to go out and hunt her up. She might be on the sidewalk outside playing. Perhaps—but this was too daring for belief—she might be spending her afternoon's earnings on another square meal.

Granny went downstairs, and through the archway into the street. There were plenty of children, living in neighboring tenement houses, gathered in groups or playing about, but no Tom was visible.

"Have you seen anything of my gal, Micky Murphy?" asked granny of a boy whom she had often seen with Tom.

"No," said Micky. "I haven't seen her."

"Haven't any of you seen her?" demanded Mrs. Walsh, making the question a general one.

"I seen her sellin' papers," said one boy.

"When was that?" asked granny, eagerly.

"'Bout four o'clock."

"Where was she?"

"Greenwich Street."

This was a clue at least, but a faint one. Tom had been seen at four o'clock, and now it was nearly eight. Long before this she must have sold her papers, and the unpleasant conviction dawned upon granny that she must have spent her earnings upon herself.

"If I could only get hold of her!" muttered granny, vengefully.

She went as far as the City Hall, and followed along down by the Park fence, looking about her in all directions, in the hope that she might espy Tom. But the latter was at this time engaging lodgings for the night, as we know, and in no danger of being caught.

Unwilling to give up the pursuit, Mrs. Walsh wandered about for an hour or more, occasionally resting on one of the seats in the City Hall Park, till the unwonted exertion began to weary her, and she realized that she was not likely to encounter Tom.

There was one chance left. Tom might have got home while she had been in search of her. Spurred by this hope, Mrs. Walsh hurried home, and mounted to her lofty room. But it was as desolate as when she left it. It was quite clear that Tom did not mean to come back that night. This was provoking; but granny still was confident that she would return in the course of the next day. So she threw herself on the bed,—not without some silent imprecations upon her rebellious charge,—and slept till morning.

Morning brought her a new realization of her loss. She found her situation by no means an agreeable one. Her appetite was excellent, but she was without food or money to buy a supply. It was certainly provoking to think that she must look out for herself. However, granny was equal to the occasion. She did not propose to work for a living, but decided that she would throw herself upon charity. To begin with, she obtained some breakfast of a poor but charitable neighbor, and then started on a walk up town. It was not till she got as far as Fourteenth Street that she commenced her round of visits.

The first house at which she stopped was an English basement house. Granny rang the basement bell.

"Is your mistress at home?" she asked.

"Yes; what's wanted?"

"I'm a poor widder," whined granny, in a lugubrious voice, "with five small children. We haven't got a bit of food in the house. Can't you give me a few pennies?"

"I'll speak to the missis, but I don't think she'll give any money."

She went upstairs, and soon returned.

"She won't give you any money, but here's a loaf of bread."

Mrs. Walsh would much have preferred a small sum of money, but muttered her thanks, and dropped the loaf into a bag she had brought with her.

She went on to the next block, and intercepted a gentleman just starting down town to his business.

"I'm a poor widder," she said, repeating her whine; "will you give me a few pennies? and may the Lord bless you!"

"Why don't you work?" asked the gentleman, brusquely.

"I'm too old and feeble," she answered, bending over to assume the appearance of infirmity. This did not escape the attention of the gentleman, who answered unceremoniously, "You're a humbug! You won't get anything from me! If I had my way, I'd have you arrested and locked up."

Granny trembled with passion, but did not think it politic to give vent to her fury.

Her next application was more successful, twenty-five cents being sent to the door by a compassionate lady, who never doubted the story of the five little children suffering at home for want of food.

Granny's eyes sparkled with joy as she hastily clutched the money. With it she could buy drink and tobacco, while food was not an object of barter.

"The missis wants to know where you live," said the servant.

Mrs. Walsh gave a wrong address, not caring to receive charitable callers, who would inevitably find out that her story was a false one, and her children mythical.

At the next house she got no money; but, on declaring that she had eaten nothing for twenty-four hours, was invited into the kitchen, where she was offered a chair, and a plate of meat and bread was placed before her. This invitation was rather an embarrassing one; for, thanks to her charitable neighbor, granny had eaten quite a hearty breakfast not long before. But, having declared that she had not tasted food for twenty-four hours, she was compelled to keep up appearances, and eat what was set before her. It was very hard work, and attracted the attention of the servants, who had supposed her half famished.

"You don't seem very hungry," said Annie, the cook.

"It's because I'm faint-like," muttered granny. At this moment her bag, containing the loaf of bread, tumbled on the floor.

"What's that?" asked the cook, suspiciously.

"It's some bread I'm goin' to carry home to the childers," said Mrs. Walsh, a little confused. "They was crying for something to ate when I come away."

"Then you'd better take it home as soon as you can," said Annie, surveying the old woman with some suspicion.

Granny was forced to leave something on her plate, nature refusing the double burden she sought to impose upon it, and went out with an uncomfortable sense of fulness. Resuming her rounds, she was repulsed at some places, at others referred to this or that charitable society, but in the end succeeded in raising twenty-five cents more in money. Fifty cents, a loaf of bread, and a little cold meat represented her gains of the morning, and with these she felt tolerably well satisfied. She had been compelled to walk up town, but now she had money and could afford to ride. She entered a Sixth Avenue car, therefore, and in half an hour or thereabouts reached the Astor House. She walked through the Park, looking about her carefully, in the hope of seeing Tom, who would certainly have fared badly if she had fallen into the clutches of the angry old woman. But Tom was nowhere visible.

So granny plodded home, and, mounting to her room, laid away the bread and meat, and, throwing herself upon the bed, indulged in a pipe. Tom was not at home, and granny began to have apprehensions that she meant to stay away longer than she had at first supposed.

"But I'll come across her some day," said granny, vindictively. "When I do I'll break every bone in her body."

The old woman lay on the bed two or three hours, and then went out, with the double purpose of investing a part of her funds in a glass of something strong, and in the hope that she might fall in with Tom. Notwithstanding the desire of vengeance, she missed her. She had not the slightest affection for the young girl who had been so long her charge, but she was used to her companionship. It seemed lonely without her. Besides, granny had one of those uncomfortable dispositions that feel lost without some one to scold and tyrannize over, and, although Tom had not been so yielding and submissive as many girls would have been under the same circumstances, Mrs. Walsh had had the satisfaction of beating her occasionally, and naturally longed for the presence of her customary victim.

So, after making the purchase she intended, granny made another visit to the Park and Printing House Square, and inspected eagerly the crowds of street children who haunt those localities as paper-venders, peddlers, and boot-blacks. But Tom, as we know, was by this time an inmate of Mrs. Merton's boarding-house,—the home found for her by her friend, the sea-captain. This was quite out of Mrs. Walsh's beat. She had not anticipated any such contingency, but supposed that Tom would be forced to earn her living by some of those street trades by means of which so many children are kept from starvation. It did not enter her calculations that, so soon after parting from her, Tom had also ceased to be a street Arab, and obtained a respectable home. Of course, therefore, disappointment was again her portion, and she was forced to return home and go to bed without the exquisite satisfaction of "breaking every bone in Tom's body."

Granny felt that she was ill-used, and that Tom was a monster of ingratitude; but on that subject there may, perhaps, be a difference of opinion.

CHAPTER XIV

TOM IS CAPTURED BY THE ENEMY

WE pass over two months, in which nothing of striking interest occurred to our heroine, or her affectionate relative, who continued to mourn her loss with more of anger than of sorrow. My readers may be interested to know how far Tom has improved in this interval. I am glad to say that she has considerably changed for the better, and is rather less of an Arab than when she entered the house. Still Mrs. Merton, on more than one occasion, had assured her intimate friend and gossip, Miss Betsy Perkins, that Tom was "a great trial," and nothing but her promise to her brother induced her to keep her.

Tom was, however, very quick and smart. She learned with great rapidity, when she chose, and was able to be of considerable service in the house before and after school. To be sure she was always getting into hot water, and from time to time indulged in impish freaks, which betrayed her street-training. At school, however, she learned very rapidly, and had already been promoted into a class higher than that which she entered. If there was one thing that Tom was ashamed of, it was to find herself the largest and oldest girl in her class. She was ambitious to stand as well as other girls of her own age, and, with this object in view, studied with characteristic energy, and as a consequence improved rapidly.

She did not get along very well with Mary Merton. Mary was languid and affected, and looked down scornfully upon her mother's hired girl, as she called her; though, as we know, money was paid for Tom's board. Tom did not care much for her taunts, being able to give as good as she sent; but there was one subject on which Mary had it in her power to annoy her. This was about her defective education.

"You don't know any more than a girl of eight," said Mary, contemptuously.

"I haven't been to school all my life as you have," said Tom.

"I know that," said Mary. "You were nothing but a beggar, or rag-picker, or something of that kind. I don't see what made my uncle take you out of the street. That was the best place for you."

"I wish you had to live with granny for a month," retorted Tom. "It would do you good to get a lick now and then."

"Your grandmother must have been a very low person," said Mary, disdainfully.

"That's where you're right," said Tom, whose affection for granny was not very great.

"I'm glad I haven't such a grandmother. I should be ashamed of it."

"She wasn't my grandmother. She only called herself so," said Tom.

"I've no doubt she was," said Mary, "and that you are just like her."

"Say that again, and I'll punch your head," said Tom, belligerently.

As Mary knew that Tom was quite capable of doing what she threatened, she prudently desisted, but instead taunted her once more with her ignorance.

"Never mind," said Tom, "wait a while and I'll catch up with you."

Mary laughed a spiteful little laugh.

"Hear her talk!" she said. "Why, I've been ever so far in English; besides, I am studying French."

"Can't I study French too?"

"That would be a great joke for a common street girl to study French! You'll be playing the piano next."

"Why not?" asked Tom, undauntedly.

"Maybe your granny, as you call her, had a piano."

"Perhaps she did," said Tom; "but it was to the blacksmith's to be mended, so I never saw it."

Tom was not in the least sensitive on the subject of granny, and however severe reflections might be indulged in upon granny's character and position, she bore them with equanimity, not feeling any particular interest in the old woman.

Still she did occasionally feel a degree of curiosity as to how granny was getting along in her absence. She enjoyed the thought that Mrs. Walsh, no longer being able to rely upon her, would be compelled to forage for herself.

"I wonder what she'll do," thought Tom. "She's such a lazy old woman that I think she'll go round beggin'. Work don't agree with her constitution."

It so happened that granny, though in her new vocation [that of begging] she made frequent excursions up town, had never fallen in with Tom. This was partly because Tom spent the hours from nine to two in school, and it was at this time that granny always went on her rounds. But one Saturday forenoon Tom was sent on an errand some half a mile distant. As she was passing through Eighteenth Street her attention was drawn to a tall, ill-dressed figure a few feet in advance of her. Though only her back was visible, Tom remembered something peculiar in granny's walk.

"That's granny," soliloquized Tom, in excitement; "she's out beggin', I'll bet a hat."

The old woman carried a basket in one hand, for the reception of cold victuals, for, though she preferred money, provisions were also acceptable, and she had learned from experience that there were some who refrained from giving money on principle, but would not refuse food.

Tom was not anxious to fall into the old woman's clutches. Still she felt like following her up, and hearing what she had to say.

She had not long to wait.

Granny turned into the area of an English basement house, and rang the basement bell.

Tom paused, and leaned her back against the railing, in such a position that she could hear what passed.

A servant answered the bell.

"What do you want?" she asked, not very ceremoniously.

"I'm a poor widder," whined granny, "with five small children. They haven't had anything to eat since yesterday. Can't you give me something? and may the Lord bless you!"

"She knows how to lie," thought Tom. "So she's got five small children?"

"You're pretty old to have five small children," said the servant, suspiciously.

"I ain't so old as I look," said Mrs. Walsh. "It's bein' poor and destitoot that makes me look old before my time."

"Where's your husband?"

"He's dead," said granny. "He treated me bad; he used to drink, and then bate me and the children."

"You look as if you drank, yourself."

"I'd scorn the action," said granny, virtuously. "I never could bear whiskey."

"Ain't she doin' it up brown?" thought Tom. "Haven't I seen her pourin' it down though?"

"Give me your basket," said the servant.

"Can't you give me some money," whined granny, "to help pay the rint?"

"We never give money," said the servant.

She went into the kitchen, and shortly returned with some cold meat and bread. Granny opened it to see what it contained.

"Haven't you got any cold chicken?" she asked, rather dissatisfied.

"She's got cheek," thought Tom.

"If you're not satisfied with what you've got, you needn't come again."

"Yes," said granny, "I'm satisfied; but my little girl is sick, and can't bear anything but chicken, or maybe turkey."

"Then you must ask for it somewhere else" said the servant. "We haven't got any for you here."

Having obtained all she was likely to get, granny prepared to go.

Tom felt that she, too, must start, for there might be danger of identification. To be sure she was now well-dressed,—quite as well as the average of girls of her age. The cap and jacket, indeed all that had made her old name of "Tattered Tom" appropriate, had disappeared, and she was very different in appearance from the young Arab whom we became acquainted with in the first chapter. In other respects, as we know, Tom had not altered quite so much. There was considerable of the Arab about her still, though there was a prospect of her eventually becoming entirely tamed.

Granny just glanced at the young girl, whose back only was visible to her, but never thought of identifying her with her lost grand-daughter. Sometimes, however, she had obtained money from compassionate school-girls, and it struck her that there might be a chance in this quarter.

She advanced, and tapped Tom on the shoulder.

"Little gal," she dolefully said, "I'm a poor widder with five small children. Can't you give me a few pennies? and may the Lord reward you!"

Tom was a little startled, but quite amused by this application from granny. She knew there was danger in answering; but there was a fascination about danger, and she thought that, even if identified, she could make her escape.

"Where do you live?" she asked, trying to disguise her voice, and looking down.

"No. 417 Bleecker Street," said granny, at random, intentionally giving the wrong address.

"I'll get my aunt to come round to-morrow and see you," said Tom.

"Give me a few pennies now," persisted granny, "to buy some bread for my children."

"How many have you got?"

"Five."

It was very imprudent, but Tom obeyed an irresistible impulse, and said, "Isn't one of them named Tom?" and she looked up in her old way.

Granny bent over eagerly, and looked in her face. She had noticed something familiar in the voice, but the dress had prevented her from suspecting anything. Now it flashed upon her that the rebellious Tom was in her clutches.

"So it's you, is it?" she said, with grim delight, clutching Tom by the arm. "I've found you at last, you trollop! Come along with me! I'll break every bone in your body!"

Tom saw that she had incautiously incurred a great peril; but she had no idea of being dragged away unresisting. She was quick-witted, and saw that, if she chose to deny all knowledge of the old woman, granny would find it hard to substantiate her claims.

"Stop that, old woman!" she said, without the least appearance of fear. "If you don't let go, I'll have you arrested!"

"You will, will you?" exclaimed granny, giving her a shake viciously. "We'll see about that. Where'd you get all them good clothes from? Come along home."

"Let me alone!" said Tom. "You've got nothing to do with me."

"Got nothing to do with you? Ain't I your granny?"

"You must be crazy," said Tom, coolly. "My grandmother don't go round the streets, begging for cold victuals."

"Do you mean to say I'm not your granny?" demanded the old woman, astounded.

"I don't know what you mean," said Tom, coolly. "You'd better go home to your five small children in Bleecker Street."

"O you trollop!" muttered granny, giving her a violent shaking; which reminded Tom of old times in not the most agreeable manner.

"Come, old woman, that's played out!" said Tom. "You'd better stop that."

"You're my gal, and I've a right to lick you," said Mrs. Walsh.

"I've got nothing to do with you."

"Come along!" said granny, attempting to drag Tom with her.

But Tom made a vigorous resistance, and granny began to fear that she had undertaken rather a hard task. The distance from Eighteenth Street to the tenement house which she called home was two miles, probably, and it would not be very easy to drag Tom that distance against her will. A ride in the horse-cars was impracticable, since she had no money with her.

The struggle was still going on, when Tom all at once espied a policeman coming around the corner. She did not hesitate to take advantage of his opportune appearance.

"Help! Police!" exclaimed Tom, in a loud voice.

This sudden appeal startled granny, whose associations with the police were not of the most agreeable nature, and she nearly released her hold. She glared at Tom in speechless rage, foreseeing that trouble was coming.

"What's the matter?" asked the officer, coming up, and regarding the two attentively.

"I think this woman must be crazy," said Tom. "She came up and asked me for a few pennies, and then grabbed me by the arm, saying she was my granny. She is trying to drag me home with her."

"What have you to say to this?" demanded the policeman.

"She's my gal," said granny, doggedly.

"You hear her," said Tom. "Do I look as if I belonged to her? She's a common beggar."

"O you ungrateful trollop!" shrieked granny, tightening her grip.

"She hurts me," said Tom. "Won't you make her let go?"

"Let her go!" said the policeman, authoritatively.

"But she's my gal."

"Let go, I tell you!" and granny was forced to obey. "Now where do you live?"

"340 Bleecker Street."

"You said it was 417 just now," said Tom, "and that you had five small children. Was I one of them?"

Granny was cornered. She was afraid that Bleecker Street might be visited, and her imposture discovered. It was hard to give up Tom, and so have the girl whom she now hated intensely, triumph over her. She would make one more attempt.

"She's my gal. She run away from me two months ago."

"If you've got five small children at home, and have to beg for a living," said the officer, who did not believe a word of her story, "you have all you can take care of. She's better off where she is."

"Can't I take her home, then?" asked granny, angrily.

"You had better go away quietly," said the policeman, "or I must take you to the station-house."

Mrs. Walsh, compelled to abandon her designs upon Tom, moved off slowly. She had got but a few steps, when Tom called out to her, "Give my love to your five small children, granny!"

The old woman, by way of reply, turned and shook her fist menacingly at Tom, but the latter only laughed and went on her way.

"Ain't she mad, though!" soliloquized Tom. "She'd lick me awful if she only got a chance. I'm glad I don't live with her. Now I get square meals every day. I'd like to see granny's five small children;" and Tom laughed heartily at what she thought a smart imposture. That Tom should be very conscientious on the subject of truth could hardly be expected. A street education, and such guardianship as she had received from granny, were not likely to make her a model; but Tom is more favorably situated now, and we may hope for gradual improvement.

CHAPTER XV

GRANNY READS SOMETHING TO HER ADVANTAGE

AFTER her unsuccessful attempt to gain possession of Tom, granny returned home, not only angry but despondent. She had been deeply incensed at Tom's triumph over her. Besides, she was tired of earning her own living, if begging from door to door can properly be called earning one's living. At any rate it required exertion, and to this Mrs. Walsh was naturally indisposed. She sighed as she thought of the years when she could stay quietly at home, and send out Tom to beg or earn money for her. She would like, since Tom was not likely to return, to adopt some boy or girl of suitable age, upon whom she could throw the burden of the common support. But such were not easy to be

met with, and Mrs. Walsh was dimly aware that no sane child would voluntarily select her as a guardian.

So granny, in rather low spirits, sought her elevated room, and threw herself upon the bed to sleep off her fatigue.

On awaking, granny seated herself at the window, and picked up mechanically the advertising sheet of the "Herald," in which a loaf of bread had been
wrapped that had been given to her the day previous. It was seldom that Mrs.
Walsh indulged in reading, not possessing very marked literary tastes; but to-
day she was seized with an idle impulse, which she obeyed, without antici-
pating that she would see anything that concerned her.

In glancing through the advertisements under the head "PERSONAL," her
attention was drawn to the following:—

"If Margaret Walsh, who left Philadelphia in the year 1855, will call at
No. - Wall Street, Room 8, she will hear of something to her advantage."

"Why, that's me!" exclaimed granny, letting the paper fall from her lap in
surprise. "It's my name, and I left Philadelphy that year. I wonder what it's
about. Maybe it's about Tom."

There were circumstances which led Mrs. Walsh to think it by no means
improbable that the inquiries to be made were about Tom, and this made her
regret more keenly that she had lost her.

"If it is," she soliloquized, "I'll get hold of her somehow."

There was one part of the advertisement which particularly interested
granny,—that in which it was suggested that she would hear something to her
advantage. If there was any money to be made, granny was entirely willing to
make it. Considering the unpromising state of her prospects, she felt that it
was a piece of extraordinary good luck.

Looking at the date of the paper, she found that it was a fortnight old, and
was troubled by the thought that it might be too late. At any rate no time was
to be lost. So, in spite of the fatigue of her morning expedition, she put on her
old cloak and bonnet, and, descending the stairs, sallied out into the street.
She made her way down Nassau Street to Wall, and, carefully looking about
her, found without difficulty the number mentioned in the advertisement. It
was a large building, containing a considerable number of offices. No. 8 was
on the third floor. On the door was a tin sign bearing the name:—

"EUGENE SELDEN,
Attorney and Counsellor."

Mrs. Walsh knocked at the door; but there was no response. She knocked
again, after a while, and then tried the door. But it was locked.

"The office closes at three, ma'am," said a young man, passing by. "You
will have to wait till to-morrow."

Mrs. Walsh was disappointed, being very anxious to ascertain what advantage she was likely to receive. She presented herself the next morning at nine,
only to find herself too early. At last she found the lawyer in. He looked up
from his desk as she entered.

"Have you business with me?" he asked.

"Are you the man that advertised for Margaret Walsh?" asked granny.

"Yes," said Mr. Selden, laying down his pen, and regarding her with interest. "Are you she?"

"Yes, your honor," said granny, thinking her extra politeness might
increase the advantage promised.

"Did you ever live in Philadelphia?"

"Yes, your honor."

"Were you in service?"

Mrs. Walsh answered in the affirmative.

"In what family?"

"In the family of Mrs. Lindsay."

"What made you leave her?" asked the lawyer, fixing his eyes searchingly upon Margaret.

Granny looked a little uneasy.

"I got tired of staying there," she said.

"When you left Philadelphia, did you come to New York?"

"Yes, your honor."

"Did you know that Mrs. Lindsay's only child disappeared at the time you left the house?" inquired the lawyer.

"If I tell the truth will it harm me?" asked granny, uneasily.

"No; but if you conceal the truth it may."

"Then I took the child with me."

"What motive had you for doing this wicked thing? Do you know that Mrs. Lindsay nearly broke her heart at the loss of the child?"

"I was mad with her," said granny, "that's one reason."

"Then there was another reason?"

"Yes, your honor."

"What was it?"

"Young Mr. Lindsay hired me to do it. He offered me a thousand dollars."

"Are you ready to swear this?"

"Yes," said granny. "I hope you'll pay me handsome for tellin'," she added. "I'm a poor—woman," she was on the point of saying "widder with five small children;" but it occurred to her that this would injure her in the present instance.

"You shall receive a suitable reward when the child is restored. It is living, I suppose?"

"Yes," said granny.

"With you?"

"No, your honor. She ran away two months ago; but I saw her this morning."

"Why should she run away? Didn't you treat her well?"

"Like as if she was my own child," said granny. "I've often and often gone without anything to eat, so that Tom might have enough. I took great care of her, your honor, and would have brought her up as a leddy if I hadn't been so poor."

"I thought it was a girl."

"So it was, your honor."

"Then why do you call her Tom?"

"Cause she was more like a boy than a gal,—as sassy a child as I ever see."

"So you have lost her?"

"Yes, your honor. She ran away from me two months since."

"But you said you saw her yesterday. Why did you not take her back?"

"She wouldn't come. She told the policeman she didn't know me,—me that have took care of her since she was a little gal,—the ungrateful hussy!"

Granny's pathos, it will be perceived, terminated in anger.

The lawyer looked thoughtful.

"The child must be got back," he said. "It is only recently that her mother ascertained the treachery by which she was taken from her, and now she is most anxious to recover her. If you will bring her to me, you shall have a suitable reward."

"How much?" asked granny, with a cunning look.

"I cannot promise in advance, but it will certainly be two hundred dollars, —perhaps more. Mrs. Lindsay will be generous."

The old woman's eyes sparkled. Such a sum promised an unlimited amount of whiskey for a considerable time. The only disagreeable feature in the case was that Tom would benefit by the restoration, since she would obtain a comfortable home, and a parent whose ideas of the parental relation differed somewhat from those of Mrs. Walsh. Still, two hundred dollars were worth the winning, and granny determined to win them. She suggested, however, that, in order to secure the co-operation of the police, she needed to be more respectably dressed; otherwise her claim would be scouted, provided Tom undertook to deny it.

This appeared reasonable, and as the lawyer had authority to incur any expense that he might consider likely to further the successful prosecution of the search, he sent out some one, in whom he had confidence, to purchase a respectable outfit for Mrs. Walsh. He further agreed to allow her three dollars a week for the present, that she might be able to devote all her time to hunting up Tom. This arrangement was very satisfactory to Mrs. Walsh, who felt like a lady in easy circumstances. Her return to the tenement house, in her greatly improved dress, created quite a sensation. She did not deign to enlighten her neighbors upon the cause of her improved fortunes, but dropped hints that she had come into a legacy.

From this time Mrs. Walsh began to frequent the up-town streets, particularly Eighteenth Street, where she had before encountered Tom. But as she still continued to make her rounds in the morning, it was many days before she caught a glimpse of the object of her search. As her expenses were paid in the mean time, she waited patiently, though she anticipated with no little pleasure the moment which should place Tom in her power. She resolved, before restoring her to her mother, to inflict upon her late ward a suitable punishment for her rebellion and flight, for which granny was not likely ever to forgive her.

"I'll give her something to remember me by," muttered granny. "See if I don't!"

CHAPTER XVI

TOM IN TROUBLE

THE reader has already obtained some idea of the character of Mary Merton. She was weak, vain, affected, and fond of dress. There was not likely to be much love lost between her and Tom, who was in all respects her opposite. Whatever might have been the defects of her street education, it had at all events secured Tom from such faults as these.

Mary sought the society of such of her companions as were wealthy or fashionable, and was anxious to emulate them in dress. But unfortunately her mother's income was limited, and she could not gratify her tastes. She was continually teasing Mrs. Merton for this and that article of finery; but, though her mother spent more for her than she could well afford, she was obliged in many cases to disappoint her. So it happened that Mary was led into temptation.

One morning she was going downstairs on her way to school. The door of Mr. Holland's room (who occupied the second floor front) chanced to be open. It occurred to Mary that the large mirror in this room would enable her to survey her figure to advantage, and, being fond of looking in the glass, she entered.

After satisfactorily accomplishing the object of her visit, Mary, in glancing about, caught sight of a pocket-book on the bureau. Curiosity led her to approach and open it. It proved to contain four five-dollar bills and a small amount of change.

"I wish the money was mine," said Mary to herself.

There was a particular object for which she wanted it. Two of her companions had handsome gold pencils, which they wore suspended by a cord around their necks. Mary had teased her mother to buy her one, but Mrs. Merton had turned a deaf ear to her request. Finally she had given up asking, finding that it would be of no avail.

"If I only had this money, or half of it," thought Mary, "I could buy a pencil for myself, and tell mother it was given me by one of my friends."

The temptation, to a vain girl like Mary, was a strong one.

"Shall I take it?" she thought.

The dishonesty of the act did not so much deter her as the fear of detection. But the idea unluckily suggested itself that Tom would be far more likely to be suspected than she.

"Mr. Holland is rich," she said to herself; "he won't feel the loss."

She held the pocket-book irresolutely in her hand, uncertain whether to take a part of the contents or the whole. Finally she opened it, drew out the bills, amounting to twenty dollars, hastily thrust them into her pocket, and, replacing the pocket-book on the bureau, went downstairs.

She met her mother in the lower hall.

"I am afraid you will be late to school, Mary," she said.

"I couldn't find my shoes for a long time," said Mary, flushing a little at the thought of the money in her pocket.

Mr. Holland's room had already been attended to, and was not again entered until half-past five in the afternoon, when Mr. Holland, who was a clerk in a down-town office, returned home.

He had missed the pocket-book shortly after leaving the house in the morning, but, being expected at the office at a certain hour, had not been able to return for it. He had borrowed money of a fellow-clerk to pay for his lunch.

As he entered the room, he saw his pocket-book lying on the bureau.

"There it is, all safe," he said to himself, quite relieved; for, though in receipt of a handsome salary, no one would care to lose twenty dollars.

He was about to put the pocket-book into his pocket unexamined, when it occurred to him to open it, and make sure that the contents were untouched. He was startled on finding less than a dollar, where he distinctly remembered that there had been nearly twenty-one dollars.

"Some one has taken it," he said to himself. "I must see Mrs. Merton about this."

He did not get an opportunity of speaking to the landlady until after dinner, when he called her aside, and told her of his loss.

"Are you quite sure, Mr. Holland," she asked, considerably disturbed, "there were twenty dollars in the pocket-book?"

"Yes, Mrs. Merton. I remember distinctly having counted the money this morning, before laying it on the bureau. It must have been taken by some one in the house. Now, who was likely to enter the room? Which of your servants makes the bed?"

"It was Jenny," said Mrs. Merton, with a sudden conviction that Tom was the guilty party.

"What, that bright little girl that I have seen about the house?"

"Yes, Mr. Holland, I am afraid it is she," said Mrs. Merton, shaking her head. "She is not exactly a servant, but a child whom my brother took out of the streets, and induced me to take charge of while he is away. She has been very ill-trained, and I am not surprised to find her dishonest. More than once I have regretted taking charge of her."

"I am sorry," said Mr. Holland. "I have noticed that she is rather different from most girls. I wish I had not exposed her to the temptation."

"She must give up the money, or I won't keep her in the house," said Mrs. Merton, who had become indignant at Tom's ingratitude, as she considered it. "My brother can't expect me to harbor a thief in the house, even for his sake. It would ruin the reputation of my house if such a thing happened again."

"She will probably give it back when she finds herself detected," said Mr. Holland.

"I will tax her with it at once," said the landlady. "Stay here, Mr. Holland, and I will call her."

Tom was called in. She looked from one to the other, and something in the expression of each led her to see that she was to be blamed for something, though what she could not conceive.

"Jane," said Mrs. Merton, sternly, "my brother will be very much grieved when he learns how badly you have behaved to-day."

"What have I been doing?" asked Tom, looking up with a fearless glance, not by any means like a girl conscious of theft.

"You have taken twenty dollars belonging to Mr. Holland."

"Who says I did it?" demanded Tom.

"It is useless to deny it. You cleared up his room this morning. His pocket-book was on the bureau."

"I know it was," said Tom. "I saw it there."

"You opened it, and took out twenty dollars."

"No, I didn't," said Tom. "I didn't touch it."

"Do not add falsehood to theft. You must have done it. There was no one else likely to do it."

"Wasn't the door unlocked all day?" demanded Tom. "Why couldn't some one else go in and take it as well as I?"

"I feel sure it was you."

"Why?" asked Tom, her eyes beginning to flash indignantly.

"I have no doubt you have stolen before. My brother took you from the street. You were brought up by a bad old woman, as you say yourself. I ought not to be surprised at your yielding to temptation. If you will restore the money to Mr. Holland, and promise not to steal again, I will overlook your offence, and allow you to remain in the house, since it was my brother's wish."

"Mrs. Merton," said Tom, proudly, "I didn't take the money, and I can't give it back. I might have stolen when I lived with granny, for I didn't get enough to eat half the time, but I wouldn't do it now."

"That sounds well," said Mrs. Merton; "but somebody must have taken the money."

"I don't care who took it," said Tom, "I didn't."

"You are more likely to have taken it than anyone else."

"You may search me if you want to," said Tom, proudly.

"Perhaps she didn't take it," said Mr. Holland, upon whom Tom's fearless bearing had made an impression.

"I will inquire if any of the servants went into your room," said Mrs. Merton. "If not, I must conclude that Jane took it."

Inquiry was made, but it appeared evident that no servant had entered the room. Tom had made the bed and attended to the chamber-work alone. Mrs. Merton was therefore confirmed in her suspicions. She summoned Tom once more, and offered to forgive her if she would make confession and restitution.

"I didn't steal the money," said Tom, indignantly. "I've told you that before."

"Unless you give it up, I cannot consent to have you remain longer in my house."

"All right!" said Tom, defiantly. "I don't want to stay if that's what you think of me."

She turned and left Mrs. Merton. Five minutes later she was in the street, going she knew not whither. She was so angry at the unfounded suspicions which had been cast upon her, that she felt glad to go. But after a while she began to think of the sudden change in her fortunes. For three months she had possessed a comfortable home, been well fed and lodged, and had been rapidly making up the deficiencies in her education. She had really tried to soften the roughness and abruptness of her manners, and become a good girl, hoping to win the approbation of her good friend, the captain, when he should return from his voyage. Now it was all over. She had lost her home, and must again wander about with no home but the inhospitable street.

"It isn't my fault," thought Tom, with a sigh. "I couldn't give back the money when I didn't take it."

CHAPTER XVII

THE GOLD PENCIL

MRS. MERTON was taken by surprise when she found that Tom had actually gone. Her conviction remained unshaken that she had stolen Mr. Holland's money, and she considered that she had been forbearing in not causing her arrest.

"Your uncle cannot blame me," she said to Mary, "for sending her away. He cannot expect me to keep a thief in my house."

"To be sure not," said Mary, promptly. "I am glad she has gone. You couldn't expect much from a girl that was brought up in the streets."

"That is true. I don't see, for my part, what your uncle saw in her."

"Nor I. She's a rude, hateful thing."

"She denied taking the money."

"Of course," said Mary. "She wouldn't mind lying any more than stealing."

Mary felt very much relieved at the way things had turned out. After taking the money, she had become frightened lest in some way suspicion might be directed towards herself. As she had hoped, her fault had been laid to Tom, and now she felt comparatively safe. She had not yet dared to use the money, but thought she might venture to do so soon.

She went up to her bedroom, and, after locking the door, opened her trunk. The four five-dollar bills were carefully laid away in one corner, underneath a pile of clothes. Mary counted them over with an air of satisfaction. Her conscience did not trouble her much as long as the fear of detection was removed.

"Mr. Holland won't miss the money," she thought, "and everybody'll think Jane took it."

The thought of her own meanness in depriving Tom of a good home, and sending her out into the street without shelter or money, never suggested itself to the selfish girl. She felt glad to be rid of her, and did not trouble herself about any discomforts or privations that she might experience.

Three days later Mary felt that she might venture to buy the pencil which she had so long coveted. Tom's disappearance was accepted by all in the house as a confirmation of the charge of theft, and no one else was likely to be suspected. Not knowing how much the pencil was likely to cost, Mary took the entire twenty dollars with her. She stopped on her way from school at a jewelry store only a few blocks distant from her mother's house. She was unwise in not going farther away, since this increased the chances of her detection.

"Let me look at your gold pencils," she asked, with an air of importance.

The salesman produced a variety of pencils, varying in price.

Mary finally made choice of one that cost twelve dollars.

She paid over the money with much satisfaction, for the pencil was larger and handsomer than those belonging to her companions, which had excited her envy. She also bought a silk chain, to which she attached it, and then hung it round her neck.

Though Mary was not aware of it, her entrance into the jewelry store had been remarked by Mrs. Carver, a neighbor and acquaintance of her mother's. Mrs. Carver, like some others of her sex, was gifted with curiosity, and wondered considerably what errand had carried Mary into the jeweller's.

Bent upon finding out, she entered the store and approached the counter.

"What did that young girl buy?" she asked.

"You mean that one who just went out?"

"Yes."

"A gold pencil-case."

"Indeed," said Mrs. Carver, looking surprised. "How expensive a pencil did she buy?"

"She paid twelve dollars."

"Will you show me one like it?"

A pencil, precisely similar, was shown Mrs. Carver, the clerk supposing she wished to purchase. But she had obtained all the information she desired.

"I won't decide to-day," she said. "I will come in again."

"There's some mystery about this," said Mrs. Carver to herself. "I wonder where Mary got so much money; surely, her mother could not have given it to her. If she did, all I have to say is, that she is very extravagant for a woman that keeps boarders for a living."

Mrs. Carver was one of those women who feel a very strong interest in the business of others. The friends with whom she was most intimate were most likely to incur her criticism. In the present instance she was determined to fathom the mystery of the gold pencil.

Mary went home with her treasure. Of course she knew that its possession would excite surprise, and she had a story prepared to account for it. She felt a little nervous, but had little doubt that her account would be believed.

As she anticipated, the pencil at once attracted her mother's attention.

"Whose pencil is that, Mary?" she asked.

"Mine, mother."

"Yours? Where did you get it?" inquired her mother, in surprise.

"Sue Cameron gave it to me. She's my bosom friend, you know."

"Let me see it. It isn't gold—is it?"

"Yes, it's solid gold," said Mary, complacently.

"But I don't understand her giving you so expensive a present. It must have cost a good deal."

"So it did. Sue said it cost twelve dollars."

"Then how came she to give it to you?"

"Oh, her father's awful rich! Besides, Sue has had another pencil given to her, and she didn't want but one; so she gave me this."

"It looks as if it were new."

"Yes, she has had it only a short time."

"When did she give it to you?"

"This morning. She promised it to me a week ago," said Mary, in a matter-of-fact manner which quite deceived her mother.

"She has certainly been very kind to you. She must like you very much."

"Yes, she does. She likes me better than any of the other girls."

"Why don't you invite her to come and see you? You ought to be polite to her, since she is so kind."

This suggestion was by no means pleasing to Mary. In the first place Sue Cameron was by no means the intimate friend she represented, and in the next, if she called and Mrs. Merton referred to the gift, it would at once let the cat out of the bag, and Mary would be in trouble. Therefore she said, "I'll invite her, mother, but I don't think she'll come."

"Why not?"

"She lives away up on Fifth Avenue, and is not allowed to make visits without some one of the family. The Camerons are very rich, you know, and stuck up. Only Sue is not."

"You'd better invite her, however, Mary, since she is such a friend of yours."

"Yes, I will, only you must not be surprised if she does not come."

The next afternoon Mrs. Carver dropped in for a call. While she was talking with Mrs. Merton, Mary came into the room. Her gold pencil was ostentatiously displayed.

"How do you do, Mary?" said the visitor. "What a handsome pencil-case you have!"

"One of her school friends gave it to her," explained Mrs. Merton.

"Indeed!" returned Mrs. Carver, with an emphasis which bespoke surprise.

"Yes," continued Mrs. Merton, unconsciously. "It was a Miss Cameron, whose father lives on Fifth Avenue. Her father is very rich, and she is very fond of Mary."

"I should think she was—uncommonly," remarked Mrs. Carver.

"There's some secret here," she thought. "I must find it out."

"Mary, my dear," she said, aloud, "come here, and let me look at your pencil."

Mary advanced reluctantly. There was something in the visitor's tone that made her feel uncomfortable. It was evident that Mrs. Carver did not accept the account she had given as readily as her mother.

"It is a very handsome pencil," said Mrs. Carver, after examination. "You are certainly very lucky, Mary. My Grace is not so fortunate. So this Mrs. Cameron lives on Fifth Avenue?"

"Yes, ma'am."

"And her father sends her to a public school. That's rather singular,—isn't it?"

"So it is," said Mrs. Merton. "I didn't think of that. And the family is very proud too, you say, Mary?"

Mary by this time was quite willing to leave the subject, but Mrs. Carver was not disposed to do so.

"I don't know why it is," said Mary. "I suppose they think she will learn more at public schools."

"Now I think of it," said Mrs. Carver, meditatively, "this pencil looks very much like one I saw at Bennett's the other day."

The color rushed to Mary's face in alarm. Her mother did not observe it, but Mrs. Carver did. But she quickly recovered herself.

"Perhaps it was bought there,—I don't know," she said.

"She carries it off well," thought Mrs. Carver. "Never mind, I'll find out some time."

Mary made some excuse for leaving the room, and the visitor asked:—

"How is that girl getting along whom your brother left with you?"

Mrs. Merton shook her head.

"She's turned out badly," she said.

"What has she done?"

"She stole twenty dollars from Mr. Holland's room. He left his pocket-book on the bureau, and she took out the money."

"Did she confess it?"

"No, she stoutly denied it. I told her, if she would confess, I would forgive her, and let her stay in the house. But she remained obstinate, and went away."

"Are you convinced that she took it?" asked Mrs. Carver, who now suspected where the gold pencil came from.

"It could have been no one else. She was in the room, making the beds, and sweeping, in the morning."

"Still, she may have been innocent."

"Then who could have taken the money?"

"Somebody that wanted a gold pencil," returned Mrs. Carver, nodding significantly.

"What!" exclaimed Mrs. Merton, aghast. "You don't mean to hint that Mary took it?"

"I mean this, that she bought the pencil herself at Bennett's, as I happen to know. Where she got the money from, you can tell better than I can."

"I can't believe it," said Mrs. Merton, very much perturbed.

"Didn't you see how she flushed up when I said I had seen a pencil like it at Bennett's? However, you can ask her."

Mrs. Merton could not rest now till she had ascertained the truth. Mary was called, and, after an attempt at denial, finally made confession in a flood of tears.

"How could you let me send Jane away on account of your fault?" asked her mother, much disturbed.

"I didn't dare to own it. You won't tell, mother?"

"I must return the money to Mr. Holland."

"You can tell him that it was accidentally found."

This Mrs. Merton finally agreed to do, not wishing to expose her own child. She was really a kindhearted woman, and was very sorry for her injustice to Tom.

"What will your uncle say?" she inquired, after Mrs. Carver had gone.

"Don't tell him," said Mary. "It's better for Jane to go, or he would be making her his heiress. Now I shall stand some chance. You can tell him that Jane went away of her own accord."

Mrs. Merton was human. She thought it only fair that one of her daughters should inherit their uncle's money in preference to a girl taken from the streets, and silently acquiesced. So the money was restored to Mr. Holland, and he was led to think that Tom had left it behind her, while the real perpetrator of the theft retained her gold pencil, and escaped exposure.

CHAPTER XVIII

IN SEARCH OF A PLACE

TOM went out into the street angry, and justly so, at the unfounded charge which had been made against her. The change in her circumstances had been so sudden, that she hardly realized, as she walked along, that she must return to her old street life. When she did realize it, it was with a feeling of disappointment, not unmixed with apprehension.

Tom had only been living at Mrs. Merton's for three months, but this short time had wrought a considerable change in her. She was no longer the wild, untamed girl who once swept the crossing. She had begun to feel the advantages of respectability, and had become ambitious of acquiring a good education. This feeling originated in the desire of surprising Captain Barnes with her improvement; but she soon began to feel an interest in learning for its own sake. She was still spirited and independent, but in a different way. Her old life looked far less attractive, since she had acquired such different tastes. Now to be suddenly thrust back into it seemed rather hard to Tom.

One thing at least could be said, she was no longer "Tattered Tom." Her old rags had been cast aside, and she was now dressed as well as most schoolgirls. She no longer looked like a child having no home but the street, but would be supposed by any who noticed her to belong to some family in good circumstances. Now, good clothes exert more influence upon the wearer than we may at first suppose. So it was with Tom. When she wore her old tatters she was quite ready to engage in a fight with any boy who jeered at her, provided he was not too large. Now she would hesitate before doing it, having an undefined idea that her respectable dress would make such a scene unbecoming.

There was one question that presented itself to Tom as she walked along, and demanded her earnest attention. This was, "How was she to live?"

She could no longer sweep the crossing; she was too well-dressed for that. Indeed she was likely to attract attention if she engaged in any of the street occupations to which she had in former times been accustomed. But something must be done. Her whole stock of money consisted of five cents, and this was not likely to last very long. It was far too little to buy such a meal as she got at Mrs. Merton's. It was doubtful, Tom reflected with a sigh, when she would get another square meal.

Suddenly the thought came to Tom, could she not hire out to do chamber-work? She had learned to do this at Mrs. Merton's. It would be a great deal better than sweeping the crossing, or selling papers.

Tom did not know how such situations were obtained, but it occurred to her that she could go from one house to another, and apply.

With this plan in her mind, she turned round, and walked up town again. When she reached Twenty-First Street she decided to try her luck. Accordingly she went up to the front door of a handsome house with a brown stone front, and rang the bell.

The door was opened by a servant, who waited respectfully for her to announce her errand, supposing her to be a school-mate of one of the children of the family. Her neat dress favored this mistake.

"Is the lady of the house at home?" inquired Tom.

"Who shall I say wishes to see her?" asked the servant, doubtfully.

"Does she want to hire a girl to do chamberwork?" continued Tom.

"Who wants the place?"

"I do," said Tom.

"Then she don't want any," said the girl, preparing to shut the door, with an entire change of manner. "Don't you know better than to come to the front door? There's the basement door below."

"One door's as good as another," said Tom, independently.

"Both are too good for you," said the servant, angry that under the influence of a mistake she had at first treated Tom with the respect due to a visitor.

"How much are you paid extra for your politeness?" asked Tom.

"Never you mind! You needn't call again."

Such was the result of Tom's first application. However, she was not discouraged. She reflected that there were a good many streets in the city, and a good many houses in each street. So she walked on, and rang the bell at the next house. She concluded to take the hint which had excited her indignation, and rang the basement bell.

"Do you want a girl to do chamber-work?" she asked.

Now it so happened that a chamber-maid was wanted here, and an order had been sent to an intelligence office for one. It was naturally supposed that Tom had come in answer to the application.

"Come in," said the servant. "I'll tell the missis that you are here."

She went upstairs, and shortly reappeared.

"You're to come up," she said.

Tom followed her upstairs, and took a seat in the hall.

Soon a lady came downstairs, with a languid step.

"Are you the girl that has applied to do chamberwork?" she said.

"Yes, ma'am," answered Tom.

"You seem very young. How old are you?"

"Twelve," answered Tom.

"Only twelve? I am surprised that so young a girl should have been sent to me. Have you any experience?"

"Yes, ma'am."

"Where have you lived?"

"At Mrs. Merton's, No. – Sixteenth Street."

"How long were you there?"

"Three months."

"Have you a recommendation from her?"

"No," answered Tom.

"Why did you leave?" asked the lady, suspiciously.

"Because she said I took some money, when I didn't," replied Tom, promptly.

A change came over the lady's face,—a change that betokened little encouragement to Tom.

"I shall not be able to take you," she said. "I wonder they should have sent you from the intelligence office."

"They didn't send me."

"You were not sent from the office? How did you know I wanted a chamber-maid?"

"I didn't know," said Tom. "I thought you might."

"If I had known that, I should have refused you at once. You can go downstairs, and the servants will let you out at the basement door,—down those stairs."

"All right," said Tom. "I can find the way; you needn't come with me."

This last remark led the lady to stare at Tom, uncertain whether she meant to be impudent or not. But Tom looked so unconscious of having said anything out of the way that she passed it over in silence.

Tom made two more applications, which proved equally unsuccessful. She began to think it would be more difficult to obtain a situation than she had supposed. At any rate, she resolved to defer further applications till the morrow. Something might turn up then, she reflected with something of her old philosophy.

CHAPTER XIX

THE OLD APPLE-WOMAN

WHEN Tom had got through her unsuccessful applications for a place, it was already nearly five o'clock. She started on her way down town. Her old street life had been spent in the neighborhood of the City Hall Park. The offices of the leading daily and weekly papers may be found within a radius of a furlong from it. It is within this limit that hundreds of homeless young Arabs swarm, and struggle for a precarious living. In returning to her old life, Tom was drawn, as by a magnet, to this centre.

She walked down Fourth Avenue, and afterwards down the Bowery. It was three months since she had been in this street, which had once been so familiar to her. As she drew near the scene of her old life, she began to see familiar faces. She passed boot-blacks and newsboys whom she had once known and still remembered; but none of them appeared to recognize her. This surprised Tom at first, until she remembered what a change there was in her dress. Neatly dressed, she looked very different from the Tom who had roamed the streets in rags and tatters. She seemed to have cut adrift from her former life and from the sympathies of her old companions. This was not a pleasant thought, since she must now go back to it. Poor Tom began to regret that she had experienced anything better, since it seemed doubtful whether she would ever again be satisfied with a street life.

She did not make herself known to any of her old acquaintances, but walked slowly along till she reached the City Hall Park. She entered the inclosure and sat down on a seat. By this time she felt hungry as well as tired. She therefore purchased, before sitting down, two apples for three cents, thus diminishing her cash capital to two. The apples were large, and satisfied her appetite tolerably well. Still it was not like the dinner she would have got at Mrs. Merton's.

Supper was provided, but it would soon be night, and she must lodge somewhere. Tom had more than once slept out, like hundreds of other street children, and not minded it; but now, after being accustomed to a good chamber and a comfortable bed, she did not feel like doing this. Besides, her clothes would be spoiled, and Tom wanted to look respectable as long as she could.

She might go back to granny, but had no disposition to do that. Whatever she might be called upon to suffer, she felt that she should be better off alone than in the power of the bad old woman who had so maltreated her.

"I wish I could earn a few pennies," said Tom to herself. "I might buy some papers if I only had money enough."

While she was thinking, a boot-black had been surveying her curiously. It was Mike Murphy, an old acquaintance of Tom's. He thought he recognized her face, but her dress puzzled him. Where could Tattered Tom have procured such a stunning outfit? That was the mystery, and it made him uncertain of her identity. However, the face looked so familiar that he determined to speak.

"Is that you, Tom?" he asked.

Tom looked up, and recognized Mike at once. It seemed good to speak to an old acquaintance.

"Yes, Mike, it's me," said Tom, whose grammar was not yet quite faultless.

"Where'd you get them clo'es? You ain't going to be married, be you?"

"Not that I know of," said Tom.

"Where've you been this long time? I haven't seen you round anywhere."

"I've been livin' up in Sixteenth Street," said Tom. "A sailor-man took me to his sister's, and got her to keep me."

"Did you like it?"

"Yes," said Tom. "I had three square meals every day. I went to school too."

"Did he buy you them clo'es?"

"Yes."

"Are you there now?"

"No, I left to-day."

"What for?"

"The old woman said I stole some money, and told me I must give it back or leave the house."

"How much did you steal?" asked Mike.

"Look here. Mike Murphy," said Tom, indignantly, "don't you say that again!"

"Didn't you take anything then?"

"Of course I didn't."

"What made her think so?"

"I don't know. Somebody took it, I s'pose, she thought it was me."

"So you had to leave?"

"Yes."

"What are you goin' to do now?"

"I don't know," said Tom. "I haven't got but two cents, and I don't know where to sleep."

"Where's the old woman you used to live with?"

"I shan't go back to her," said Tom, firmly. "I hate her."

"You've got some good clo'es," said Mike. "I didn't know you, at first. I thought you was a young lady."

"Did you?" asked Tom, rather pleased.

The time had been when she did not want to look like a young lady,—when she would have preferred to be a boy. But her tastes had changed considerably since then. Something of the instinct of her sex had sprung up in her, as she was brought to a closer knowledge of more refined ways of life. She was no longer a young Arab in her feelings, as before. Three months had wrought a great change in Tom.

"If you haven't any place to sleep, Tom," said Mike, "you can come along of me."

"Can I?" asked Tom. "What'll your mother say?"

"Oh, she won't mind. Only you'll maybe have to sleep on the floor."

"I don't mind," said Tom. "It'll be better than sleeping in the street. Where do you live?"

"In Mulberry Street."

"I guess I'll get something to do to-morrow," said Tom.

"What did you use to do?"

"Sweep the crossings sometimes. I won't do that again. It's too dirty."

"It would sp'ile them nice clo'es of yours."

"Yes," said Tom. "Besides, I wouldn't want Mrs. Merton, or Mary, to see me doin' that."

"Who's Mary?"

"It's her child."

"Did you like her?"

"No, I didn't. She hated me too."

"Well, I'm goin' home. Come along, Tom."

Tom got up from her seat with alacrity, and prepared to accompany Mike. It was a great burden off her mind to think she was likely to have a shelter for the night. Perhaps something would turn up for her the next day. This thought brought back some of her old courage and confidence.

Mike Murphy's home was neither elegant nor spacious. Mulberry Street is not an aristocratic locality, and its residents do not in general move in fashionable society. Mrs. Murphy was a retail merchant, being the proprietor of an apple-stand on Nassau, near Spruce Street. Several years' exposure to the weather had made her face nearly as red as the apples she dealt in, and a sedentary life had enlarged her proportions till she weighed close upon two hundred pounds. In nearly all weathers she was to be found at her post, sometimes sheltered by a huge cotton umbrella, whose original color had been changed by the sun to a pale brown. Though she had not yet been able to retire from trade upon a competence, she had earned enough, with Mike's assistance, to support a family of six children,—in Mulberry Street style, to be sure, but they had never been obliged to go to bed hungry, and the younger children had been kept at the public school.

When Mike entered, his mother was already at home. She usually closed up her business about five o'clock, and went home to get supper.

She looked up as Mike entered, and regarded his companion with some surprise.

"What young leddy have you got with you, Mike?" asked Mrs. Murphy.

"She thinks you are a young lady, Tom," said Mike, laughing.

"Don't you know me, Mrs. Murphy?" asked Tom, who had known Mike's mother for several years.

"By the powers, if it ain't Tom. Shure and you've had a rise in the world, I'm thinkin'. Why, you're dressed like a princess!"

"Maybe I am," said Tom; "but if I was one I'd be richer'n I am now."

"Tom was took up by a lady," explained Mike, "but she's sent her away, and she's got nothing barrin' her clo'es. I told her you'd let her sleep here to-night, mother."

"To be sure I will," said the kind-hearted woman. "It isn't much of a bed I can offer you, Tom, but it's better than sleepin' out."

"I can lie on the floor," said Tom. "I don't mind that."

"But why did the leddy turn you out?" inquired the apple-merchant.

Tom told her story, which Mrs. Murphy never thought of doubting.

"She's a hard, cruel woman. I'll say that for her, Tom dear," said Mrs. Murphy. "But never you mind. You're welcome to stay here, though its a poor place. We're going to have some supper directly, and you must take some with us."

"I've eaten supper," said Tom.

"What did you have?"

"Two apples."

"I don't say nothin' ag'in' apples, for it's them I live by, but tay and toast is better for supper. Biddy, toast the bread, and I'll set the table. When a body's tired, a cup of tay goes to the right spot, and you'll find it so, Tom dear."

The good-hearted woman bustled about, and set the table, while Biddy, a girl of ten, toasted a large number of slices of bread, for the young Murphys were all blessed with good appetites. The tea soon diffused a fragrant aroma about the little room. Mrs. Murphy, humble as were her means, indulged in one solitary extravagance. She always purchased the best quality of "tay," as she called it, no matter what might be the price.

"It's a dale chaper than whiskey," she used to say, in extenuation of her extravagance. "It's mate and drink to me both, and warms me up besides, when I've got chilled by rason of stayin' out all day."

There was a plate of cold meat placed on the table. This, with the tea and toast, constituted Mrs. Murphy's evening repast.

"You can sit by me, Tom dear," she said, her face beaming with hospitality. "It isn't much I've got, but you are heartily welcome to what there is. Children, set up to the table, all of you. Mike, see that Tom has enough to ate. There's one thing I can give you, and that's a cup of illigant tay, that a quane might not turn up her nose at."

In spite of the two apples, Tom made room for a fair share of Mrs. Murphy's supper. Once more she felt that she had a home, humble enough, to be sure, but made attractive by kindness.

"I wish I could stay here," thought Tom; and it occurred to her that she might be able to make such an arrangement with the old apple-woman, on condition of paying a certain sum towards the family expenses.

CHAPTER XX

TOM SPECULATES IN GOLD

DURING the evening some of the neighbors came in, and received a hearty greeting from Mrs. Murphy.

"And who is this young leddy?" asked Mrs. O'Brien, looking at Tom.

"It's a friend of mine," said Mrs. Murphy.

"Don't you know me?" asked Tom, who, in the days of her rags and tatters, had known Mrs. O'Brien.

"Shure and it isn't Tom?" said Mrs. O'Brien, in surprise.

"Did ye iver see such a change?" said Mrs. Murphy. "Shure and I didn't know her meself when she came in wid my Mike."

"It's mighty fine you're dressed, Tom," said Mrs. O'Brien. "Your granny ain't come into a fortun', has she?"

"I don't live with granny now," answered Tom. "She's a bad old woman, and she isn't my granny either."

"It was only yesterday I saw her, and fine she was dressed too, wid a nice shawl to her back, and quite the leddy, barrin' a red nose. She says she's come into some money."

Tom opened wide her eyes in astonishment. She had speculated more than once on granny's circumstances, but it had never entered her thoughts that she had taken a step upwards in respectability.

"Where did you see her?" asked Tom.

"She was gettin' out of a Third Avenue car. She said she had just come from up town."

"She was lookin' after me, it's likely," said Tom.

"Where did she get her new clothes from?" Tom wondered.

"Maybe she's been adopted by a rich family in Fifth Avenoo," remarked Mike,—a sally which nearly convulsed his mother with laughter.

"Shure, Mike, and you'll be the death of me some time," she said.

"She'd make an interestin' young orphan," continued Mike.

"Hadn't you better marry her, Mike? and then you'd be my grandfather," suggested Tom.

"Such a beauty ain't for the likes of me," answered Mike. "Besides, mother wouldn't want her for a daughter-in-law. She'd likely get jealous of her good looks."

"Mike, you're a case!" said Mrs. Murphy, with a smile on her broad, good-humored face.

So the evening passed, enlivened with remarks, not very intellectual or refined, it is true, but good-natured, and at times droll. Tom enjoyed it. She had a home-feeling, which she had never had at Mrs. Merton's; and above all she was cheered by the thought that she was welcome, though the home was humble enough.

By and by the callers departed, and the family made preparations for bed.

"I can't give you a very nice bed, Tom," said Mrs. Murphy, "but I'll fix you up a place to slape on the floor wid my Biddy."

"That'll be jolly," said Tom. "If it wasn't for you, I'd have to sleep out in the street."

"That would be a pity, entirely, as long as I have a roof over me. There's room enough for you, Tom, and it won't be robbin' any of us."

Tom slept comfortably. Her bed was not one of the softest; but she had never been used to beds of down, sleeping on a hard straw bed even at Mrs. Merton's. She woke, feeling refreshed, and in much better spirits than when she set out from Mrs. Merton's.

When breakfast was over, Mrs. Murphy set out for her place of business, and Mike for his daily occupation. Biddy remained at home to take charge of the younger children. With the rest Tom went too.

"Come back to-night, Tom," said Mrs. Murphy.

"I should like to," said Tom, "if you'll let me pay for my board."

"Shure we won't quarrel about that. And what are you goin' to do, Tom, the day?"

"I don't know," said Tom. "If I had any money I'd buy some papers."

"How much wud you want?"

"Twenty-five cents would give me a start."

Mrs. Murphy dived into the recesses of a capacious pocket, and drew out a handful of currency.

"I'll lind it to you," she said. "Why didn't you ask me before?"

"Thank you," said Tom. "I'll bring it back tonight. You're very kind to me, Mrs. Murphy," she added, gratefully.

"It's the poor that knows how to feel for the poor," said the apple-woman. "It's I that'll trust you, Tom, dear."

Three months before Tom would have told Mrs. Murphy that she was a trump; but though some of her street phrases clung to her, she was beginning to use less of the slang which she had picked up during her long apprenticeship to a street life. Though her position, even at Mrs. Merton's, had not been as favorable as it might have been elsewhere, the influences were far better than in the home (if it deserved the name) in which she had been reared, and the association of the school which she attended had, likewise, been of advantage to her. I do not wish it to be understood that Tom had in three months changed from a young Arab into a refined young lady. That would hardly be possible; but she had begun to change, and she could never again be quite the wild, reckless girl whose acquaintance we made at the street-crossing.

Tom went out with Mrs. Murphy, helping her to carry her basket of apples. Leaving her at her accustomed stand, she went to the newspaper offices, and laid in a small supply. With these she went to Fulton Ferry, partly because she fancied that there was no danger of granny's coming there in pursuit of her. Even if the encounter did take place she was resolved not to go back. Still it was better to avoid it altogether.

Tom was rather late in the field. Most of her competitors had been selling papers for an hour, and some had already sold quite a number. However, not being in the least bashful, she managed to obtain her share of the trade that remained. The boats came in at frequent intervals, loaded down with passengers,—clerks, shop-boys, merchants, bankers, book-keepers, operatives, who made a home in Brooklyn, but spent the day in the busy metropolis.

"Morning papers, sir?" asked Tom, to a rather portly gentleman, who did business in Wall Street.

"Yes; give me the 'Herald.'"

He drew a coin from his pocket, and handed to Tom.

"Never mind about the change," he said.

Tom was about to put it in her pocket, supposing from the size that it was a five-cent piece; but, chancing to glance at it more particularly, she saw that it was a five-dollar gold piece.

Her eyes sparkled with joy. To her it was an immense fortune. She had never, in all her life, had so much money before. "But did he mean to give her so much?" was the question that suggested itself to her immediately. He had, to be sure, told her to keep the change, but Tom knew too much of human nature and the ways of the world to think it likely that anybody would pay five dollars in gold for a morning paper, without asking for a return of the change.

Now I am quite aware that in three cases out of four the lucky news-vender would have profited by the mistake, and never thought of offering to correct it. Indeed, I am inclined to think that Tom herself would have done the same three months before. Even now she was strongly tempted to do so. But she remembered the false charge that had been made against her by Mrs. Merton the day before, and the indignation she felt.

"If I keep this, and it's ever found out, she'll be sure I took the twenty dollars," thought Tom. "I won't do it. I won't let her call me a thief. I'll give it back."

The purchaser of the paper was already half through Fulton Market before Tom made up her mind to return the money. She started on a run, afraid her resolution might give way if she stopped to consider.

She easily recognized the man who had paid her the money.

"Mister," said Tom, touching him to attract his attention.

"What's wanted?" he inquired, looking at our heroine.

"Did you mean to give me this?" and Tom displayed the gold piece.

"Did I give it to you?"

"Yes, you bought a 'Herald,' you know, and told me to keep the change."

"Well, why didn't you?" he asked, in some curiosity.

"I thought you made a mistake."

"I shouldn't have found it out. Didn't you want to keep it?"

"Yes," said Tom, unhesitatingly.

"Why didn't you?"

"I thought it would be stealing."

"You're a natural phenomenon!"

"Is that a bad name?" demanded Tom.

"No, not in this case. So I told you to keep the change, did I?"

"Yes, sir."

"Then you'd better do it."

"Do you mean it?" asked Tom, astonished.

"To be sure. I never break my word."

"Then I'll do it," said Tom. "Ain't I in luck this morning, though?"

"Yes, I think you are. As I probably know more of business than you, my young friend, will you permit me to give you a piece of advice?"

"All right," said Tom.

"Then, as gold is at a premium, you had better sell that gold piece, and take the value in currency."

"Where can I sell it?" asked Tom.

"I don't, in general, solicit business, but, if you have confidence in my integrity, you may call at my office, No. – Wall Street, any time to-day, and I will give you the market value of the gold."

"I don't understand all them big words," said Tom, rather puzzled, "but I'll go as soon as I have sold my papers."

"Very good. You may ask for Mr. Dunbar. Can you remember the name?"

Tom said she could, repeating it two or three times, to become familiar with it.

An hour later she entered the broker's office, looking about her for her acquaintance of the morning.

"Ah, there you are," said the broker, recognizing her. "So you want to sell your gold?"

"Yes, sir."

"Gold sells at 141 to-day. Will that be satisfactory?"

"Yes, sir."

"Mr. Johnson," said Mr. Dunbar, addressing a clerk, "give that young lady value in currency for five dollars in gold."

Tom handed in the gold, and received in return seven dollars and five cents. She could hardly credit her good luck, not being familiar with the mysteries of banking.

"Thank you, sir," said she gratefully, to the broker.

"I hope you will favor us with any future business you may have in our line," said Mr. Dunbar, with a friendly smile.

"Yes, sir," answered Tom, rather mystified by his manner, but mentally deciding that he was one of the jolliest gentlemen she had ever met.

When Tom emerged from the office, and was once more in the hurry and bustle of Wall Street, it is very doubtful whether, in that street of millionaires and men striving to become such, there was a single one who felt so fabulously wealthy as she.

CHAPTER XXI

TOM FALLS INTO THE ENEMY'S HANDS

TOM found herself the possessor of seven dollars and fifty cents, including the quarter which she owed to Mrs. Murphy for money advanced. It was not yet eleven o'clock. She decided to call on Mrs. Murphy, pay back the loan, and inform her of her good luck.

Mrs. Murphy was seated at her stand, keeping a sharp lookout for customers, when she espied Tom approaching.

"Have you sold your papers, Tom?" she asked.

"Yes, Mrs. Murphy. Here's the money I borrowed of you."

"Keep it longer; you'll maybe nade it. I ain't afraid to trust you."

"I don't need it. I have been lucky. See there!" and Tom displayed a roll of bills.

"Where'd ye get all them?" asked the applewoman, in amazement.

"A gentleman paid me a gold piece for a 'Herald,' and wouldn't take any change."

"Is it truth you're tellin', Tom?"

"Of course it is. Do you think I'd tell you a lie?"

"Tell me all about it, Tom."

Tom did so, to the intense interest of Mrs. Murphy, who, after ejaculations as to Tom's luck, added, "I wish he'd buy some apples of me, and trate me in the same way. And what are you goin' to do wid your money, Tom, dear?"

"I'm going to get a square meal pretty soon, Mrs. Murphy. If you'll come along, I'll treat you."

"Thank you, Tom, all the same, but I can't lave my business. You'd better put it in the savings bank, where it'll be safe. Maybe you might lose it."

"Have you got any money in the savings-bank?"

"No, Tom, dear. It takes all I earn for the rint and atin' for the childers."

"I want to live with you, Mrs. Murphy, if you'll take me."

"Shure and I'd be glad to have you, Tom, if you'll put up wid my poor room."

"I'd rather be there than at Mrs. Merton's," said Tom.

After some negotiation, Mrs. Murphy agreed to take Tom as a boarder, furnishing her with lodging, breakfast and supper, for a dollar and a half a week. It seemed a small sum, but it would be a welcome addition to the applewoman's weekly income, while it would take Tom from the streets, and give her a cheerful and social home.

"I'll pay you now for a week," said Tom. "Then I'll be all right even if I lose the money."

After some persuasion, Mrs. Murphy was induced to accept the payment in advance.

"Now I'll go and get some dinner," said Tom.

Tom directed her steps to the Belmont House Restaurant, on Fulton Street. It has two rooms, one for ladies, the other for gentlemen; and is well-patronized by a very respectable class, chiefly clerks and business men. It was of a higher grade than the restaurants which those in Tom's line of business were accustomed to frequent. Her dress, however, prevented any surprise being felt at her entrance. She sat down at a table, and looked over a bill of fare. She observed that roast turkey was marked forty cents. This was rather a large price for one in her circumstances to pay. However, she had been in luck, and felt that she could afford an unusual outlay.

"Roast turkey and a cup of coffee!" ordered Tom, as the waiter approached the table.

"All right, miss," said that functionary.

Soon the turkey was set before her, with a small dish of cranberry sauce, and a plate of bread and butter. Two potatoes and the cup of coffee made up Tom's dinner. She surveyed it with satisfaction, and set to with an appetite.

"I should like to live this way every day," thought Tom; "but I can't afford it."

The waiter brought a check, and laid it beside her plate. It was marked 45 cents.

Tom walked up to the desk near the door, and paid her bill in an independent manner, as if she were accustomed to dine there every day. In making the payment she had drawn out her whole stock of money, and still held it in her hand as she stood on the sidewalk outside. She little guessed the risk she ran in doing so, or that the enemy she most dreaded was close at hand. For just at the moment Tom stood with her face towards Broadway, granny turned the corner of Nassau and Fulton Streets, and bore down upon her, her eyes sparkling with joy and anticipated triumph. She was not alone. With her was a man of thirty-five, bold and reckless in expression, but otherwise with the dress and appearance of a gentleman.

"There's the gal now!" said granny, in excitement.

"Where?" said her companion, sharing her excitement.

"There, in front of that eating-house."

"The one with her back towards us?"

"Yes. Don't say a word, and I'll creep up and get hold of her."

Tom was about to put back her money in her pocket, when she felt her arm seized in a firm grasp. Turning in startled surprise, she met the triumphant glance of her old granny.

"Let me alone!" said Tom, fiercely, trying to snatch away her arm.

"I've got you, have I?" said granny. "I knowed I'd get hold of you at last, you young trollop! Come home with me, right off!"

"I won't go with you," said Tom, resolutely. "I don't want to have anything to do with you. You haven't got anything to do with me."

"Haven't I, I should like to know? Ain't I your granny?"

"No, you ain't."

"What do you mean by that?" demanded Mrs. Walsh, rather taken aback.

"You ain't any relation of mine. I don't know where you got hold of me; but I won't own such an old drunkard for a granny."

"Come along!" said granny, fiercely. "You'll pay for this, miss."

"Help!" exclaimed Tom, finding that she was likely to be carried away against her will, at the same time struggling violently.

"What's the matter?" asked a gentleman, who had just come out of the restaurant.

"It's my grand-child, sir," said Mrs. Walsh, obsequiously. "She run away from me, and now she don't want to go back."

"She hasn't got anything to do with me," said Tom. "Help!"

This last exclamation was intended to attract the attention of a policeman who was approaching.

"What's the trouble?" he demanded, authoritatively.

Mrs. Walsh repeated her story.

"What is the child's name?" asked the policeman.

"Jane," answered the old woman, who was at first on the point of saying "Tom."

"How long has she lived with you?"

"Ever since she was born, till a few weeks ago."

"What do you say to this?" asked the officer.

"I did live with her; but she beat me, so I left her. She says she is my granny, but she isn't."

"Where do you live now?"

"With Mrs. Murphy, in Mulberry Street."

This intelligence rather astonished granny, who heard it for the first time.

"Is the child related to you?" asked the officer.

"She's my grandchild, but she's always been a wild, troublesome child. Many's the time I have kept awake all night thinkin' of her bad ways," said granny, virtuously. "It was only yesterday," she added, with a sudden thought suggested by the sight of the money which she had seen Tom counting, "that she came to my room, and stole some money. She's got it in her pocket now."

"Have you taken any money from your grandmother?" demanded the policeman.

"No, I haven't," said Tom, boldly.

"I saw her put it in her pocket," said granny.

"Show me what you have in your pocket."

"I've got some money," said Tom, feeling in rather a tight place; "but it was given me this morning by a gentleman at Fulton Ferry."

"Show it," said the officer, authoritatively.

Tom was reluctantly compelled to draw out the money she had left,—a little over five dollars.

Granny's eyes sparkled as she saw it.

"It's the money I lost," said she. "Give it to me;" and she clutched Tom's hand.

"Not for Joe!" said Tom, emphatically. "It's mine, and I'll keep it."

"Will you make her give it up?" asked granny, appealing to the policeman. "It's some of my hard earnings, which that wicked girl took from me."

"That's a lie!" retorted Tom. "You never saw the money. There was a gentleman down to Fulton Ferry that give it to me this morning."

"That's a likely story," said granny, scornfully.

"If you don't believe it you can ask him. He's got an office on Wall Street, No. – and his name is Mr. Dunbar. Take me round there, and see if he don't say so."

"Don't believe her," said granny. "She can lie as fast as she can talk."

"Ask Mrs. Murphy then. She keeps an apple-stand corner of Nassau and Spruce Streets."

"You are sure she took this money from you?" inquired the policeman.

"Yes," said Mrs. Walsh. "I put it in my drawer yesterday forenoon, and when I come to look for it it was gone. Mrs. Molloy, that lives on the next floor, told me she saw Tom, I mean Jane, come in about three o'clock, when I was out to work. It was then that she took it."

If granny had been dressed in her old fashion, she would have inspired less confidence; but it must be remembered that, through money advanced by the lawyer, she was now, in outward appearance, a very respectable old woman; and appearances go a considerable way. The officer was, therefore, disposed to believe her. If he had any doubt on the subject it was settled by the interference of Mr. Lindsay, who had hitherto kept aloof, but who now advanced, saying, "I know this woman, Mr. Officer, and I can assure you that her story is correct. The child has been wild and rebellious, and stolen money. But her grandmother does not wish to have her arrested, as she might rightfully do. She prefers to take her back, and do what she can to redeem her."

Mr. Lindsay was in outward appearance a gentleman. His manner was quiet, and calculated to inspire confidence.

"That is sufficient," said the officer, respectfully. "Hark you," he added, addressing Tom, "you had better go away quietly with your grandmother, or I shall advise her to give you in charge for theft."

Granny had conquered. Tom saw that further immediate resistance would be unavailing; without a word, therefore, she allowed herself to be led away, mentally resolving, however, that her stay with granny would be brief.

CHAPTER XXII

THE LAWYER AND HIS CLIENT

MR. SELDEN, the lawyer who has already been introduced to the reader, sat in his office with a pile of papers before him, when a knock was heard at the door. His clerk being absent, he arose and opened it. A lady stood before him.

"Will you enter, madam?" he said.

"Is this Mr. Selden?" she asked.

"That is my name, madam."

"My name will probably be familiar to you. I am Mrs. Lindsay."

"I am glad to see you, madam. Will you be seated?"

She sat down, and the lawyer regarded with interest the client whom he now saw for the first time. She was still young, less than forty probably, and, though her face bore the impress of sorrow, she was still beautiful.

"I suppose you have no news for me," she said.

"I am sorry to say that I have as yet no trace of the child. Margaret Walsh is on the lookout for her, and, as you have made it worth her while, I do not doubt that she will eventually find her for you."

"Do you think my child is still in the city?" asked Mrs. Lindsay, anxiously.

"I have no doubt of it. A child, bred as she has been, does not often leave the city voluntarily, unless in the case of those children who are from time to time carried away to homes in the West, through the agency of the Children's Aid Society."

"But may she not be of the number of these?"

"I thought it possible, and have accordingly inquired particularly of the officers of the society whether any child answering to her description has been under their charge, and I am assured that this is not the case. She is probably earning a living for herself somewhere in the streets, though we cannot tell in what way, or in what part of the city. Having run away from Mrs. Walsh, whom I suspect she did not like, she probably keeps out of the way, to avoid falling again into her hands."

"It is terrible to think that my dear child is compelled to wander about the streets homeless, and no doubt often suffering severe privations," said Mrs. Lindsay, with a sigh.

"Have good courage, madam," said the lawyer. "I am convinced that we shall find her very soon."

"I hope indeed that your anticipations may be realized," said the mother. "But I have not yet told you what brings me to New York at this time."

Mr. Selden bowed and assumed an air of attention.

"It is not pleasant," said Mrs. Lindsay, after a slight pause, "to speak ill of a relative; but I am obliged to tell you that the worst foe I have is my brother-in-law, a younger brother of my late husband. It was he who in the first place contrived the abduction of the child, and, though he witnessed my distress, he has never relented, though it was doubtless in his power, at any time, to restore her to me."

"How lately have you become aware of his connection with the affair?"

"Only a few months since. One day I opened a desk belonging to him, in search of an envelope, when I accidentally came upon a letter from Margaret Walsh, written some years since, giving an account of her arrival in New York with my dear child, and claiming from him a sum of money which it appears he had promised as a compensation for her services. This discovery astounded me. It was the first intimation I had of my brother-in-law's perfidy. He had always offered me such a delicate and unobtrusive sympathy, and appeared to share so sincerely in my sorrow, that I could scarcely believe the testimony of my senses. I read the letter three times before I could realize his treachery. Of course I did not make known to him the discovery I had made, but, calling on a lawyer, I asked him to recommend to me some trustworthy gentleman in his profession in this city. Your name was suggested, and I at once authorized him to communicate with you, and employ you in the matter."

"I trust I shall prove worthy of the recommendation," said the lawyer, inclining his head.

"There is one question which I should like to ask," he continued. "In what manner would your brother-in-law be likely to derive advantage from your child's disappearance?"

"My husband left a large property," said Mrs Lindsay. "Half of this was bequeathed to me, the remaining half I was to hold in trust for my child. If, however, she should die before reaching her majority my brother-in-law, Mr. James Lindsay, was to receive my child's portion."

"That constitutes a very powerful motive," said the lawyer. "The love of money is the root of all evil, you know."

"I do not like to suspect my brother-in-law of such baseness," said Mrs. Lindsay, "but I fear I must."

"How are his own means? Has he considerable property?"

"He had. Both my husband and himself inherited a large property; but I have reason to think that, at the time I speak of, he had lost large sums by gambling. He had passed two years abroad, and I heard from acquaintances, who met him there, that he played for high stakes at Baden Baden and other German gambling resorts, and lost very heavily. I suspect that he must have reduced his means very much in this way."

"You are probably correct, and this supplies what we lawyers always seek—the motive. I can quite understand that to a man so situated a hundred thousand dollars must have been a powerful temptation. I must ask you another question. Has Mr. James Lindsay derived any advantage from your child's property thus far?"

"He has, though it was legally decided that he could not come into absolute possession, since my child's death was not definitely ascertained; at least, until such time as, if living, she would have attained her majority, it was decreed that the income derived from the property should be paid to him, this payment to cease only in case of Jenny's restoration."

"And has this been done?"

"It has."

"Then Mr. James Lindsay has for the last six years received the income of a hundred thousand dollars."

Mrs. Lindsay inclined her head.

"And you never suspected his agency in the affair, in spite of all this?"

"Never. I knew James profited by my dear child's loss, but I was not prepared to suspect him of such baseness."

"I should have thought of it at once; but then we lawyers see so much of the bad side of human nature that we are prone to suspect evil."

"Then I should not wish to be a lawyer. It pains me to think ill of others."

"I respect you for the sentiment, madam, though in my profession I am compelled to repudiate it. May I inquire whether your brother-in-law yet suspects that you have discovered his complicity in the plot against your child?"

"It is that which brings me to see you to-day. I feel sure that in some way he has gained a knowledge of my secret, though I endeavored to conceal it from him."

"That is not surprising. He might accidentally have seen the advertisement for Margaret Walsh, which, under your directions, I inserted in the leading New York daily papers."

"He must have found out in this way."

"He will now doubtless do what he can to prevent your recovering possession of her."

"I fear he has already commenced. Three days since, he told me that he was about to go to Washington, and possibly further south for a few weeks. He added that, having much business to occupy him, he doubted if he should be able to write often. I supposed this to be true, until yesterday I heard that, instead of taking the cars to Baltimore, he had bought a ticket for New York. This attempt to deceive me convinces me that he has penetrated my secret."

"Do you know where he is staying in New York?"

"No, I do not. I only reached the city to-day, and came at once to your office to inform you of the new danger which menaced our cause."

"The information is important, Mrs. Lindsay," said the lawyer, thoughtfully. "I must endeavor to guard against his machinations. No doubt he will first try to find out Margaret Walsh, and when he has found her will seek to buy her over to his interest. From what I know of the woman, he will have no difficulty in succeeding."

"What can we do?" asked Mrs. Lindsay, anxiously.

"I don't care to bid against him, for, having such large interests at stake, he will take care to go as high as we. We must do what we can to keep them apart."

"Will that be possible?"

"We can at least try. I must have time to think what methods are to be used."

"When shall you see Margaret?"

"To-morrow, probably. That is the day on which she has been accustomed to come for her weekly allowance, and I must do her the justice to say that she has never yet failed to present herself punctually. You will remain in New York?"

"Yes," said Mrs. Lindsay. "In my present state of mind I could not be contented away from here."

"What will be your address?"

"I have not thought."

"Let me advise you not to stop at a hotel. Your arrival would in that way become known to Mr. James Lindsay, as it would probably be published in the 'Evening Express.'"

"Can you recommend me a good boarding-house, Mr. Selden?"

"I know an excellent one on West Twenty-Fifth Street, where you will have a fine room and every comfort. I will, if you desire it, give you a letter to Mrs. Thurston, with whom I once boarded myself."

"I shall feel much indebted to you, Mr. Selden, if you will do so."

The lawyer turned to his desk, and wrote a brief note, which he handed to his client. She took it, and rose from her seat, saying, "May I hope to see you this evening, Mr. Selden? I am sorry to trespass upon your time to such an extent, but you will appreciate a mother's anxiety."

"I can and I do," said the lawyer; "and you may rest assured that my best energies shall be devoted to your service."

Within two hours Mrs. Lindsay found herself installed in a handsome apartment at Mrs. Thurston's boarding-house.

"I shall feel better," she reflected, "now that I am in the city where my child in all probability is leading a life of poverty and privation. God grant that she may be restored to me, and that I may be able to make up to her the care of which she has so cruelly been deprived for six long years!"

CHAPTER XXIII

HOW GRANNY AND TOM BECAME SEPARATED

IT will be understood why Mr. Lindsay had visited New York, and opened communication with Margaret Walsh. The knowledge that his sister-in-law had discovered his agency in the disappearance of her child, and the fear that she might recover her, and so deprive him of the large property for which he had intrigued, alarmed him, and led him to exert himself to frustrate, if possible, his sister's plans.

Only two days after reaching the city, he had met Margaret in the street. He recognized her at once, and discovered without much difficulty the steps Mrs. Lindsay had this far taken. He at once offered Margaret double the reward if she would serve his interests; and granny consented, nothing loath. The first object was still to get possession of Tom. How that was effected has already been told. We will now resume our story where we left it at the end of the twenty-first chapter.

Tom walked quietly away with granny, feeling that there was no chance of immediate escape. She meant to bide her time, and break away as soon as she could. Mr. Lindsay walked on the other side of granny until they reached the Astor House.

"Stop here a minute," he said, "I will go in and inquire when the next train starts on the Erie Road."

The old woman did as directed. Tom could not help wondering how there should be an acquaintance between granny and a well-dressed gentleman like Mr. Lindsay. It seemed strange, yet there was an evident understanding between them.

Mr. Lindsay came out in less than five minutes.

"A train starts in an hour," he said. "We had better go to the depot at once."

Granny made some objection to the short notice, but he over-ruled it.

"It must be done," he said, decidedly. "It is the only safe way."

"I ain't used to travellin'," said Margaret.

"You've got a tongue in your head," he said, roughly. "All you've got to do is to inquire when you are in doubt. I will go to the depot with you, and buy your tickets."

Mrs. Walsh made no further objection, and they took their way to the depot.

"I wonder what's up," thought Tom.

They reached the depot and went into the reception-room. Mr. Lindsay went out, and returned shortly with two strips of tickets, which he gave to granny, explaining in what way they would be called for. He then took out a roll of bills, and gave her. Then ensued a whispered conversation, of which Tom only heard detached words, from which she was unable to gather a definite idea. Then they entered the cars, and Mr. Lindsay left them, with a last injunction, "Mind she don't escape."

"I'll take care," nodded granny.

Soon the cars were on their way. It was the first time within her remembrance that Tom had ridden in the cars, and she looked out of the window with great interest, enjoying the rapid motion and the changing views. At last, yielding to curiosity, she turned and addressed the old woman.

"Where are we goin', granny?"

"Never you mind!" said granny.

"But I do mind. Are we goin' far?"

"None of your business!"

"Who was that man that gave you money? Has he got anything to do with me?"

"No," said granny.

"Why did he give you money?"

"Because he's a relation of mine," said granny. "He's my nephew."

Tom was not in the least deceived. She knew that, if granny had a nephew, he would be a far different man from Mr. Lindsay. However, she had a curiosity to hear what granny would say, and continued asking questions.

"Then he's a relation of mine," said Tom.

"No he isn't," said granny, sharply.

"Why isn't he? Ain't you my granny?"

Mrs. Walsh could not gainsay this argument. "He's a little of a relation to you," she said. "He's give me some money, so I can live with you out West. You won't have to sweep streets no longer."

The mystery seemed to deepen. What truth there might be in granny's representations Tom could not tell. One thing was clear, however. Relation or not, this man had given granny money, and would probably give her more. Probably, if Tom remained with her, she would not fare as hard as formerly; but this she did not intend to do. She had come to dislike granny, who, she felt instinctively, was not really her relation, and still cherished the intention of running away as soon as there was a good opportunity.

Meanwhile the cars sped on till seventy-five miles separated them from the city. Broad fields extended on either side of the railway track. To Tom, who was a true child of the city, who had rarely seen green grass, since the round of her life had been spent within a short distance of City Hall Park, it seemed strange. She wondered how it would seem to live in the country, and rather thought she should not like it.

At length they came to a station where supper was to be obtained. Granny was hungry and rose with alacrity.

"Shall I go with you?" asked Tom.

"No," said Mrs. Walsh, "set right here. I'll go and buy something for you."

They were so far away from the city now that granny had no fear of Tom's escaping, particularly as she had no money.

Tom retained her seat, therefore, and granny entered the station-house, where some of her fellow-passengers were already hurrying down their suppers.

She stepped up to the counter, and soon was engaged in a similar way.

"Will you have a cup of coffee, maam?" inquired the waiter.

"Haven't you got some whiskey?" inquired the old woman.

"No, we don't keep it."

Granny looked disappointed. She was very fond of whiskey, and, having plenty of money, saw no reason why she should be deprived of her favorite beverage.

"Ain't there any to be got near by?" she asked.

"There's a saloon a few rods up the road," was the reply.

"Could I find it easy?"

"Yes, there's a sign outside. It's a small one-story building. You can't miss it."

Mrs. Walsh hastily bought a couple of cakes for Tom, and hurried out of the building. There stood the cars, liable to start at any time. It was the part of prudence to get in and granny hesitated. But the desire for a dram was strong within her, and she thought she could run over and get a glass, and be back in time. The train stopped ten minutes for refreshments, and she had not consumed more than five. The temptation proved too strong for her to resist.

She reached the saloon, and, entering, said, "Give me a glass of whiskey, quick. I'm going right off in the train."

The whiskey was poured out, and granny drank it with a sense of exquisite enjoyment.

"Give me another," she said.

Another was poured out, and she had half drunk it, when the whistle was heard. This recalled the old woman to the risk she incurred of being left by the train. Setting down the glass hastily, she was hurrying out of the saloon, when she was stopped by the bar-tender.

"You haven't paid for your drinks, ma'am," he said bluntly.

Granny saw the train just beginning to move.

"I can't stop," she said desperately. "I shall be left."

"That don't go down!" said the bar-tender, roughly; "you must pay for your drinks."

"I'll send it to you," said granny, trying to break away.

"That trick won't work," said the man, and he clutched the old woman by the arm.

"I've got a gal aboard," screamed granny, desperately, trying at the same time to break away.

"I don't care if you've got forty gals aboard, you must pay."

Mrs. Walsh drew a bill from her pocket, and, throwing it down, rushed for the train without waiting for the change. But too much time had already been lost. The cars were now speeding along at a rate which made it quite impossible for her to catch them, and get aboard.

"Stop!" she shrieked frantically, running with a degree of speed of which she would have been thought incapable. "I've got a gal aboard. I shall lose her."

Some of the passengers saw her from the windows, and were inclined to laugh rather than sympathize with her evident distress.

"Serves her right!" said a grouty old fellow.

"Why didn't she come back in time?"

"There's a woman left behind," said another passenger to the conductor.

He shrugged his shoulders, and said, indifferently, "That's her lookout. If she didn't choose to come to time, she must take the consequences."

"Couldn't you stop the train?" asked a kindhearted little woman.

"No ma'am. Quite impossible. We're behind time already."

So the train sped on, leaving granny frantic and despairing, waving her arms and screaming hoarsely, "Stop! I've got a gal aboard!"

"What would Mr. Lindsay say?" she could not help thinking. Only four hours had passed since Tom had been placed in her charge, and they were separated. She cared little or nothing for Tom, or her welfare, but for her own interests, which were likely to be seriously affected, she cared a great deal. She was to have a comfortable annuity as long as she kept Tom safe in custody, and that was at an end unless she could manage to get her back.

She went into the station-house, and inquired when the next train would leave. She learned that several hours must elapse. Having plenty of time, therefore, she went back to the saloon, and recovered the change due her, taking an additional glass of whiskey, to drown her chagrin and disappointment.

CHAPTER XXIV

TOM'S ADVENTURES

AMONG those who looked out of the window, and witnessed granny's frantic gesticulations was Tom.

"Ain't that rich?" she uttered, in high delight.

"What's the matter?" asked an old lady, who sat just in front, bending over and speaking to Tom.

"It's my granny," said Tom, laughing afresh. "She's left behind. You ought to see her shakin' her fist at the cars."

"Are you laughing at your grandmother's disappointment?" asked the old lady's daughter, a prim-visaged maiden lady. "For shame, child!"

"I'm glad to get rid of her," said Tom, coolly. "She ain't my granny; she only pretends to be."

"Hasn't she had the care of you?"

"No," said Tom. "I've had the care of her. She took all the money I earned, and spent it for rum."

"What are you going to do?" inquired the old maid.

"I don't know," said Tom, her attention being now first called to the embarrassment of her situation. She was nearly eighty miles from New York, and this distance was fast increasing. She had no railway ticket and no money. What was she to do?

"Have you had any supper, child?" asked the old lady.

"No," answered Tom. "Granny went out to get some."

"Priscilla," said the old lady, "haven't you got some of them cookies left?"

"Yes, ma," said the daughter.

"You'd better give some of them to the child."

The younger lady took several hard seed-cakes from a paper bag, and offered them to Tom, who accepted and ate them with avidity.

Meanwhile she was considering what was best to be done. She wanted to get back to New York, where she felt at home. Then she could go back to Mrs. Murphy's, whom she had paid for a week's board in advance. She had no money, for granny had forcibly taken from her what she had left after paying for her dinner. How she was to get back seemed rather a problem. One thing, however, appeared evident: every moment carried her farther away from the city. So Tom concluded that the sooner she got off, the better.

When the cars reached the next stopping-place, Tom got up and went to the door.

"Where are you going?" asked the old lady.

"I'm going to look out," answered Tom, fearing that some impediment might be placed in her way.

"Don't you get off, or you may get lost too."

"All right."

Tom stepped on the platform, and, quietly jumping from the cars, ran round the depot, to escape notice. The stop was a short one, and directly she heard the noise of the departing train. When it was fairly on the way, Tom began to look around her and consider her situation.

It was a small station, and there was scarcely a house near the depot. It was already twilight, and to Tom, who was accustomed to the crowded city, it appeared very lonely and desolate. She knew not where she should pass the night. She had often been in that position in the city, and it did not trouble her. Here, however, she was rather startled at the unwonted solitude. Besides, being wholly ignorant of the country, it occurred to her that she might meet some wild animal prowling around.

Just as this thought came into her mind, she saw advancing towards her a cow, followed by a farmer's boy, about two years older than herself. Now Tom was brave enough constitutionally, but this was the first cow she had ever seen, and the branching horns led her to suppose it fierce and dangerous, like a lion, for example.

She rushed with headlong speed to a stone wall and climbed over.

"Ho! ho!" laughed the boy; "are you afraid of a cow?"

"Won't she kill me?" asked Tom, a little reassured.

"She wouldn't kill a fly. Didn't you ever see a cow afore?"

"No, I didn't," said Tom. "I thought it was something like a lion."

"Where've you lived all your life?" asked the boy, astonished at Tom's greenness, as he considered it.

"In New York."

"I thought everybody'd seen cows. Where are you going?"

"I don't know," answered Tom.

"You ain't stoppin' to Doctor Simpson's, be you?"

"I'm stoppin' on this fence," said Tom, rather humorously.

"Taint a fence; it's a stone wall."

"What's the odds?"

"How did you come here?"

"By the cars," said Tom. "I got left."

"You did? Where are you going to sleep tonight?"

"I don't know."

"There's a tavern in the village."

"What's that?"

"A tavern. Don't you know? A hotel."

"I haven't got any money."

"That's queer," said the boy, staring. "Where are you goin' to sleep?"

"On the grass," said Tom; "only I'm afraid of the wild animals."

"Pooh! there ain't no wild animals round here. But you mustn't sleep outdoors. You'll catch cold. If you'll come home with me, mother'll let you sleep in our house."

"Thank you," said Tom. "You're a brick."

"You talk queer for a girl. What's your name?"

"Tom."

"Tom? That's a boy's name."

"They call me so. My right name is Jane."

"Well, Jane, come along, and I'll show you where we live."

The two walked together, soon becoming sociable. The boy, James Hooper, was amazed at Tom's ignorance of the most common things pertaining to country life, but found that in other ways she was sharp enough.

"You talk just like a boy," he said.

"Do I?" said Tom. "I used to wish I was a boy, but I don't know now. I think I'd like to grow up a lady,—a tip-top one, you know,—and dress fine."

"Are all the girls in New York like you?" asked James, curiously.

"No," said Tom. "There's Mary Merton, she isn't a bit like me. This is the way she walks," and Tom imitated Mary's languid, mincing gait.

"I like you best," said James. "But here we are. Do you see that house down the lane?"

"Yes," said Tom.

"That's where we live."

It was a large, square, comfortable farm-house, such as we often see in farming towns. The farmer's wife, a stout, comely woman, stood at the door.

"Who've you got with you, James?" she asked.

"It's a girl that got left by the train," said James. "She's got no money to pay for her lodging. I told her you would let her sleep here."

"Of course I will. Come right in, child. How did you get left?"

"I just got out a minute," said Tom, "and the cars went off and left me."

"What a pity! Who was travelling with you?"

"My granny," answered Tom.

"What'll she do? She'll be very much frightened."

"I expect she will," said Tom, who had made up her mind not to tell too much.

"Were you going back to the city?"

Tom answered in the affirmative. I do not mean to defend the lie, for a lie it was, but I have not represented Tom as perfect in any respect. In the future she will improve, I hope, when placed under more favorable circumstances. Her object in saying what she did was to prevent any opposition being made to her return to the city.

"You haven't had any supper, have you?" asked Mrs. Hooper.

"I ate a few cakes," answered Tom.

"That isn't hearty enough for a growing girl," said the good woman. "You must take some supper with us."

The family supper had been eaten, but a tempting array of dishes was soon set before Tom, whose appetite was always ready to answer any reasonable demands upon it.

In the evening Tom's best course was discussed. She expressed a strong desire to return at once to the city, saying she would be all right there.

"If your grandmother would not feel anxious about you," said Mrs. Hooper, "we should be glad to have you stop with us a day or two."

"I guess I'd better go back," said Tom, for, knowing that granny had been left by the cars only five miles away, she was under some apprehensions that she might find her way thither.

"You can take the nine-o'clock train to-morrow morning," said James, "and get to the city before night."

"Before night? She'll get there by one o'clock," said his mother.

"I haven't got any money to buy a ticket," said Tom.

"We will lend you the necessary amount," said the farmer, "and your grandmother can pay it back whenever it is convenient."

Tom felt a little reluctant to accept this money, for she knew that there was no hope of repayment by granny; but she determined to accept it, and work hard till she could herself save up money enough to pay the debt incurred. She felt grateful to the farmer's family for their kindness, and was resolved that they should not suffer by it.

In the evening they gathered in the plain sitting room, covered with a rag-carpet. Tom helped James make a kite. She was ignorant, but learned readily. In her interest, she occasionally let slip some street phrases which rather surprised James, who was led to wonder whether Tom was a fair specimen of New York girls. He had always fancied that he should feel bashful in their society; but with Tom he felt perfectly at home.

In the morning he accompanied Tom to the depot, and paid for her ticket, being supplied with money for the purpose by his mother.

"Good-by," he said, shaking her hand as she entered the cars.

"Good-by, old fellow," said Tom. "I'll pay you back that money if granny don't."

The train started and was soon whirling along at the rate of twenty miles an hour. Half-way between this and the next station they passed a train bound in an opposite direction. Looking through the window on the side towards the other train, Tom caught a glimpse of granny's face. The old woman had been compelled to stop till morning, and had taken the first train bound westward. She did not see Tom, who quickly moved her head from the window.

"Sold again!" thought Tom, in high delight, "When granny catches me again, she'll know it."

CHAPTER XXV

TOM FINDS HER MOTHER

TOM sat back in her seat and enjoyed the prospect from the windows, as the train sped along. She felt in unusually good spirits, knowing that she had put granny entirely off the track, and that there was no immediate chance of her recapture.

"If I only had that money granny took from me, I'd be all right," she said to herself. However, her board and lodging were paid at Mrs. Murphy's for a week in advance, and that was something.

About forty miles from New York a number of passengers got into the cars. The seats were mostly occupied, but the one beside Tom was untaken. A gentleman advanced up the aisle with a lady, looking about him for a seat.

"Is this seat engaged?" he inquired of Tom.

"No," answered Tom.

"Then you had better sit here, Rebecca," said the gentleman. "I think you will have no trouble. You won't forget where you are to go,—Mrs. Thurston's, West Twenty-Fifth Street. I can't recall the number, but a glance in the Directory will settle that."

"I wish you knew the number," said the lady.

"It was very careless of me to lose it, I confess. Still, I think you will have no trouble. But good-by, I must hurry out, or I shall be left."

"Good-by. Let me see you soon."

The gentleman got out, and the lady settled down into her seat, and looked about her. Finally her glance rested on her young companion. She was inclined to be social, and accordingly opened a conversation with Tom.

"Are you going to New York?" she inquired.

"Yes, ma'am."

"I suppose you live there?"

"Yes."

"I have never been there, and know nothing at all about the city."

"It's a big place," remarked Tom.

"Yes, I suppose so. I have always lived in the country, and I am afraid I shan't feel at home there. But my sister, who is boarding with a Mrs. Thurston, who keeps a large boarding-house on West Twenty-Fifth Street, has invited me to come up and spend a few weeks, and so I have got started."

"I guess you'll like it," said Tom.

"Do you live anywhere near West Twenty-Fifth Street?"

"Not now," said Tom. "I did live in West Sixteenth Street, but I don't now."

"Are you travelling alone?"

"Yes," said Tom.

"I suppose you live with your father and mother?"

"I haven't got any," answered Tom, laconically.

"I suppose you are well acquainted with the city?"

"Yes," said Tom. "I know it like a book."

The fact was, that Tom knew it a great deal better than a book, for her book-knowledge, as we very well know, was by no means extensive.

"Do you board?"

"Yes," said Tom. "I board with Mrs. Murphy, in Mulberry Street."

It struck the lady that Murphy was an Irish name, but the name of the street suggested nothing to her. She judged from Tom's appearance that she belonged to a family in comfortable circumstances.

"I wish I knew the number of Mrs. Thurston's house," said the lady rather anxiously. "I'm so afraid I shan't find it."

"I'll tell you what," said Tom, "I'll go with you, if you want me to."

"I wish you would," said the lady, much relieved. "It would be a great favor."

"I s'pose you won't mind givin' me a quarter," added Tom, with a sharp eye to the main chance; not unreasonably, since she was penniless.

"I'll give you double that amount," said the lady, "and thank you into the bargain. I'm not much used to travelling, and feel as helpless as a child."

"I'll take care of you," said Tom, confidently. "I'll take you to Mrs. Thurston's right side up with care."

"She talks rather singularly," thought the lady; but Tom's confident tone inspired her with corresponding confidence, and she enjoyed the rest of her journey much more than she would otherwise have done. Tom's request for compensation did not surprise her, for she reflected that children have always a use for money.

At length they reached the city, and Tom and her companion got out of the cars.

"Come right along," said Tom, taking the lady by the hand as if she were a child.

"Carriage, ma'am?" asked several hackmen.

"Perhaps I'd better take a carriage," said the lady, whose name, by the way, was Mrs. Parmenter.

"Just as you say," said Tom.

"I've got a nice carriage, ma'am. This way, please," said a burly driver.

"Look here, mister, what are you going to charge?" demanded Tom.

"Where do you want to go?"

"To Mrs. Thurston's, West Twenty-Fifth Street."

"Whereabouts in the street? What number?"

"The lady don't know."

"Then how am I to carry you there?"

"Look into the Directory," said Tom. "If it's too much trouble for you, we'll take another man."

The hackman made no further objections, but resolved to increase his charge to compensate for the extra trouble. But here again Tom defeated him, compelling him to agree to a price considerably less than he at first demanded.

"Young lady," said he, paying an involuntary tribute to Tom's shrewdness, "you're about as sharp as they make 'em."

"That's so," said Tom. "You're right the first time."

Mrs. Parmenter and Tom entered the carriage, and the driver mounted his box.

"I don't see how you dared to talk to that man so," said the lady. "I should have paid him whatever he asked."

"Then you'd have got awfully cheated," said Tom. "I know their tricks."

"I'm sure I'm much obliged to you. I don't know how I should have got along without you."

"I've always lived in the city," said Tom; "so I've got my eye-teeth cut. They can't cheat me easy."

"I'm afraid I'm selfish in taking you with me," said Mrs. Parmenter. "I hope your friends won't be alarmed at your coming home late."

"I don't think they will," said Tom, laughing.

"You said you had no relatives living in the city?"

"Not now. My granny's just left New York. She's travellin' for her health," added Tom, with a burst of merriment, at which Mrs. Parmenter was rather surprised.

"Where has she gone?"

"Out West. I went a little way with her, just to oblige. She was awful sorry to part with me, granny was," and Tom laughed again in a manner that quite puzzled her companion, who mentally decided that Tom was a very odd girl indeed.

"After we get to Mrs. Thurston's," said Mrs. Parmenter, "I'll tell the driver to carry you home. Shall I?"

Tom fancied the sensation she would produce in Mulberry Street, if she should drive up to the door of the humble tenement house in which she boarded, and declined the offer. She might have accepted, for the joke of it, but she saw that the hackman took her for a young lady, and she did not wish to let him discover the unfashionable locality in which she made her home.

"Never mind," said Tom. "I'd just as lieves ride in the cars."

They stopped at a drug-store, and the driver, going in, ascertained without difficulty, by an examination of the Directory, the number of Mrs. Thurston's boarding-house. A few minutes later, he drew up in front of a very good-looking house, and, jumping from the box, opened the door.

"Is this Mrs. Thurston's?" asked Mrs. Parmenter.

"Yes, ma'am; it's the number that's put down in the Directory."

"I'll ring the bell and see," said Tom.

She ran up the steps, and rang a loud peal, which was quickly answered.

"Is this Mrs. Thurston's?" she asked.

"Yes."

"Then here's a lady that's coming in," said Tom. "It's the right place," she added, going back to the carriage where Mrs. Parmenter was engaged in paying the driver.

"Now, my dear," said Mrs. Parmenter, "I hope you'll accept this for your kindness in guiding me."

She drew a dollar from her purse, and handed it to Tom.

"Thank you," said Tom, quite elated. "I'm glad I come with you."

Mrs. Parmenter was about to enter the house, when another lady descended the steps. It was Mrs. Lindsay, who had been recommended to this house, as the reader may remember, by the Wall Street lawyer. She no sooner saw Tom than she became excited, and grasped the balustrade for support.

"Child," she said, eagerly, "what is your name?"

"Tom," answered our heroine, surprised.

"Tom?"

"That's what they call me. Jane is my real name."

"Do you know a woman named Margaret Walsh?" continued Mrs. Lindsay, her emotion increasing.

"Why, that's my granny," said Tom, surprised.

There was no more room for doubt. Mrs. Lindsay opened her arms.

"Found at last!" she exclaimed. "My dear, dear child!"

"Are you my mother?" asked Tom, in amazement.

"Yes, Jenny, your own mother, never again, I hope, to be separated from you;" and Mrs. Lindsay clasped the astonished girl to her arms.

"You don't look a bit like granny," she said, scanning the refined and beautiful features of her mother.

"You mean Margaret," said Mrs. Lindsay, with a shudder. "She is a wicked woman. It was she who stole you away from me years ago."

"I played such a trick on her," said Tom, laughing. "She wanted to carry me off out West; but I left her, and she's goin' on alone."

"Come in, my darling," said Mrs. Lindsay. "Your home is with your mother henceforth. You have much to tell me. I want to know how you have passed all these years of cruel separation."

She took Tom up to her own chamber, and drew from her the whole story. Many parts gave her pain, as Tom recounted her privations and ill-treatment; but deep thankfulness came at the end, because the child so long-lost was at last restored.

"To-morrow I must buy you some new clothes," said she. "Are these all you have?"

"Yes," said Tom, "they are a good deal nicer than I used to wear."

"You shall have better still. I will try to make up to you for your past privations."

"I want to go out a little while," said Tom. "I'd like to tell Mrs. Murphy what's happened to me. You see, I paid her for a week's board, and she'll wonder where I am."

"I can't trust you out of my sight," said Mrs Lindsay; "but I'll go with you if you wish it."

"Yes, I should like that."

Great was the astonishment of worthy Mrs. Murphy, when Tom came up to her stand with a handsomely dressed and stylish lady, whom she introduced as her mother. I will not attempt to repeat the ejaculations in which she indulged, nor her delight when Mrs. Lindsay bought one of her apples for Tom, and paid for it with a ten-dollar bill, refusing change.

"Shure, your mother's a rale leddy, Tom dear," she said; "and it's I that's glad of it, for your sake."

Mrs. Lindsay ordered dinner for herself and Tom in her own room, not wishing to introduce her to her fellow-boarders until she had supplied her with a more suitable wardrobe, for Tom's dress was by this time soiled and dirty. When the lawyer came up in the evening, his surprise was great to find the child, whom he had exhausted his legal skill to discover, already restored to her mother. He offered his sincere congratulations, and, it may here be remarked, was handsomely paid for the trouble he had taken in the matter.

By the next post, at Tom's request, a letter was sent by Mrs. Lindsay to the farmer's wife who had sheltered Tom, enclosing the amount of money paid for the railroad ticket, and thanking her earnestly for the kindness shown to her child. Much to Tom's delight, an extra ten dollars was enclosed as a present to James Hooper from her.

CHAPTER XXVI

CONCLUSION

WHEN Tom was suitably dressed, it was easy to perceive a strong resemblance between her mother and herself. This resemblance was affected, to be sure, by a careless, independent expression produced by the strange life she had led as a street Arab. No doubt her new life would soften and refine her manners, and make her more like girls of her own age.

Having no further occasion to remain in New York, Mrs. Lindsay took the train for Philadelphia the next day, where Tom, whom we must now call Jane Lindsay found herself in an elegant home, surrounded by all that wealth could supply. Her mother lost no time in supplying her with teachers, that the defects of her education might be remedied. These were great, as we know, but Jane—I had nearly said Tom—was quick, and her ambition was excited, so that the progress which she made was indeed remarkable. At the end of the year she was as far advanced as most girls of her age.

At first our heroine found the change in her life not altogether agreeable. She missed the free life of the streets, which, in spite of all its privations and discomforts, is not without a charm to the homeless young Arabs that swarm about the streets. But in a short time she acquired new tastes, never, however, losing that fresh and buoyant spirit, and sturdy independence, which had enabled her to fight her way when she was compelled to do so. It was evident that Jane, whether from her natural tendencies or her past experiences, was not likely to settle down into one of those average, stereotyped, uninteresting young ladies that abound in our modern society. Nature was sure to assert itself in a certain piquancy and freshness of manner, which, added to her personal attraction, will, I think, eventually make Tom—the name slipped from my pen unintentionally—a great favorite in society. Her faults, at some of which I have hinted, she did not at once get rid of; but the influence of an excellent mother will, I am convinced, in time eradicate most of them.

When James Lindsay learned that his sister-in-law had recovered her child, he went abroad without seeing her, being ashamed no doubt to meet one whom he had so deeply injured, and there was no difficulty in reclaiming the property, the income of which had for some years been wrongly diverted to his use.

Such of my readers as have conceived an admiration for granny may be interested to learn that she kept on in her western journey, hoping to come upon Tom somewhere; but of course she was disappointed. She arrived at length in Chicago, and, having a considerable sum of money in her possession, decided to stay there. She did not venture to open communication with James Lindsay, lest he should take from her the money she had at present, on account of her careless guardianship. Hiring a room, she gave herself up to the delights of drinking and smoking. The last habit proved fatal, when, one afternoon, she lay down with her lighted pipe in her mouth. Falling asleep, the pipe fell upon the bed, setting on fire the bedclothes, and next the clothing of Margaret herself. Whether she was suffocated before awakening, or whether she awoke too late for rescue, was never ascertained. Certain it is, however, that when the smell of smoke called in the neighbors, granny was quite dead, expiating by her tragical end the sins of her miserable career.

I must sketch one more scene, and then this chronicle of Tom's adventurous life will close.

Fifteen months after Tom made the acquaintance of Captain Barnes, that worthy officer returned to New York. He at once repaired to the house of his sister, Mrs. Merton, expecting to find Tom. He had thought of her very often while at sea, and pictured with pleasure the improvement which she would exhibit after a year's training and education.

"I have no child. I probably shall never have one," he said to himself. "If Jenny has become such a girl as I hope, I will formally adopt her, and when I have become too old to go to sea, we will make a pleasant and cosey little home together, and she shall cheer my declining years."

Such thoughts as these warmed the heart of the sailor, and made him anxious for the voyage to close.

He had heard nothing from his sister since he left, and was, therefore, ignorant of the fact that Tom was no longer in her charge.

When he reached his sister's house, and had kissed her and his nieces, he inquired eagerly:—

"Where's Jane? Has she improved?"

"Then you haven't heard, Albert," said his sister, not without embarrassment, for she was about to deceive him.

"Heard! What is there to hear?" he said impatiently.

"Jane has not been with me for a year."

"What has become of her?"

"Indeed I don't know. She remained with me three months after you left, and then suddenly disappeared. She must have got tired of a life so different from that she had been accustomed to lead, and determined to go back to her street life."

"I am deeply grieved to hear it," said Captain Barnes. "I have anticipated meeting her with so much pleasure. And have you never seen her since?"

"Never."

"I thought you might accidentally have met her in the street."

"No."

"Had she improved while she did stay?"

"Yes," said Mrs. Merton, with hesitation, "that is, a little. She was not quite so wild and rude as at first; but I don't think she would ever have made up the deficiencies of her early training."

Captain Barnes paced the floor, deeply disturbed. His disappointment was a great one.

"I shall try to trace her," he said at length. "I will apply to the police for help."

"That's the best thing to do, uncle," said Mary, with a sneer. "Very likely you'll find her at Blackwell's Island."

"For shame, niece," said her uncle, sternly. "You might have a little more charity for a poor girl who has not had your advantages."

Mary was abashed, and regretted that she had spoken so unguardedly, for she hoped to produce a favorable impression upon her uncle, in the hope of becoming his heiress.

The silence was broken by the stopping of a carriage before the door. Mary flew to the window.

"O mother," she said, "there's a beautiful carriage at the door, with a coachman in livery, and there's a lady and a young girl, elegantly dressed, getting out."

Quite a sensation was produced by the intelligence.

A moment later, and the servant brought in the cards of Mrs. Lindsay and Miss Lindsay.

"I don't remember the name," said Mrs. Merton, "but you may show the ladies in, Hannah."

Directly afterwards Mrs. Lindsay and our heroine entered the room. They were visiting friends in New York, and Jane had induced her mother to call at the house where she had learned her first lessons in civilization. She was very different now from the young Arab of fifteen months since. She was now a young lady in manners, and her handsome dress set off a face which had always been attractive. Neither Mrs. Merton nor Mary dreamed of associating this brilliant young lady with the girl whom they had driven from the house by a false charge.

"Good morning, Mrs. Lindsay," said Mrs. Merton, deferentially. "Won't you and the young lady take seats?"

"You are no doubt surprised to see me," said Mrs. Lindsay, "but my daughter wished me to call. She was for three months, she tells me, a member of your family."

"Indeed," said Mrs. Merton, in surprise, "I think there must be some mistake. I don't remember that Miss Lindsay ever boarded with me."

"Don't you remember Tom?" asked Jane, looking up, and addressing Mrs. Merton in something of her old tone.

"Good gracious! You don't mean to say—" ejaculated the landlady, while Mary opened wide her eyes in astonishment and dismay.

"For years," explained Mrs. Lindsay, "my daughter was lost to me through the cruel schemes of one whom I deemed a faithful friend; but, thank God, she was restored to me within a week after she left your house."

"Was that the reason of your leaving, Jane?" asked Captain Barnes.

"Mother," said Jane, cordially grasping the hand of the captain, "this is the kind gentleman who first found me in the street, and provided me with a home."

"Accept a mother's gratitude," said Mrs. Lindsay simply, but with deep feeling.

"I was sure you would turn out right, Jane," said the captain, his face glowing with pleasure. "Then you left my sister, because you found your mother?"

"No, that was not the reason," said Jane, looking significantly at Mrs. Merton, who, knowing that she had suspected her of what was really her daughter's fault, felt confused and embarrassed.

"There was a—a little misunderstanding," she stammered, "for which I hope Miss Lindsay will excuse me. I found out my mistake afterwards."

No further explanation was then given, but Captain Barnes required and obtained an explanation afterwards. He blamed his sister severely, and Mary even more, and that young lady's prospects of becoming her uncle's heiress are now very slender.

"I hope, Captain Barnes," said Mrs. Lindsay, "you will come to Philadelphia and pass a few days at my house. Nothing would please my daughter more, nor myself."

The good captain finally accepted this invitation, though with diffidence, and henceforth never arrived in port without visiting his former protégée where he always found a warm welcome.

And so my story ends. My heroine is now a young lady, not at all like the

"Tattered Tom" whose acquaintance we first made at the street-crossing. For her sake, her mother loses no opportunity of succoring those homeless waifs, who, like her own daughter, are exposed to the discomforts and privations of the street, and through her liberality and active benevolence more than one young Arab has been reclaimed, and is likely to fill a respectable place in society.

RAGGED DICK

OR

Street Life

in New York

with the Boot-Blacks

PREFACE

"RAGGED DICK" was contributed as a serial story to the pages of the SCHOOL-MATE, a well-known juvenile magazine, during the year 1867. While in course of publication, it was received with so many evidences of favor that it has been rewritten and considerably enlarged, and is now presented to the public as the first volume of a series intended to illustrate the life and experiences of the friendless and vagrant children who are now numbered by thousands in New York and other cities.

Several characters in the story are sketched from life. The necessary information has been gathered mainly from personal observation and conversations with the boys themselves. The author is indebted also to the excellent Superintendent of the Newsboys' Lodging House, in Fulton Street, for some facts of which he has been able to make use. Some anachronisms may be noted. Wherever they occur, they have been admitted, as aiding in the development of the story, and will probably be considered as of little importance in an unpretending volume, which does not aspire to strick historical accuracy.

The author hopes that, while the volumes in this series may prove interesting as stories, they may also have the effect of enlisting the sympathies of his readers in behalf of the unfortunate children whose life is described, and of leading them to cooperate with the praiseworthy efforts now making [sic] by the Children's Aid Society and other organziations to ameliorate their condition.

[Horatio Alger]
New York, April, 1868.

CHAPTER I

RAGGED DICK IS INTRODUCED TO THE READER

"WAKE up there, youngster," said a rough voice

Ragged Dick opened his eyes slowly, and stared stupidly in the face of the speaker, but did not offer to get up.

"Wake up, you young vagabond!" said the man a little impatiently; "I suppose you'd lay there all day, if I hadn't called you."

"What time is it?" asked Dick.

"Seven o'clock."

"Seven o'clock! I oughter've been up an hour ago. I know what 'twas made me so precious sleepy. I went to the Old Bowery last night, and didn't turn in till past twelve."

"You went to the Old Bowery? Where'd you get your money?" asked the man, who was a porter in the employ of a firm doing business on Spruce Street.

"Made it by shines, in course. My guardian don't allow me no money for theatres, so I have to earn it."

"Some boys get it easier than that," said the porter significantly.

"You don't catch me stealin', if that's what you mean," said Dick.

"Don't you ever steal, then?"

"No, and I wouldn't. Lots of boys does it, but I wouldn't."

"Well, I'm glad to hear you say that. I believe there's some good in you, Dick, after all."

"Oh, I'm a rough customer!" said Dick. "But I wouldn't steal. It's mean."

"I'm glad you think so, Dick," and the rough voice sounded gentler than at first. "Have you got any money to buy your breakfast?"

"No, but I'll soon get some."

While this conversation had been going on, Dick had got up. His bedchamber had been a wooden box half full of straw, on which the young bootblack had reposed his weary limbs, and slept as soundly as if it had been a bed of down. He dumped down into the straw without taking the trouble of undressing.

Getting up too was an equally short process. He jumped out of the box, shook himself, picked out one or two straws that had found their way into rents in his clothes, and, drawing a well-worn cap over his uncombed locks, he was all ready for the business of the day.

Dick's appearance as he stood beside the box was rather peculiar. His pants were torn in several places, and had apparently belonged in the first instance to a boy two sizes larger than himself. He wore a vest, all the buttons of which were gone except two, out of which peeped a shirt which looked as if it had been worn a month. To complete his costume he wore a coat too long for him, dating back, if one might judge from its general appearance, to a remote antiquity.

Washing the face and hands is usually considered proper in commencing the day, but Dick was above such refinement. He had no particular dislike to dirt, and did not think it necessary to remove several dark streaks on his face and hands. But in spite of his dirt and rags there was something about Dick that was attractive. It was easy to see that if he had been clean and well dressed he would have been decidedly good-looking. Some of his companions were sly, and their faces inspired distrust; but Dick had a frank, straightforward manner that made him a favorite.

Dick's business hours had commenced. He had no office to open. His little blacking-box was ready for use, and he looked sharply in the faces of all who passed, addressing each with, "Shine yer boots, sir?"

"How much?" asked a gentleman on his way to his office.

"Ten cents," said Dick, dropping his box, and sinking upon his knees on the sidewalk, flourishing his brush with the air of one skilled in his profession.

"Ten cents! Isn't that a little steep?"

"Well, you know 'taint all clear profit," said Dick, who had already set to work. "There's the *blacking* costs something, and I have to get a new brush pretty often."

"And you have a large rent too," said the gentleman quizzically, with a glance at a large hole in Dick's coat.

"Yes, sir," said Dick, always ready to joke, "I have to pay such a big rent for my manshun up on Fifth Avenoo, that I can't afford to take less than ten cents a shine. I'll give you a bully shine, sir."

"Be quick about it, for I am in a hurry. So your house is on Fifth Avenue, is it?"

"It isn't anywhere else," said Dick, and Dick spoke the truth there.

"What tailor do you patronize?" asked the gentleman, surveying Dick's attire.

"Would you like to go to the same one?" asked Dick, shrewdly.

"Well, no; it strikes me that he didn't give you a very good fit."

"This coat once belonged to General Washington," said Dick, comically. "He wore it all through the Revolution, and it got torn some, 'cause he fit so hard. When he died he told his widder to give it to some smart young feller that hadn't got none of his own; so she gave it to me. But if you'd like it, sir, to remember General Washington by, I'll let you have it reasonable."

"Thank you, but I wouldn't want to deprive you of it. And did your pants come from General Washington too?"

"No, they was a gift from Lewis Napoleon. Lewis had outgrown 'em and sent 'em to me,—he's bigger than me, and that's why they don't fit."

"It seems you have distinguished friends. Now, my lad, I suppose you would like your money."

"I shouldn't have any objection," said Dick.

"I believe," said the gentleman, examining his pocket-book, "I haven't got anything short of twenty-five cents. Have you got any change?"

"Not a cent," said Dick. "All my money's invested' in the Erie Railroad."

"That's unfortunate."

"Shall I get the money changed, sir?"

"I can't wait; I've got to meet an appointment immediately. I'll hand you twenty-five cents, and you can leave the change at my office any time during the day."

"All right, sir. Where is it?"

"No. 125 Fulton Street. Shall you remember?"

"Yes, sir. What name?"

"Greyson,—office on second floor."

"All right, sir; I'll bring it."

"I wonder whether the little scamp will prove honest," said Mr. Greyson to himself, as he walked away. "If he does, I'll give him my custom regularly. If he don't, as is most likely, I shan't mind the loss of fifteen cents."

Mr. Greyson didn't understand Dick. Our ragged hero wasn't a model boy in all respects. I am afraid he swore sometimes, and now and then he played tricks upon unsophisticated boys from the country, or gave a wrong direction to honest old gentlemen unused to the city. A clergyman in search of the Cooper Institute he once directed to the Tombs Prison, and, following him unobserved, was highly delighted when the unsuspicious stranger walked up the front steps of the great stone building on Centre Street, and tried to obtain admission.

"I guess he wouldn't want to stay long if he did get in," thought Ragged Dick, hitching up his pants. "Leastways I shouldn't. They're so precious glad to see you that they won't let you go, but board you gratooitous, and never send in no bills."

Another of Dick's faults was his extravagance. Being always wide-awake and ready for business, he earned enough to have supported him comfortably and respectably. There were not a few young clerks who employed Dick from time to time in his professional capacity, who scarcely earned as much as he, greatly as their style and dress exceeded his. But Dick was careless of his earnings. Where they went he could hardly have told himself. However much he managed to earn during the day, all was generally spent before morning. He was fond of going to the Old Bowery Theatre, and to Tony Pastor's, and if he had any money left afterwards, he would invite some of his friends in somewhere to have an oyster stew; so it seldom happened that he commenced the day with a penny.

Then I am sorry to add that Dick had formed the habit of smoking. This cost him considerable, for Dick was rather fastidious about his cigars, and wouldn't smoke the cheapest. Besides, having a liberal nature, he was generally ready to treat his companions. But of course the expense was the smallest objection. No boy of fourteen can smoke without being affected injuriously. Men are frequently injured by smoking, and boys always. But large numbers of the newsboys and boot-blacks form the habit. Exposed to the cold and wet they find that it warms them up, and the self-indulgence grows upon them. It is not uncommon to see a little boy, too young to be out of his mother's sight, smoking with all the apparent satisfaction of a veteran smoker.

There was another way in which Dick sometimes lost money. There was a noted gambling-house on Baxter Street, which in the evening was sometimes crowded with these juvenile gamesters, who staked their hard earnings, generally losing of course, and refreshing themselves from time to time with a vile mixture of liquor at two cents a glass. Sometimes Dick strayed in here, and played with the rest.

I have mentioned Dick's faults and defects, because I want it understood, to begin with, that I don't consider him a model boy. But there were some good points about him nevertheless. He was above doing anything mean or dishonorable. He would not steal, or cheat, or impose upon younger boys, but was frank and straight-forward, manly and self-reliant. His nature was a noble one, and had saved him from all mean faults. I hope my young readers will like him as I do, without being blind to his faults. Perhaps, although he was only a boot-black, they may find something in him to imitate.

And now, having fairly introduced Ragged Dick to my young readers, I must refer them to the next chapter for his further adventures.

CHAPTER II

JOHNNY NOLAN

AFTER Dick had finished polishing Mr. Greyson's boots he was fortunate enough to secure three other customers, two of them reporters in the Tribune establishment, which occupies the corner of Spruce Street and Printing House Square.

When Dick had got through with his last customer the City Hall clock indicated eight o'clock. He had been up an hour, and hard at work, and naturally began to think of breakfast. He went up to the head of Spruce Street, and turned into Nassau. Two blocks further, and he reached Ann Street. On this street was a small, cheap restaurant, where for five cents Dick could get a cup of coffee, and for ten cents more, a plate of beefsteak with a plate of bread thrown in. These Dick ordered, and sat down at a table.

It was a small apartment with a few plain tables unprovided with cloths, for the class of customers who patronized it were not very particular. Our hero's breakfast was soon before him. Neither the coffee nor the steak were as good as can be bought at Delmonico's; but then it is very doubtful whether, in the present state of his wardrobe, Dick would have been received at that aristocratic restaurant, even if his means had admitted of paying the high prices there charged.

Dick had scarcely been served when he espied a boy about his own size standing at the door, looking wistfully into the restaurant. This was Johnny Nolan, a boy of fourteen, who was engaged in the same profession as Ragged Dick. His wardrobe was in very much the same condition as Dick's.

"Had your breakfast, Johnny?" inquired Dick, cutting off a piece of steak.

"No."

"Come in, then. Here's room for you."

"I ain't got no money," said Johnny, looking a little enviously at his more fortunate friend.

"Haven't you had any shines?"

"Yes, I had one, but I shan't get any pay till to-morrow."

"Are you hungry?"

"Try me, and see."

"Come in. I'll stand treat this morning."

Johnny Nolan was nowise slow to accept this invitation, and was soon seated beside Dick.

"What'll you have, Johnny?"

"Same as you."

"Cup o' coffee and beefsteak," ordered Dick.

These were promptly brought, and Johnny attacked them vigorously.

Now, in the boot-blacking business, as well as in higher avocations, the same rule prevails, that energy and industry are rewarded, and indolence suffers. Dick was energetic and on the alert for business, but Johnny the reverse. The consequence was that Dick earned probably three times as much as the other.

"How do you like it?" asked Dick, surveying Johnny's attacks upon the steak with evident complacency.

"It's hunky."

I don't believe "hunky" is to be found in either Webster's or Worcester's big dictionary; but boys will readily understand what it means.

"Do you come here often?" asked Johnny.

"Most every day. You'd better come too."

"I can't afford it."

"Well, you'd ought to, then," said Dick. "What do you do with your money, I'd like to know?"

"I don't get near as much as you, Dick."

"Well, you might if you tried. I keep my eyes open,—that's the way I get jobs. You're lazy, that's what's the matter."

Johnny did not see fit to reply to this charge. Probably he felt the justice of it, and preferred to proceed with the breakfast, which he enjoyed the more as it cost him nothing.

Breakfast over, Dick walked up to the desk, and settled the bill. Then, followed by Johnny, he went out into the street.

"Where are you going, Johnny?"

"Up to Mr. Taylor's, on Spruce Street, to see if he don't want a shine."

"Do you work for him reg'lar?"

"Yes. Him and his partner wants a shine most every day. Where are you goin'?"

"Down front of the Astor House. I guess I'll find some customers there."

At this moment Johnny started, and, dodging into an entry way, hid behind the door, considerably to Dick's surprise.

"What's the matter now?" asked our hero.

"Has he gone?" asked Johnny, his voice betraying anxiety.

"Who gone, I'd like to know?"

"That man in the brown coat."

"What of him. You ain't scared of him, are you?"

"Yes, he got me a place once."

"Where?"

"Ever so far off."

"What if he did?"

"I ran away."

"Didn't you like it?"

"No, I had to get up too early. It was on a farm, and I had to get up at five to take care of the cows. I like New York best."

"Didn't they give you enough to eat?"

"Oh, yes, plenty."

"And you had a good bed?"

"Yes."

"Then you'd better have stayed. You don't get either of them here. Where'd you sleep last night?"

"Up an alley in an old wagon."

"You had a better bed than that in the country, didn't you?"

"Yes, it was as soft as—as cotton."

Johnny had once slept on a bale of cotton, the recollection supplying him with a comparison.

"Why didn't you stay?"

"I felt lonely," said Johnny.

Johnny could not exactly explain his feelings, but it is often the case that the young vagabond of the streets, though his food is uncertain, and his bed may be any old wagon or barrel that he is lucky enough to find unoccupied when night sets in, gets so attached to his precarious but independent mode of life, that he feels discontented in any other. He is accustomed to the noise and bustle and ever-varied life of the streets, and in the quiet scenes of the country misses the excitement in the midst of which he has always dwelt.

Johnny had but one tie to bind him to the city. He had a father living, but he might as well have been without one. Mr. Nolan was a confirmed drunkard, and spent the greater part of his wages for liquor. His potations made him ugly, and inflamed a temper never very sweet, working him up sometimes to such a pitch of rage that Johnny's life was in danger. Some months before, he had thrown a flat-iron at his son's head with such terrific force that unless Johnny had dodged he would not have lived long enough to obtain a place in our story. He fled the house, and from that time had not dared to re-enter it. Somebody had given him a brush and box of blacking, and he had set up in business on his own account. But he had not energy enough to succeed, as has already been stated, and I am afraid the poor boy had met with many hardships, and suffered more than once from cold and hunger. Dick had befriended him more than once, and often given him a breakfast or dinner, as the case might be.

"How'd you get away?" asked Dick, with some curiosity. "Did you walk?"

"No, I rode on the cars."

"Where'd you get your money? I hope you didn't steal it."

"I didn't have none."

"What did you do, then?"

"I got up about three o'clock, and walked to Albany."

"Where's that?" asked Dick, whose ideas on the subject of geography were rather vague.

"Up the river."

"How far?"

"About a thousand miles," said Johnny, whose conceptions of distance were equally vague.

"Go ahead. What did you do then?"

"I hid on top of a freight car, and came all the way without their seeing me. That man in the brown coat was the man that got me the place, and I'm afraid he'd want to send me back."

"Well," said Dick, reflectively, "I dunno as I'd like to live in the country. I couldn't go to Tony Pastor's or the Old Bowery. There wouldn't be no place to spend my evenings. But I say, it's tough in winter, Johnny, 'specially when your overcoat's at the tailor's, an' likely to stay there."

"That's so, Dick. But I must be goin', or Mr. Taylor'll get somebody else to shine his boots."

Johnny walked back to Nassau Street, while Dick kept on his way to Broadway.

"That boy," soliloquized Dick, as Johnny took his departure, "ain't got no ambition. I'll bet he won't get five shines to-day. I'm glad I ain't like him. I couldn't go to the theatre, nor buy no cigars, nor get half as much as I wanted to eat.—Shine yer boots, sir?"

Dick always had an eye to business, and this remark was addressed to a young man, dressed in a stylish manner, who was swinging a jaunty cane.

"I've had my boots blacked once already this morning, but this confounded mud has spoiled the shine."

"I'll make 'em all right, sir, in a minute."

"Go ahead, then."

The boots were soon polished in Dick's best style, which proved very satisfactory, our hero being a proficient in the art.

"I haven't got any change," said the young man, fumbling in his pocket, "but here's a bill you may run somewhere and get changed. I'll pay you five cents extra for your trouble."

He handed Dick a two-dollar bill, which our hero took into a store close by. "Will you please change that, sir?" said Dick, walking up to the counter.

The salesman to whom he proffered it took the bill, and, slightly glancing at it, exclaimed angrily, "Be off, you young vagabond, or I'll have you arrested."

"What's the row?"

"You've offered me a counterfeit bill."

"I didn't know it," said Dick.

"Don't tell me. Be off, or I'll have you arrested."

CHAPTER III
DICK MAKES A PROPOSITION

THOUGH Dick was somewhat startled at discovering that the bill he had offered was counterfeit, he stood his ground bravely.

"Clear out of this shop, you young vagabond," repeated the clerk.

"Then give me back my bill."

"That you may pass it again? No, sir, I shall do no such thing."

"It doesn't belong to me," said Dick. "A gentleman that owes me for a shine gave it to me to change."

"A likely story," said the clerk; but he seemed a little uneasy.

"I'll go and call him," said Dick.

He went out, and found his late customer standing on the Astor House steps.

"Well, youngster, have you brought back my change? You were a precious long time about it. I began to think you had cleared out with the money."

"That ain't my style," said Dick, proudly.

"Then where's the change?"

"I haven't got it."

"Where's the bill then?"

"I haven't got that either."

"You young rascal!"

"Hold on a minute, mister," said Dick, "and I'll tell you all about it. The man what took the bill said it wasn't good, and kept it."

"The bill was perfectly good. So he kept it, did he? I'll go with you to the store, and see whether he won't give it back to me."

Dick led the way, and the gentleman followed him into the store. At the reappearance of Dick in such company, the clerk flushed a little, and looked nervous. He fancied that he could browbeat a ragged boot-black, but with a gentleman he saw that it would be a different matter. He did not seem to notice the new-comers, but began to replace some goods on the shelves.

"Now," said the young man, "point out the clerk that has my money."

"That's him," said Dick, pointing out the clerk.

The gentleman walked up to the counter.

"I will trouble you," he said a little haughtily, "for a bill which that boy offered you, and which you still hold in your possession."

"It was a bad bill," said the clerk, his cheek flushing, and his manner nervous.

"It was no such thing. I require you to produce it, and let the matter be decided."

The clerk fumbled in his vest-pocket, and drew out a bad-looking bill.

"This is a bad bill, but it is not the one I gave the boy."

"It is the one he gave me."

The young man looked doubtful.

"Boy," he said to Dick, "is this the bill you gave to be changed?"

"No, it isn't."

"You lie, you young rascal!" exclaimed the clerk, who began to find himself in a tight place, and could not see the way out.

This scene naturally attracted the attention of all in the store, and the proprietor walked up from the lower end, where he had been busy.

"What's all this, Mr. Hatch?" he demanded.

"That boy," said the clerk, "came in and asked change for a bad bill. I kept the bill, and told him to clear out. Now he wants it again to pass on somebody else."

"Show the bill."

The merchant looked at it. "Yes, that's a bad bill," he said. "There is no doubt about that."

"But it is not the one the boy offered," said Dick's patron. "It is one of the same denomination, but on a different bank."

"Do you remember what bank it was on?"

"It was on the Merchant's Bank of Boston."

"Are you sure of it?"

"I am."

"Perhaps the boy kept it and offered the other."

"You may search me if you want to," said Dick, indignantly.

"He doesn't look as if he was likely to have any extra bills. I suspect that your clerk pocketed the good bill, and has substituted the counterfeit note. It is a nice little scheme of his for making money."

"I haven't seen any bill on the Merchant's Bank," said the clerk, doggedly.

"You had better feel in your pockets."

"This matter must be investigated," said the merchant firmly. "If you have the bill, produce it."

"I haven't got it," said the clerk; but he looked guilty notwithstanding.

"I demand that he be searched," said Dick's patron.

"I tell you I haven't got it."

"Shall I send for a police officer, Mr. Hatch, or will you allow yourself to be searched quietly?" said the merchant.

Alarmed at the threat implied in these words, the clerk put his hand into his vest-pocket, and drew out a two-dollar bill on the Merchants' Bank.

"Is this your note?" asked the shopkeeper, showing it to the young man.

"It is."

"I must have made a mistake," faltered the clerk.

"I shall not give you a chance to make such another mistake in my employ," said the merchant sternly. "You may go up to the desk and ask for what wages are due you. I shall have no further occasion for your services."

"Now, youngster," said Dick's patron, as they went out of the store, after he had finally got the bill changed. "I must pay you something extra for your trouble. Here's fifty cents."

"Thank you, sir," said Dick. "You're very kind. Don't you want some more bills changed?"

"Not to-day," said he with a smile. "It's too expensive."

"I'm in luck," thought our hero complacently. "I guess I'll go to Barnum's to-night, and see the bearded lady, the eight-foot giant, the two-foot dwarf, and the other curiosities, too numerous to mention."

Dick shouldered his box and walked up as far as the Astor House. He took his station on the sidewalk, and began to look about him.

Just behind him were two persons,—one, a gentleman of fifty; the other, a boy of thirteen or fourteen. They were speaking together, and Dick had no difficulty in hearing what was said.

"I am sorry, Frank, that I can't go about, and show you some of the sights of New York, but I shall be full of business to-day. It is your first visit to the city too."

"Yes, sir."

"There's a good deal worth seeing here. But I'm afraid you'll have to wait till next time. You can go out and walk by yourself, but don't venture too far, or you may get lost."

Frank looked disappointed.

"I wish Tom Miles knew I was here," he said. "He would go around with me."

"Where does he live?"

"Somewhere up town, I believe."

"Then, unfortunately, he is not available. If you would rather go with me than stay here, you can, but as I shall be most of the time in merchants' counting-rooms, I am afraid it would not be very interesting."

"I think," said Frank, after a little hesitation, "that I will go off by myself. I won't go very far, and if I lose my way, I will inquire for the Astor House."

"Yes, anybody will direct you here. Very well, Frank, I am sorry I can't do better for you."

"Oh, never mind, uncle. I shall be amused in walking around, and looking at the shop-windows. There will be a great deal to see."

Now Dick had listened to all this conversation. Being an enterprising young man, he thought he saw a chance for a speculation, and determined to avail himself of it.

Accordingly he stepped up to the two just as Frank's uncle was about leaving, and said, "I know all about the city, sir; I'll show him around, if you want me to."

The gentleman looked a little curiously at the ragged figure before him.

"So you are a city boy, are you?"

"Yes, sir," said Dick, "I've lived here ever since I was a baby."

"And you know all about the public buildings, I suppose?"

"Yes, sir."

"And the Central Park?"

"Yes, sir. I know my way all round."

The gentleman looked thoughtful.

"I don't know what to say, Frank," he remarked after a while. "It is rather a novel proposal. He isn't exactly the sort of guide I would have picked out for you. Still he looks honest. He has an open face, and I think can be depended upon."

"I wish he wasn't so ragged and dirty," said Frank, who felt a little shy about being seen with such a companion.

"I'm afraid you haven't washed your face this morning," said Mr. Whitney, for that was the gentleman's name.

"They didn't have no wash-bowls at the hotel where I stopped," said Dick.

"What hotel did you stop at?"

"The Box Hotel."

"The Box Hotel?"

"Yes, sir, I slept in a box on Spruce Street."

Frank surveyed Dick curiously.

"How did you like it?" he asked.

"I slept bully."

"Suppose it had rained."

"Then I'd have wet my best clothes," said Dick.

"Are these all the clothes you have?"

"Yes, sir."

Mr. Whitney spoke a few words to Frank, who seemed pleased with the suggestion.

"Follow me, my lad," he said.

Dick in some surprise obeyed orders, following Mr. Whitney and Frank into the hotel, past the office, to the foot of the staircase. Here a servant of the hotel stopped Dick, but Mr. Whitney explained that he had something for him to do, and he was allowed to proceed.

They entered a long entry, and finally paused before a door. This being opened a pleasant chamber was disclosed.

"Come in, my lad," said Mr. Whitney.

Dick and Frank entered.

CHAPTER IV

DICK'S NEW SUIT

"NOW," said Mr. Whitney to Dick, "my nephew here is on his way to a boarding-school. He had a suit of clothes in his trunk about half worn. He is willing to give them to you. I think they will look better than those you have on."

Dick was so astonished that he hardly knew what to say. Presents were something that he knew very little about, never having received any to his knowledge. That so large a gift should be made to him by a stranger seemed very wonderful.

The clothes were brought out, and turned out to be a neat gray suit.

"Before you put them on, my lad, you must wash yourself. Clean clothes and a dirty skin don't go very well together. Frank, you may attend to him. I am obliged to go at once. Have you got as much money as you require?"

"Yes, uncle."

"One more word, my lad," said Mr. Whitney, addressing Dick; "I may be rash in trusting a boy of whom I know nothing, but I like your looks, and I think you will prove a proper guide for my nephew."

"Yes I will, sir," said Dick, earnestly. "Honor bright!"

"Very well. A pleasant time to you."

The process of cleansing commenced. To tell the truth Dick needed it, and the sensation of cleanliness he found both new and pleasant. Frank added to his gift a shirt, stockings, and an old pair of shoes. "I am sorry I haven't any cap," said he.

"I've got one," said Dick.

"It isn't so new as it might be," said Frank, surveying an old felt hat, which had once been black, but was now dingy, with a large hole in the top and a portion of the rim torn off.

"No," said Dick; "my grandfather used to wear it when he was a boy, and I've kep' it ever since out of respect for his memory. But I'll get a new one now. I can buy one cheap on Chatham Street."

"Is that near here?"

"Only five minutes' walk."

"Then we can get one on the way."

When Dick was dressed in his new attire, with his face and hands clean, and his hair brushed, it was difficult to imagine that he was the same boy.

He now looked quite handsome, and might readily have been taken for a young gentleman, except that his hands were red and grimy.

"Look at yourself," said Frank, leading him before the mirror.

"By gracious!" said Dick, starting back in astonishment, "that isn't me, is it?"

"Don't you know yourself?" asked Frank, smiling.

"It reminds me of Cinderella," said Dick, "when she was changed into a fairy princess. I see it one night at Barnum's. What'll Johnny Nolan say when he sees me? He won't dare to speak to such a young swell as I be now. Ain't it rich?" and Dick burst into a loud laugh. His fancy was tickled by the anticipation of his friend's surprise. Then the thought of the valuable gifts he had received occurred to him, and he looked gratefully at Frank.

"You're a brick," he said.

"A what?"

"A brick! You're a jolly good fellow to give me such a present."

"You're quite welcome, Dick," said Frank, kindly. "I'm better off than you are, and I can spare the clothes just as well as not. You must have a new hat though. But that we can get when we go out. The old clothes you can make into a bundle."

"Wait a minute till I get my handkercher," and Dick pulled from the pocket of the pants a dirty rag, which might have been white once, though it did not look like it, and had apparently once formed a part of a sheet or shirt.

"You mustn't carry that," said Frank.

"But I've got a cold," said Dick.

"Oh, I don't mean you to go without a handkerchief. I'll give you one."

Frank opened his trunk and pulled out two, which he gave to Dick.

"I wonder if I ain't dreamin'," said Dick, once more surveying himself doubtfully in the glass. "I'm afraid I'm dreamin', and shall wake up in a barrel, as I did night afore last."

"Shall I pinch you so you can wake here?" asked Frank, playfully.

"Yes," said Dick, seriously, "I wish you would."

He pulled up the sleeve of his jacket, and Frank pinched him pretty hard, so that Dick winced.

"Yes, I guess I'm awake," said Dick; " you've got a pair of nippers, you have. But what shall I do with my brush and blacking?" he asked.

"You can leave them here till we come back," said Frank. "They will be safe."

"Hold on a minute," said Dick, surveying Frank's boots with a professional eye, "you ain't got a good shine on them boots. I'll make 'em shine so you can see your face in 'em."

And he was as good as his word.

"Thank you," said Frank; "now you had better brush your own shoes."

This had not occurred to Dick, for in general the professional boot-black considers his blacking too valuable to expend on his own shoes or boots, if he is fortunate enough to possess a pair.

The two boys now went downstairs together. They met the same servant who had spoken to Dick a few minutes before, but there was no recognition.

"He don't know me," said Dick. "He thinks I'm a young swell like you."

"What's a swell?"

"Oh, a feller that wears nobby clothes like you."

"And you, too, Dick."

"Yes," said Dick, "who'd ever have thought as I should have turned into a swell?"

They had now got out on Broadway, and were slowly walking along the west side by the Park, when who should Dick see in front of him, but Johnny Nolan?

Instantly Dick was seized with a fancy for witnessing Johnny's amazement at his change in appearance. He stole up behind him, and struck him on the back.

"Hallo, Johnny, how many shines have you had?"

Johnny turned round expecting to see Dick, whose voice he recognized, but his astonished eyes rested on a nicely dressed boy (the hat alone excepted) who looked indeed like Dick, but so transformed in dress that it was difficult to be sure of his identity.

"What luck, Johnny?" repeated Dick.

Johnny surveyed him from head to foot in great bewilderment.

"Who be you?" he said.

"Well, that's a good one," laughed Dick; "so you don't know Dick?"

"Where'd you get all them clothes?" asked Johnny. "Have you been stealin'?"

"Say that again, and I'll lick you. No, I've lent my clothes to a young feller as was goin' to a party, and didn't have none fit to wear, and so I put on my second-best for a change."

Without deigning any further explanation, Dick went off, followed by the astonished gaze of Johnny Nolan, who could not quite make up his mind whether the neat-looking boy he had been talking with was really Ragged Dick or not.

In order to reach Chatham Street it was necessary to cross Broadway. This was easier proposed than done. There is always such a throng of omnibuses, drays, carriages, and vehicles of all kinds in the neighborhood of the Astor House, that the crossing is formidable to one who is not used to it. Dick made nothing of it, dodging in and out among the horses and wagons with perfect self-possession. Reaching the opposite sidewalk, he looked back, and found that Frank had retreated in dismay, and that the width of the street was between them.

"Come across!" called out Dick.

"I don't see any chance," said Frank, looking anxiously at the prospect before him. "I'm afraid of being run over."

"If you are, you can sue 'em for damages," said Dick.

Finally Frank got safely over after several narrow escapes, as he considered them.

"Is it always so crowded?" he asked.

"A good deal worse sometimes," said Dick. "I knowed a young man once who waited six hours for a chance to cross, and at last got run over by an omnibus, leaving a widder and a large family of orphan children. His widder, a beautiful young woman, was obliged to start a peanut and apple stand. There she is now."

"Where?"

Dick pointed to a hideous old woman, of large proportions, wearing a bonnet of immense size, who presided over an apple-stand close by. Frank laughed.

"If that is the case," he said, "I think I will patronize her."

"Leave it to me," said Dick, winking.

He advanced gravely to the apple-stand, and said, "Old lady, have you paid your taxes?"

The astonished woman opened her eyes.

"I'm a gov'ment officer," said Dick, "sent by the mayor to collect your taxes. I'll take it in apples just to oblige. That big red one will about pay what you're owin' to the gov'ment."

"I don't know nothing about no taxes," said the old woman, in bewilderment.

"Then," said Dick, "I'll let you off this time. Give us two of your best apples, and my friend here, the President of the Common Council, will pay you."

Frank smiling, paid three cents apiece for the apples, and they sauntered on, Dick remarking, "If these apples ain't good, old lady, we'll return 'em, and get our money back." This would have been rather difficult in his case, as the apple was already half consumed.

Chatham Street, where they wished to go, being on the East side, the two boys crossed the Park. This is an enclosure of about ten acres, which years ago was covered with a green sward, but is now a great thoroughfare for pedestrians and contains several important public buildings. Dick pointed out the City Hall, the Hall of Records, and the Rotunda. The former is a white building of large size, and surmounted by a cupola.

"That's where the mayor's office is," said Dick. "Him and me are very good friends. I once blacked his boots by partic'lar appointment. That's the way I pay my city taxes." . . .

CHAPTER VIII

DICK'S EARLY HISTORY

"HAVE you always lived in New York, Dick?" asked Frank, after a pause.

"Ever since I can remember."

"I wish you'd tell me a little about yourself. Have you got any father or mother?"

"I ain't got no mother. She died when I wasn't but three years old. My father went to sea; but he went off before mother died, and nothin' was ever heard of him. I expect he got wrecked, or died at sea."

"And what became of you when your mother died?"

"The folks she boarded with took care of me, but they was poor, and they couldn't do much. When I was seven the woman died, and her husband went out West, and then I had to scratch for myself."

"At seven years old!" exclaimed Frank, in amazement.

"Yes," said Dick, "I was a little feller to take care of myself, but," he continued with pardonable pride, "I did it."

"What could you do?"

"Sometimes one thing, and sometimes another," said Dick. "I changed my business accordin' as I had to. Sometimes I was a newsboy, and diffused intelligence among the masses, as I heard somebody say once in a big speech he made in the Park. Them was the times when Horace Greeley and James Gordon Bennett made money."

"Through your enterprise?" suggested Frank.

"Yes," said Dick; "but I give it up after a while."

"What for?"

"Well, they didn't always put news enough in their papers, and people wouldn't buy 'em as fast as I wanted 'em to. So one mornin' I was stuck on a lot of Heralds, and I thought I'd make a sensation. So I called out 'GREAT NEWS! QUEEN VICTORIA ASSASSINATED!' All my Heralds went off like hot cakes, and I went off, too, but one of the gentlemen what got sold remembered me, and said he'd have me took up, and that's what made me change my business."

"That wasn't right, Dick," said Frank.

"I know it," said Dick; "but lots of boys does it."

"That don't make it any better."

"No," said Dick, "I was sort of ashamed at the time, 'specially about one poor old gentleman,—a Englishman he was. He couldn't help cryin' to think the queen was dead, and his hands shook when he handed me the money for the paper."

"What did you do next?"

"I went into the match business," said Dick, "but it was small sales and small profits. Most of the people I called on had just laid in a stock, and didn't want to buy. So one cold night, when I hadn't money enough to pay for a lodgin', I burned the last of my matches to keep me from freezin'. But it cost too much to get warm that way, and I couldn't keep it up."

"You've seen hard times, Dick," said Frank, compassionately.

"Yes," said Dick, "I've knowed what it was to be hungry and cold, with nothin' to eat or to warm me; but there's one thing I never could do," he added proudly.

"What's that?"

"I never stole," said Dick. "It's mean and I wouldn't do it."

"Were you ever tempted to?"

"Lots of times. Once I had been goin' round all day, and hadn't sold any matches, except three cents' worth early in the mornin'. With that I bought an apple, thinkin' I should get some more bimeby. When evenin' come I was awful hungry. I went into a baker's just to look at the bread. It made me feel kind o' good just to look at the bread and cakes, and I thought maybe they would give me some. I asked 'em wouldn't they give me a loaf, and take their pay in matches. But they said they'd got enough matches to last three months; so there wasn't any chance for a trade. While I was standin' at the stove warmin' me, the baker went into a back room, and I felt so hungry I thought I would take just one loaf, and go off with it. There was such a big pile I don't think he'd have known it."

"But you didn't do it?"

"No, I didn't, and I was glad of it, for when the man came in ag'in, he said he wanted some one to carry some cake to a lady in St. Mark's Place. His boy was sick, and he hadn't no one to send; so he told me he'd give me ten cents if I would go. My business wasn't very pressin' just then, so I went, and when

I come back, I took my pay in bread and cakes. Didn't they taste good, though?"

"So you didn't stay long in the match business, Dick?"

"No, I couldn't sell enough to make it pay. Then there was some folks that wanted me to sell cheaper to them; so I couldn't make any profit. There was one old lady—she was rich, too, for she lived in a big brick house—beat me down so, that I didn't make no profit at all; but she wouldn't buy without, and I hadn't sold none that day; so I let her have them. I don't see why rich folks should be so hard upon a poor boy that wants to make a livin'."

"There's a good deal of meanness in the world, I'm afraid, Dick."

"If everybody was like you and your uncle," said Dick, "there would be some chance for poor people. If I was rich I'd try to help 'em along."

"Perhaps you will be rich sometime, Dick."

Dick shook his head.

"I'm afraid all my wallets will be like this," said Dick, indicating, the one he had received from the dropper [a scam artist], "and will be full of papers what ain't of no use to anybody except the owner."

"That depends very much on yourself, Dick," said Frank. "Stewart wasn't always rich, you know."

"Wasn't he?"

"When he first came to New York as a young man he was a teacher, and teachers are not generally very rich. At last he went into business, starting in a small way, and worked his way up by degrees. But there was one thing he determined in the beginning; that he would be strictly honorable in all his dealings, and never overreach any one for the sake of making money. If there was a chance for him, Dick, there is a chance for you."

"He knowed enough to be a teacher, and I'm awful ignorant," said Dick.

"But you needn't stay so."

"How can I help it?"

"Can't you learn at school?"

"I can't go to school 'cause I've got my livin' to earn. It wouldn't do me much good if I learned to read and write, and just as I'd got learned I starved to death."

"But are there no night-schools?"

"Yes."

"Why don't you go? I suppose you don't work in the evenings."

"I never cared much about it," said Dick, "and that's the truth. But since I've got to talkin' with you, I think more about it. I guess I'll begin to go."

"I wish you would, Dick. You'll make a smart man if you only get a little education."

"Do you think so?" asked Dick, doubtfully.

"I know so. A boy who has earned his own living ever since he was seven years old must have something in him. I feel very much interested in you, Dick. You've had a hard time of it so far in life, but I think better times are in store. I want you to do well, and I feel sure you can if you only try."

"You're a good fellow," said Dick, gratefully. "I'm afraid I'm a pretty rough customer, but I ain't as bad as some. I mean to turn over a new leaf, and try to grow up 'spectable."

"There've been a great many boys begin as low down as you, Dick, that have grown up respectable and honored. But they had to work pretty hard for it."

"I'm willin' to work hard," said Dick.

"And you must not only work hard, but work in the right way."

"What's the right way?"

"You began in the right way when you determined never to steal, or do anything mean or dishonorable, however strongly tempted to do so. That will make people have confidence in you when they come to know you. But, in order to succeed well, you must manage to get as good an education as you can. Until you do, you cannot get a position in an office or counting-room, even to run errands."

"That's so," said Dick, soberly. "I never thought how awful ignorant I was till now."

"That can be remedied with perseverance," said Frank. "A year will do a great deal for you."

"I'll go to work and see what I can do," said Dick, energetically. . . .

CHAPTER X

INTRODUCES A VICTIM OF MISPLACED CONFIDENCE

"WHAT a queer chap you are, Dick!" said Frank laughing. "You always seem to be in good spirits."

"No, I ain't always. Sometimes I have the blues."

"When?"

"Well, once last winter it was awful cold, and there was big holes in my shoes, and my gloves and all my warm clothes was at the tailor's. I felt as if life was sort of tough, and I'd like it if some rich man would adopt me, and give me plenty to eat and drink and wear, without my havin' to look so sharp after it. Then agin' when I've seen boys with good homes, and fathers, and mothers, I've thought I'd like to have somebody to care for me."

Dick's tone changed as he said this, from his usual levity, and there was a touch of sadness in it. Frank, blessed with a good home and indulgent parents, could not help pitying the friendless boy who had found life such up-hill work.

"Don't say you have no one to care for you, Dick," he said, lightly laying his hand on Dick's shoulder. "I will care for you."

"Will you?"

"If you will let me."

"I wish you would," said Dick, earnestly. "I'd like to feel that I have one friend who cares for me."

Central Park was now before them, but it was far from presenting the appearance which it now exhibits. It had not been long since work had been commenced upon it, and it was still very rough and unfinished. A rough tract of land, two miles and a half from north to south, and a half a mile broad, very rocky in parts, was the material from which the Park Commissioners have made the present beautiful enclosure. There were no houses of good appearance near it, buildings being limited mainly to rude temporary huts used by the workmen who were employed in improving it. The time will undoubtedly come when the Park will be surrounded by elegant residences, and compare favorably in this respect with the most attractive parts of any city in the world. But at the time when Frank and Dick visited it, not much could be said in favor either of the Park or its neighborhood.

"If this is Central Park," said Frank, who naturally felt disappointed, "I don't think much of it. My father's got a large pasture that is much nicer."

"It'll look better some time," said Dick. "There ain't much to see now but rocks. We will take a walk over it if you want to."

"No," said Frank, "I've seen as much of it as I want to. Besides, I feel tired."

"Then we'll go back. We can take the Sixth Avenue cars. They will bring us out at Vesey Street, just beside the Astor House."

"All right," said Frank. "That will be the best course. . . . Is that the right car, Dick?"

"Yes, jump in, and I'll follow."

The Sixth Avenue is lined with stores, many of them of very good appearance, and would make a very respectable principal street for a good-sized city. But it is only one of several long business streets which run up the island, and illustrate the extent and importance of the city to which they belong.

No incidents worth mentioning took place during their ride down town. In about three-quarters of an hour the boys got out of the car beside the Astor House.

"Are you goin' in now, Frank?" asked Dick.

"That depends upon whether you have anything else to show me."

"Wouldn't you like to go to Wall Street?"

"That's the street where there are so many bankers and brokers,—isn't it?"

"Yes, I s'pose you ain't afraid of bulls and bears,—are you?"

"Bulls and bears?" repeated Frank, puzzled.

"Yes."

"What are they?"

"The bulls is what tries to make the stocks go up, and the bears is what try to growl 'em down."

"Oh, I see. Yes, I'd like to go."

Accordingly they walked down on the west side of Broadway as far as Trinity Church, and then, crossing, entered a street not very wide or very long, but of very great importance. The reader would be astonished if he could know the amount of money involved in the transactions which take place in a single day in this street. It would be found that although Broadway is much greater in length, and lined with stores, it stands second to Wall Street in this respect.

"What is that large marble building?" asked Frank, pointing to a massive structure on the corner of Wall and Nassau Streets. It was in the form of a parallelogram, two hundred feet long by ninety wide, and about eighty feet in height, the ascent to the entrance being by eighteen granite steps.

"That's the Custom House," said Dick.

"It looks like pictures I've seen of the Parthenon at Athens," said Frank, meditatively.

"Where's Athens?" asked Dick. "It ain't in York State,—is it?"

"Not the Athens I mean, at any rate. It is in Greece, and was a famous city two thousand years ago."

"That's longer than I can remember," said Dick. "I can't remember distinctly more'n about a thousand years."

"What a chap you are, Dick! Do you know if we can go in?"

The boys ascertained, after a little inquiry, that they would be allowed to do so. They accordingly entered the Custom House and made their way up to the roof, from which they had a fine view of the harbor, the wharves crowded with shipping, and the neighboring shores of Long Island and New Jersey. Towards the north they looked down for many miles upon continuous lines of streets, and thousands of roofs, with here and there a church-spire rising above its neighbors. Dick had never before been up there, and he, as well as Frank, was interested in the grand view spread before them.

At length they descended, and were going down the granite steps on the outside of the building, when they were addressed by a young man, whose appearance is worth describing.

He was tall, and rather loosely put together, with small eyes and rather a prominent nose. His clothing had evidently not been furnished by a city tailor. He wore a blue coat with brass buttons, and pantaloons of rather scanty dimensions, which were several inches too short to cover his lower limbs. He held in his hand a piece of paper, and his countenance wore a look of mingled bewilderment and anxiety.

"Be they a-payin' out money inside there?" he asked, indicating the interior by a motion of his hand."

"I guess so," said Dick. "Are you a goin' in for some?"

"Wal, yes. I've got an order here for sixty dollars,—made a kind of speculation this morning."

"How was it?" asked Frank.

"Wal, you see I brought down some money to put in the bank, fifty dollars it was, and I hadn't justly made up my mind what bank to put it into, when a chap came up in a terrible hurry, and said it was very unfortunate, but the bank wasn't open, and he must have some money right off. He was obliged to go out of the city by the next train. I asked him how much he wanted. He said fifty dollars. I told him I'd got that, and he offered me a check on the bank for sixty, and I let him have it. I thought that was a pretty easy way to earn ten dollars, so I counted out the money and he went off. He told me I'd hear a bell ring when they began to pay out money. But I've waited most two hours, and I hain't heard it yet. I'd ought to be goin', for I told dad I'd be home to-night. Do you think I can get the money now?"

"Will you show me the check?" asked Frank, who had listened attentively to the countryman's story, and suspected that he had been made the victim of a swindler. It was made out upon the "Washington Bank," in the sum of sixty dollars, and was signed "Ephraim Smith."

"Washington Bank!" repeated Frank. "Dick, is there such a bank in the city?"

"Not as I knows on," said Dick. "Leastways I don't own any shares in it."

"Ain't this the Washington Bank?" asked the countryman, pointing to the building on the steps of which the three were now standing.

"No, it's the Custom House."

"And won't they give me any money for this?" asked the young man, the perspiration standing on his brow.

"I am afraid the man who gave it to you was a swindler," said Frank, gently.

"And won't I ever see my fifty dollars again?" asked the youth in agony.

"I am afraid not."

"What'll dad say?" ejaculated the miserable youth. "It makes me feel sick to think of it. I wish I had the feller here. I'd shake him out of his boots."

"What did he look like? I'll call a policeman and you shall describe him. Perhaps in that way you can get track of your money."

Dick called a policeman, who listened to the description, and recognized the operator as an experienced swindler. He assured the countryman that there was very little chance of his ever seeing his money again. The boys left the miserable youth loudly bewailing his bad luck, and proceeded on their way down the street.

"He's a baby," said Dick, contemptuously. "He'd ought to know how to take care of himself and his money. A feller has to look sharp in this city, or he'll lose his eye-teeth before he knows it."

"I suppose you never got swindled out of fifty dollars, Dick?"

"No, I don't carry no such small bills. I wish I did," he added.

"So do I, Dick. What's that building there at the end of the street?"

"That's the Wall-Street Ferry to Brooklyn."

"How long does it take to go across?"

"Not more'n five minutes."

"Suppose we just ride over and back."

"All right!" said Dick. "It's rather expensive; but if you don't mind, I don't."

"Why, how much does it cost?"

"Two cents apiece."

"I guess I can stand that. Let us go."

They passed the gate, paying the fare to a man who stood at the entrance, and were soon on the ferry-boat, bound for Brooklyn.

They had scarcely entered the boat, when Dick, grasping Frank by the arm, pointed to a man just outside of the gentlemen's cabin.

"Do you see that man, Frank?" he inquired.

"Yes, what of him?"

"He's the man that cheated the country chap out of his fifty dollars."

CHAPTER XI
DICK AS A DETECTIVE

DICK'S ready identification of the rogue who had cheated the countryman, surprised Frank.

"What makes you think it is he?" he asked.

"Because I've seen him before, and I know he's up to them kind of tricks. When I heard how he looked, I was sure I knowed him."

"Our recognizing him won't be of much use," said Frank. "It won't give back the countryman his money."

"I don't know," said Dick, thoughtfully. "May be I can get it."

"How?" asked Frank, incredulously.

"Wait a minute, and you'll see."

Dick left his companion, and went up to the man whom he suspected.

"Ephraim Smith," said Dick, in a low voice.

The man turned suddenly, and looked at Dick uneasily.

"What did you say?" he asked.

"I believe your name is Ephraim Smith," continued Dick.

"You're mistaken," said the man, and was about to move off.

"Stop a minute," said Dick. "Don't you keep your money in the Washington Bank?"

"I don't know any such bank. I'm in a hurry, young man, and I can't stop to answer any foolish questions."

The boat had by this time reached the Brooklyn pier, and Mr. Ephraim Smith seemed in a hurry to land.

"Look here," said Dick, significantly; "you'd better not go on shore unless you want to jump into the arms of a policeman."

"What do you mean?" asked the man, startled.

"That little affair of yours is known to the police," said Dick; "about how you got fifty dollars out of a greenhorn on a false check, and it mayn't be safe for you to go ashore."

"I don't know what you're talking about," said the swindler with affected boldness, though Dick could see that he was ill at ease.

"Yes you do," said Dick. "There isn't but one thing to do. Just give me back that money, and I'll see that you're not touched. If you don't, I'll give you up to the first p'liceman we meet."

Dick looked so determined, and spoke so confidently, that the other, overcome by his fears, no longer hesitated, but passed a roll of bills to Dick and hastily left the boat.

All this Frank witnessed with great amazement, not understanding what influence Dick could have obtained over the swindler sufficient to compel restitution.

"How did you do it?" he asked eagerly.

"I told him I'd exert my influence with the president to have him tried by habeas corpus," said Dick.

"And of course that frightened him. But tell me, without joking, how you managed."

Dick gave a truthful account of what occurred, and then said, "Now we'll go back and carry the money."

"Suppose we don't find the poor countryman?"

"Then the p'lice will take care of it."

They remained on board the boat, and in five minutes were again in New York. Going up Wall Street, they met the countryman a little distance from the Custom House. His face was marked with the traces of deep anguish; but in his case even grief could not subdue the cravings of appetite. He had purchased some cakes of one of the old women who spread out for the benefit of passers-by an array of apples and seed-cakes, and was munching them with melancholy satisfaction.

"Hilloa!" said Dick. "Have you found your money?"

"No," ejaculated the young man, with a convulsive gasp. "I sha'n't ever see it again. The mean skunk's cheated me out of it. Consarn his picter! It took me most six months to save it up. I was workin' for Deacon Pinkham in our place. Oh, I wish I'd never come to New York! The deacon, he told me he'd keep it for me; but I wanted to put it in the bank, and now it's all gone, boo hoo!"

And the miserable youth, having despatched his cakes, was so overcome by the thought of his loss that he burst into tears.

"I say," said Dick, "dry up, and see what I've got here."

The youth no sooner saw the roll of bills, and comprehended that it was indeed his lost treasure, than from the depths of anguish he was exalted to the most ecstatic joy. He seized Dick's hand, and shook it with so much energy that our hero began to feel rather alarmed for its safety.

" 'Pears to me you take my arm for a pump-handle," said he. "Couldn't you show your gratitood some other way? It's just possible I may want to use my arm ag'in some time."

The young man desisted, but invited Dick most cordially to come up and stop a week with him at his country home, assuring him that he wouldn't charge him anything for board.

"All right!" said Dick. "If you don't mind I'll bring my wife along, too. She's delicate, and the country air might do her good."

Jonathan stared at him in amazement, uncertain whether to credit the fact of his marriage. Dick walked on with Frank, leaving him in an apparent state of stupefaction, and it is possible that he has not yet settled the affair to his satisfaction.

"Now," said Frank, "I think I'll go back to the Astor House. Uncle has probably got through his business and returned."

"All right," said Dick.

The two boys walked up to Broadway, just where the tall steeple of Trinity faces the street of bankers and brokers, and walked leisurely to the hotel. When they arrived at the Astor House, Dick said, "Good-by, Frank."

"Not yet," said Frank; "I want you to come in with me."

Dick followed his young patron up the steps. Frank went to the reading-room, where, as he had thought probable, he found his uncle already arrived, and reading a copy of "The Evening Post," which he had just purchased outside.

"Well, boys," he said, looking up, "have you had a pleasant jaunt?"

"Yes, sir," said Frank. "Dick's a capital guide."

"So this is Dick," said Mr. Whitney, surveying him with a smile. "Upon my word, I should hardly have known him. I must congratulate him on his improved appearance."

"Frank's been very kind to me," said Dick, who, rough street-boy as he was, had a heart easily touched by kindness, of which he had never experienced much. "He's a tip-top fellow."

"I believe he is a good boy," said Mr. Whitney. "I hope, my lad, you will prosper and rise in the world. You know in this free country poverty in early life is no bar to a man's advancement. I haven't risen very high myself," he added, with a smile, "but have met with moderate success in life; yet there was a time when I was as poor as you."

"Were you, sir?" asked Dick, eagerly.

"Yes, my boy, I have known the time when I have been obliged to go without my dinner because I didn't have enough money to pay for it."

"How did you get up in the world?" asked Dick, anxiously.

"I entered a printing-office as an apprentice, and worked for some years. Then my eyes gave out and I was obliged to give that up. Not knowing what else to do, I went into the country, and worked on a farm. After a while I was lucky enough to invent a machine, which has brought me in a great deal of money. But there was one thing I got while I was in the printing-office which I value more than money."

"What was that, sir?"

"A taste for reading and study. During my leisure hours I improved myself by study, and acquired a large part of the knowledge which I now possess. Indeed, it was one of my books that first put me on the track of the invention, which I afterwards made. So you see, my lad, that my studious habits paid me in money, as well as in another way."

"I'm awful ignorant," said Dick, soberly.

"But you are young, and, I judge, a smart boy. If you try to learn, you can, and if you ever expect to do anything in the world, you must know something of books."

"I will," said Dick, resolutely. "I ain't always goin' to black boots for a livin'."

"All labor is respectable, my lad, and you have no cause to be ashamed of any honest business; yet when you can get something to do that promises better for your future prospects, I advise you to do so. Till then earn your living in the way you are accustomed to, avoid extravagance, and save up a little money if you can."

"Thank you for your advice," said our hero. "There ain't many that takes an interest in Ragged Dick."

"So that's your name," said Mr. Whitney. "If I judge you rightly, it won't be long before you change it. Save your money, my lad, buy books, and determine to be somebody, and you may yet fill an honorable position."

"I'll try," said Dick. "Good-night, sir."

"Wait a minute, Dick," said Frank. "Your blacking-box and old clothes are upstairs. You may want them."

"In course," said Dick. "I couldn't get along without my best clothes, and my stock in trade."

"You may go up to the room with him, Frank," said Mr. Whitney. "The clerk will give you the key. I want to see you, Dick, before you go."

"Yes, sir," said Dick.

"Where are you going to sleep to-night, Dick?" asked Frank, as they went upstairs together.

"P'r'aps at the Fifth Avenue Hotel—on the outside," said Dick.

"Haven't you any place to sleep, then?"

"I slept in a box, last night."

"In a box?"

"Yes, on Spruce Street."

"Poor fellow!" said Frank, compassionately.

"Oh, 'twas a bully bed—full of straw! I slept like a top."

"Don't you earn enough to pay for a room, Dick?"

"Yes," said Dick; "only I spend my money foolish, goin' to the Old Bowery, and Tony Pastor's, and sometimes gamblin' in Baxter Street."

"You won't gamble any more,—will you, Dick?" said Frank, laying his hand persuasively on his companion's shoulder.

"No, I won't," said Dick.

"You'll promise?"

"Yes, and I'll keep it. You're a good feller. I wish you was goin' to be in New York."

"I am going to a boarding-school in Connecticut. The name of the town is Barnton. Will you write to me, Dick?"

"My writing would look like hens' tracks," said our hero.

"Never mind. I want you to write. When you write you can tell me how to direct, and I will send you a letter."

"I wish you would," said Dick. "I wish I was more like you."

"I hope you will make a much better boy, Dick. Now we'll go in to my uncle. He wishes to see you before you go."

They went into the reading-room. Dick had wrapped up his blacking-brush in a newspaper with which Frank had supplied him, feeling that a guest of the Astor House should hardly be seen coming out of the hotel displaying such a professional sign.

"Uncle, Dick's ready to go," said Frank.

"Good-by, my lad," said Mr. Whitney. "I hope to hear good accounts of you sometime. Don't forget what I have told you. Remember that your future position depends mainly upon yourself, and that it will be high or low as you choose to make it."

He held out his hand, in which was a five-dollar bill. Dick shrunk back. "I don't like to take it," he said. "I haven't earned it." "Perhaps not," said Mr. Whitney; "but I give it to you because I remember my own friendless youth. I hope it may be of service to you. Sometime when you are a prosperous man, you can repay it in the form of aid to some poor boy, who is struggling upward as you are now."

"I will, sir," said Dick, manfully.

He no longer refused the money, but took it gratefully, and, bidding Frank and his uncle good-by, went out into the street. A feeling of loneliness came over him as he left the presence of Frank, for whom he had formed a strong attachment in the few hours he had known him.

CHAPTER XII

DICK HIRES A ROOM ON MOTT STREET

GOING out into the fresh air Dick felt the pangs of hunger. He accordingly went to a restaurant and got a substantial supper. Perhaps it was the new clothes he wore, which made him feel a little more aristocratic. At all events, instead of patronizing the cheap restaurant where he usually procured his meals, he went into the refectory attached to Lovejoy's Hotel, where the prices were higher and the company more select. In his ordinary dress, Dick would have been excluded, but now he had the appearance of a very respectable, gentlemanly boy, whose presence would not discredit any establishment. His orders were therefore received with attention by the waiter and in due time a good supper was placed before him.

"I wish I could come here every day," thought Dick. "It seems kind o' nice and 'spectable, side of the other place. There's a gent at that other table that I've shined boots for more'n once. He don't know me in my new clothes. Guess he don't know his boot-black patronizes the same establishment."

His supper over, Dick went up to the desk, and, presenting his check, tendered in payment his five-dollar bill, as if it were one of a large number which he possessed. Receiving back his change he went out into the street.

Two questions now arose: How should he spend the evening, and where should he pass the night? Yesterday, with such a sum of money in his possession, he would have answered both questions readily. For the evening, he would have passed it at the Old Bowery, and gone to sleep in any out-of-the-way place that offered. But he had turned over a new leaf, or resolved to do so. He meant to save his money for some useful purpose,—to aid his advancement in the world. So he could not afford the theatre. Besides, with his new clothes, he was unwilling to pass the night out of doors.

"I should spile 'em," he thought, "and that wouldn't pay."

So he determined to hunt up a room which he could occupy regularly, and consider as his own, where he could sleep nights, instead of depending on boxes and old wagons for a chance shelter. This would be the first step towards respectability, and Dick determined to take it.

He accordingly passed through the City Hall Park, and walked leisurely up Centre Street.

He decided that it would hardly be advisable for him to seek lodgings in Fifth Avenue, although his present cash capital consisted of nearly five dollars in money, besides the valuable papers, [actually worthless pieces of tissue], contained in his wallet. Besides, he had reason to doubt whether any in his line of business lived on that aristocratic street. He took his way to Mott Street, which is considerably less pretentious, and halted in front of a shabby brick lodging-house kept by a Mrs. Mooney, with whose son Tom, Dick was acquainted.

Dick rang the bell, which sent back a shrill metallic response.

The door was opened by a slatternly servant, who looked at him inquiringly, and not without curiosity. It must be remembered that Dick was well dressed, and that nothing in his appearance bespoke his occupation. Being naturally a good-looking boy, he might readily be mistaken for a gentleman's son.

"Well, Queen Victoria," said Dick, "is your missus at home?"

"My name's Bridget," said the girl.

"Oh, indeed!" said Dick. "You looked so much like the queen's picter what she gave me last Christmas in exchange for mine, that I couldn't help calling you by her name."

"Oh, go along wid ye!" said Bridget. "It's makin' fun ye are."

"If you don't believe me," said Dick, gravely, "all you've got to do is to ask my partic'lar friend, the Duke of Newcastle."

"Bridget!" called a shrill voice from the basement.

"The missus is calling me," said Bridget, hurriedly. "I'll tell her ye want her."

"All right!" said Dick.

The servant descended into the lower regions, and in a short time a stout, red-faced woman appeared on the scene.

"Well, sir, what's your wish?" she asked.

"Have you got a room to let?" asked Dick.

"Is it for yourself you ask?" questioned the woman, in some surprise.

Dick answered in the affirmative.

"I haven't got any very good rooms vacant. There's a small room in the third story."

"I'd like to see it," said Dick.

"I don't know as it would be good enough for you," said the woman, with a glance at Dick's clothes.

"I ain't very partic'lar about accommodations," said our hero. "I guess I'll look at it."

Dick followed the landlady up two narrow staircases, uncarpeted and dirty, to the third landing, where he was ushered into a room about ten feet square. It could not be considered a very desirable apartment. It had once been covered with an oilcloth carpet, but this was now very ragged, and looked worse than none. There was a single bed in the corner, covered with an indiscriminate heap of bed-clothing, rumpled and not over-clean. There was a bureau, with the veneering scratched and in some parts stripped off, and a small glass, eight inches by ten, cracked across the middle; also two chairs in rather a disjointed condition. Judging from Dick's appearance, Mrs. Mooney thought he would turn from it in disdain.

But it must be remembered that Dick's past experience had not been of a character to make him fastidious. In comparison with a box, or an empty wagon, even this little room seemed comfortable. He decided to hire it if the rent proved reasonable.

"Well, what's the tax?" asked Dick.

"I ought to have a dollar a week," said Mrs. Mooney, hesitatingly.

"Say seventy-five cents, and I'll take it," said Dick.

"Every week in advance?"

"Yes."

"Well, as times is hard, and I can't afford to keep it empty, you may have it. When will you come?"

"To-night," said Dick.

"It ain't lookin' very neat. I don't know as I can fix it up to-night."

"Well, I'll sleep here to-night, and you can fix it up to-morrow."

"I hope you'll excuse the looks. I'm a lone woman, and my help is so shiftless, I have to look after everything myself; so I can't keep things as straight as I want to."

"All right!" said Dick.

"Can you pay me the first week in advance?" asked the landlady, cautiously.

Dick responded by drawing seventy-five cents from his pocket, and placing it in her hand.

"What's your business, sir, if I may inquire?" said Mrs. Mooney.

"Oh, I'm professional!" said Dick.

"Indeed!" said the landlady, who did not feel much enlightened by this answer.

"How's Tom?" asked Dick.

"Do you know my Tom?" said Mrs. Mooney in surprise. "He's gone to sea,—to Californy. He went last week."

"Did he?" said Dick. "Yes, I knew him."

Mrs. Mooney looked upon her new lodger with increased favor, on finding that he was acquainted with her son, who, by the way, was one of the worst young scamps in Mott Street, which is saying considerable.

"I'll bring over my baggage from the Astor House this evening," said Dick in a tone of importance.

"From the Astor House!" repeated Mrs. Mooney, in fresh amazement.

"Yes, I've been stoppin' there a short time with some friends," said Dick.

Mrs. Mooney might be excused for a little amazement at finding that a guest from the Astor House was about to become one of her lodgers—such transfers not being common.

"Did you say you was purfessional?" she asked.

"Yes, ma'am," said Dick, politely.

"You ain't a—a—," Mrs. Mooney paused, uncertain what conjecture to hazard.

"Oh, no, nothing of the sort," said Dick, promptly. "How could you think so, Mrs. Mooney?"

"No offense, sir," said the landlady, more perplexed than ever.

"Certainly not," said our hero. "But you must excuse me now, Mrs. Mooney, as I have business of great importance to attend to."

"You'll come round this evening?"

Dick answered in the affirmative, and turned away.

"I wonder what he is!" thought the landlady, following him with her eyes as he crossed the street. "He's got good clothes on, but he don't seem very particular about his room. Well; I've got all my rooms full now. That's one comfort."

Dick felt more comfortable now that he had taken the decisive step of hiring a lodging, and paying a week's rent in advance. For seven nights he was sure of a shelter and a bed to sleep in. The thought was a pleasant one to our young vagrant, who hitherto had seldom known when he rose in the morning where he should find a resting-place at night.

"I must bring my traps round," said Dick to himself. "I guess I'll go to bed early to-night. It'll feel kinder good to sleep in a reg'lar bed. Boxes is rather hard to the back, and ain't comfortable in case of rain. I wonder what Johnny Nolan would say if he knew I'd got a room of my own."

. . . It will be seen that Dick was getting ambitious. Hitherto he had thought very little of the future, but was content to get along as he could, dining as well as his means would allow, and spending the evenings in the pit of the Old Bowery, eating peanuts between the acts if he was prosperous, and if unlucky supping on dry bread or an apple, and sleeping in an old box or a wagon. Now, for the first time, he began to reflect that he could not black boots all his life. In seven years he would be a man, and, since his meeting with Frank, he felt he would like to be a respectable man. He could see and appreciate the difference between Frank and such a boy as Micky Maguire [a common bully], and it was not strange that he preferred the society of the former.

In the course of the next morning, in pursuance of his new resolutions for the future, he called at a savings bank, and held out four dollars in bills besides another dollar in change [recently earned]. There was a high railing, and a number of clerks busily writing at desks behind it. Dick, never having been in a bank before, did not know where to go. He went, by mistake, to the desk where money was paid out.

"Where's your book?" asked the clerk.

"I haven't got any."

"Have you any money deposited here?"

"No, sir, I want to leave some here."

"Then go to the next desk."

Dick followed directions, and presented himself before an elderly man with gray hair, who looked at him over the rims of his spectacles.

"I want you to keep that for me," said Dick, awkwardly emptying his money out on the desk.

"How much is there?"

"Five dollars."

"Have you got an account here?"

"No, sir."

"Of course you can write?"

The "of course" was said on account of Dick's neat dress.

"Have I got to do any writing?" asked our hero, a little embarrassed.

"We want you to sign your name in this book," and the old gentleman shoved round a large folio volume containing the names of depositors.

Dick surveyed the book with some awe.

"I ain't much on writin'," he said.

"Very well, write as well as you can."

The pen was put into Dick's hand, and, after dipping it in the inkstand, he succeeded after a hard effort, accompanied by many contortions of the face, in inscribing upon the book of the bank the name

DICK HUNTER.

"Dick!—that means Richard, I suppose," said the bank officer, who had some difficulty in making out the signature.

"No; Ragged Dick is what folks call me."

"You don't look very ragged."

"No, I've left my rags to home. They might get wore out if I used 'em too common."

"Well, my lad, I'll make out a book in the name of Dick Hunter, since you seem to prefer Dick to Richard. I hope you will save up your money and deposit more with us."

Our hero took his bank-book, and gazed on the entry "Five Dollars" with a new sense of importance. He had been accustomed to joke about Erie shares, but now, for the first time, he felt himself a capitalist; on a small scale, to be sure, but still it was no small thing for Dick to have five dollars which he could call his own. He firmly determined that he would lay by every cent he could spare from his earnings towards the fund he hoped to accumulate.

But Dick was too sensible not to know that there was something more than money needed to win a respectable position in the world. He felt that he was very ignorant. Of reading and writing he only knew the rudiments, and that, with a slight acquaintance with arithmetic, was all he did know of books. Dick knew he must study hard, and he dreaded it. He looked upon learning as attended with greater difficulties than it really possesses. But Dick had good pluck. He meant to learn, nevertheless, and resolved to buy a book with his first spare earnings.

When Dick went home at night he locked up his bank-book in one of the drawers of the bureau. It was wonderful how much more independent he felt whenever he reflected upon the contents of that drawer, and with what an important air of joint ownership he regarded the bank building in which his small savings were deposited.

CHAPTER XV

DICK SECURES A TUTOR

THE next morning Dick was unusually successful, having plenty to do, and receiving for one job twenty-five cents,—the gentleman refusing to take change. Then flashed upon Dick's mind the thought that he had not yet returned the change due to the gentleman whose boots he had blacked on the morning of his introduction to the reader.

"What'll he think of me?" said Dick to himself. "I hope he won't think I'm mean enough to keep the money."

Now Dick was scrupulously honest, and though the temptation to be otherwise had often been strong, he had always resisted it. He was not willing on any account to keep money which did not belong to him, and he immediately started for 125 Fulton Street (the address which had been given him) where he found Mr. Greyson's name on the door of an office. . . .

The door being open, Dick walked in.

"Is Mr. Greyson in?" he asked of a clerk who sat on a high stool before a desk.

"Not just now. He'll be in soon. Will you wait?"

"Yes," said Dick.

"Very well; take a seat then."

Dick sat down and took up the morning "Tribune," but presently came to a word of four syllables, which he pronounced to himself a "sticker," and laid it down. But he had not long to wait, for five minutes later Mr. Greyson entered.

"Did you wish to speak to me, my lad?" said he to Dick, whom in his new clothes he did not recognize.

"Yes, sir," said Dick. "I owe you some money."

"Indeed!" said Mr. Greyson, pleasantly; "that's an agreeable surprise. I didn't know but you had come for some. So you are a debtor of mine, and not a creditor?"

"I b'lieve that's right," said Dick, drawing fifteen cents from his pocket, and placing in Mr. Greyson's hand.

"Fifteen cents!" repeated he, in some surprise. "How do you happen to be indebted to me in that amount?"

"You gave me a quarter for a-shinin' your boots, yesterday mornin', and couldn't wait for the change. I meant to have brought it before, but I forgot all about it till this mornin'."

"It had quite slipped my mind also. But you don't look like the boy I employed. If I remember rightly he wasn't as well dressed as you."

"No," said Dick. "I was dressed for a party, then, but the clo'es was too well ventilated to be comfortable in cold weather."

"You're an honest boy," said Mr. Greyson. "Who taught you to be honest?"

"Nobody," said Dick. "But it's mean to cheat and steal. I've always knowed that."

"Then you've got ahead of some of our business men. Do you read the Bible?"

"No," said Dick. "I've heard it's a good book, but I don't know much about it."

"You ought to go to some Sunday School. Would you be willing?"

"Yes," said Dick, promptly. "I want to grow up 'spectable. But I don't know where to go."

"Then I'll tell you. The church I attend is at the corner of Fifth Avenue and Twenty-first Street."

"I've seen it," said Dick.

"I have a class in the Sunday School there. If you'll come next Sunday, I'll take you into my class, and do what I can to help you."

"Thank you," said Dick, "but p'r'aps you'll get tired of teaching me. I'm awful ignorant."

"No, my lad," said Mr. Greyson, kindly. "You evidently have some good principles to start with, as you have shown by your scorn of dishonesty. I shall hope good things of you in the future."

"Well, Dick," said our hero, apostrophizing himself, as he left the office; "you're gettin' up in the world. You've got money invested, and are goin' to attend church, by partic'lar invitation, on Fifth Avenue. I shouldn't wonder much if you should find cards, when you get home, from the Mayor, requestin' the honor of your company to dinner, along with other distinguished guests."

Dick felt in very good spirits. He seemed to be emerging from the world in which he had hitherto lived, into a new atmosphere of respectability, and the change seemed very pleasant to him.

At six o'clock Dick went into a restaurant on Chatham Street, and got a comfortable supper. He had been so successful during the day that, after paying for this, he still had ninety cents left. While he was despatching his supper, another boy came in, smaller and slighter than Dick, and sat down beside him. Dick recognized him as a boy who three months before had entered the ranks of the boot-blacks, but who, from a natural timidity, had not been able to earn much. He was ill-fitted for the coarse companionship of the street boys, and shrank from the rude jokes of his present associates. Dick had never troubled him; for our hero had a certain chivalrous feeling which would not allow him to bully or disturb a younger and weaker boy than himself.

"How are you, Fosdick?" said Dick, as the other seated himself.

"Pretty well," said Fosdick. "I suppose you're all right."

"Oh, yes, I'm right side up with care. I've been havin' a bully supper. What are you goin' to have?"

"Some bread and butter."

"Why don't you get a cup o' coffee?"

"Why," said Fosdick, reluctantly, "I haven't got money enough to-night."

"Never mind," said Dick; "I'm in luck to-day. I'll stand treat."

"That's kind in you," said Fosdick, gratefully.

"Oh, never mind that," said Dick.

Accordingly he ordered a cup of coffee, and a plate of beefsteak, and was gratified to see that his young companion partook of both with evident relish. When the repast was over, the boys went out into the street together, Dick pausing at the desk to settle for both suppers.

"Where are you going to sleep to-night, Fosdick?" asked Dick, as they stood on the sidewalk.

"I don't know," said Fosdick, a little sadly. "In some door-way, I expect. But I'm afraid the police will find me out, and make me move on."

"I'll tell you what," said Dick, "you must go home with me. I guess my bed will hold two."

"Have you got a room?" asked the other, in surprise.

"Yes," said Dick, rather proudly, and with a little excusable exultation. "I've got a room over on Mott Street; there I can receive my friends. That'll be better than sleepin' in a door-way,—won't it?"

"Yes, indeed it will," said Fosdick. "How lucky I was to come across you! It comes hard to me living as I do. When my father was alive I had every comfort."

"That's more'n I ever had," said Dick. "But I'm goin' to try to live comfortable now. Is your father dead?"

"Yes," said Fosdick, sadly. "He was a printer; but he was drowned one dark night from a Fulton ferry-boat, and, as I had no relations in the city, and no money, I was obliged to go to work as quick as I could. But I don't get on very well."

"Didn't you have no brothers nor sisters?" asked Dick.

"No," said Fosdick; "father and I used to live alone. He was always so much company to me that I feel very lonesome without him. There's a man out West somewhere that owes him two thousand dollars. He used to live in the city, and father lent him all his money to help him go into business; but he failed, or pretended to, and went off. If father hadn't lost that money he would have left me well off; but no money would have made up his loss to me."

"What's the man's name that went off with your father's money?"

"His name is Hiram Bates."

"P'r'aps you'll get the money again, sometime."

"There isn't much chance of it," said Fosdick. "I'd sell out my chances of that for five dollars."

"Maybe I'll buy you out sometime," said Dick. "Now, come round and see what sort of a room I've got. I used to go to the theatre evenings, when I had money; but now I'd rather go to bed early, and have a good sleep."

"I don't care much about theatres," said Fosdick. "Father didn't use to let me go very often. He said it wasn't good for boys."

"I like to go to the Old Bowery sometimes. They have tip-top plays there. Can you read and write well?" he asked, as a sudden thought came to him.

"Yes," said Fosdick. "Father always kept me at school when he was alive, and I stood pretty well in my classes. I was expecting to enter at the Free Academy next year."

"Then I'll tell you what," said Dick; "I'll make a bargain with you. I can't read much more'n a pig; and my writin' looks like hens' tracks. I don't want to grow up knowin' no more'n a four-year-old boy. If you'll teach me readin' and writin' evenin's, you shall sleep in my room every night. That'll be better'n door-steps or old boxes, where I've slept many a time."

"Are you in earnest?" said Fosdick, his face lighting up hopefully.

"In course I am," said Dick. "It's fashionable for young gentlemen to have private tootors to introduce 'em into the flower-beds of literatoor and science, and why shouldn't I foller the fashion? You shall be my perfessor; only you must promise not to be very hard if my writin' looks like a rail-fence on a bender."

"I'll try not to be too severe," said Fosdick, laughing. "I shall be thankful for such a chance to get a place to sleep. Have you got anything to read out of?"

"No," said Dick. "My extensive and well-selected library was lost overboard in a storm, when I was sailin' from the Sandwich Islands to the desert of Sahara. But I'll buy a paper. That'll do me a long time."

Accordingly Dick stopped at a paper-stand, and bought a copy of a weekly paper, filled with the usual variety of reading matter,—stories sketches, poems, etc.

They soon arrived at Dick's lodging-house. Our hero, procuring a lamp from the landlady, led the way into his apartment, which he entered with the proud air of a proprietor.

"Well, how do you like it, Fosdick?" he asked, complacently.

The time was when Fosdick would have thought it untidy and not particularly attractive. But he had served a severe apprenticeship in the streets, and it was pleasant to feel himself under shelter, and he was not disposed to be critical.

"It looks very comfortable, Dick," he said.

"The bed ain't very large," said Dick; "but I guess we can get along."

"Oh, yes," said Fosdick, cheerfully. "I don't take up much room."

"Then that's all right. There's two chairs, you see, one for you and one for me. In case the mayor comes in to spend the evenin' socially, he can sit on the bed."

The boys seated themselves, and five minutes later, under the guidance of his young tutor, Dick had commenced his studies.

CHAPTER XVI

THE FIRST LESSON

FORTUNATELY for Dick, his young tutor was well qualified to instruct him. Henry Fosdick, though only twelve years old, knew as much as many boys of fourteen. He had always been studious and ambitious to excel. His father, being a printer, employed in an office where books were printed, often brought home new books in sheets, which Henry was always glad to read. Mr. Fosdick had been, besides, a subscriber to the Mechanics' Apprentices'

Library, which contains many thousands of well-selected and instructive books. Thus Henry had acquired an amount of general information, unusual in a boy of his age. Perhaps he had devoted too much time to study, for he was not naturally robust. All this, however, fitted him admirably for the office to which Dick had appointed him,—that of his private instructor.

The two boys drew up their chairs to the rickety table, and spread out the paper before them.

"The exercises generally commence with ringin' the bell," said Dick; "but as I ain't got none, we'll have to do without."

"And the teacher is generally provided with a rod," said Fosdick. "Isn't there a poker handy, that I can use in case my scholar doesn't behave well?"

" 'Tain't lawful to use fire-arms," said Dick.

"Now, Dick," said Fosdick, "before we begin, I must find out how much you already know. Can you read any?"

"Not enough to hurt me," said Dick. "All I know about readin' you could put in a nutshell, and there'd be room left for a small family."

"I suppose you know your letters?"

"Yes," said Dick, "I know 'em all, but not intimately. I guess I can call 'em all by name."

"Where did you learn them? Did you ever go to school?"

"Yes; I went two days."

"Why did you stop?"

"It didn't agree with my constitution."

"You don't look very delicate," said Fosdick.

"No," said Dick, "I ain't troubled much that way; but I found lickin's didn't agree with me."

"Did you get punished?"

"Awful," said Dick.

"What for?"

"For indulgin' in a little harmless amoosement," said Dick. "You see the boy that was sittin' next to me fell asleep, which I considered improper in school-time; so I thought I'd help the teacher a little by wakin' him up. So I took a pin and stuck into him; but I guess it went a little too far, for he screeched awful. The teacher found out what it was that made him holler, and whipped me with a ruler till I was black and blue. I thought 'twas about time to take a vacation; so that's the last time I went to school."

"You didn't learn to read in that time, of course?"

"No," said Dick; "but I was a newsboy a little while; so I learned a little, just so's to find out what the news was. Sometimes I didn't read straight and called the wrong news. One mornin' I asked another boy what the paper said, and he told me the King of Africa was dead. I thought it was all right till folks began to laugh."

"Well, Dick, if you'll only study well, you won't be liable to make such mistakes."

"I hope so," said Dick. "My friend Horace Greeley told me the other day that he'd get me to take his place now and then when he was off makin' speeches if my edication hadn't been neglected."

"I must find a good piece for you to begin on," said Fosdick, looking over the paper.

"Find an easy one," said Dick, "with words of one story."

Fosdick at length found a piece which he thought would answer. He discovered on trial that Dick had not exaggerated his deficiencies. Words of two syllables he seldom pronounced right, and was much surprised when he was told how "through" was sounded.

"Seems to me it's throwin' away letters to use all them," he said.

"How would you spell it?" asked his young teacher.

"T-h-r-u," said Dick.

"Well," said Fosdick, "there's a good many other words that are spelt with more letters than they need to have. But it's the fashion, and we must follow it."

But if Dick was ignorant, he was quick, and had an excellent capacity. Moreover he had a perseverance, and was not easily discouraged. He had made up his mind he must know more, and was not disposed to complain of the difficulty of his task. Fosdick had occasion to laugh more than once at his ludicrous mistakes; but Dick laughed too, and on the whole both were quite interested in the lesson.

At the end of an hour and a half the boys stopped for the evening

"You're learning fast, Dick," said Fosdick. "At this rate you will soon learn to read well."

"Will I?" asked Dick with an expression of satisfaction. "I'm glad of that. I don't want to be ignorant. I didn't use to care, but I do now. I want to grow up 'spectable."

"So do I, Dick. We will both help each other, and I am sure we can accomplish something. But I am beginning to feel sleepy."

"So am I," said Dick. "Them hard words make my head ache. I wonder who made 'em all?"

"That's more than I can tell. I suppose you've seen a dictionary."

"That's another of 'em. No, I can't say I have, though I may have seen him in the street without knowin' him."

"A dictionary is a book containing all the words in the language."

"How many are there?"

"I don't rightly know; but I think there are about fifty thousand."

"It's a pretty large family," said Dick. "Have I got to learn 'em all?"

"That will not be necessary. There are a large number which you would never find occasion to use."

"I'm glad of that," said Dick; "for I don't expect to live to be more'n a hundred, and by that time I wouldn't be more'n half through."

By this time the flickering lamp gave a decided hint to the boys that unless they made haste they would have to undress in the dark. They accordingly drew off their clothes, and Dick jumped into bed. But Fosdick, before doing so, knelt down by the side of the bed, and said a short prayer.

"What's that for?" asked Dick, curiously.

"I was saying my prayers," said Fosdick, as he rose from his knees. "Don't you ever do it?"

"No," said Dick. "Nobody ever taught me."

"Then I'll teach you. Shall I?"'

"I don't know," said Dick, dubiously. "What's the good?"

Fosdick explained as well as he could, and perhaps his simple explanation was better adapted to Dick's comprehension than one from an older person would have been. Dick felt more free to ask questions, and the example of his new friend, for whom he was beginning to feel a warm attachment, had considerable effect upon him. When, therefore, Fosdick asked again if he should teach him a prayer, Dick consented, and his young bedfellow did so. Dick was not naturally irreligious. If he had lived without a knowledge of God and of religious things, it was scarcely to be wondered at in a lad who, from an early age, had been thrown upon his own exertions for the means of living, with no one to care for him or give him good advice. But he was so far good that he could appreciate goodness in others, and this it was that had drawn him to Frank in the first place, and now to Henry Fosdick. He did not, therefore, attempt to ridicule his companion, as some boys better brought up might have done, but was willing to follow his example in what something told him was right. Our young hero had taken an important step toward securing that genuine respectability which he was ambitious to attain.

Weary with the day's work, and Dick perhaps still more fatigued by the unusual mental effort he had made, the boys soon sank into a deep and peaceful slumber, from which they did not awaken till six o'clock the next morning. Before going out Dick sought Mrs. Mooney, and spoke to her on the subject of taking Fosdick as a room-mate. He found that she had no objection, provided he would allow her twenty-five cents a week extra, in consideration of the extra trouble which his companion might be expected to make. To this Dick assented, and the arrangement was definitely concluded.

This over, the two boys went out and took stations near each other. Dick had more of a business turn than Henry, and less shrinking from publicity, so that his earnings were greater. But he had undertaken to pay the entire expenses of the room, and needed to earn more. Sometimes, when two customers presented themselves at the same time, he was able to direct one to his friend. So at the end of the week both boys found themselves with surplus earnings. Dick had the satisfaction of adding two dollars and a half to his deposits in the Savings Bank, and Fosdick commenced an account by depositing seventy-five cents.

On Sunday morning Dick bethought himself of his promise to Mr. Greyson to come to the church on Fifth Avenue. To tell the truth, Dick recalled it with some regret. He had never been inside a church since he could remember, and he was not much attracted by the invitation he had received. But Henry, finding him wavering, urged him to go, and offered to go with him. Dick gladly accepted the offer, feeling that he required someone to lend him countenance under such unusual circumstances.

Dick dressed himself with scrupulous care, giving his shoes a "shine" so brilliant that it did him great credit in a professional point of view, and endeavored to clean his hands thoroughly; but, in spite of all he could do, they were not so white as if his business had been of a different character.

Having fully completed his preparations, he descended into the street, and, with Henry by his side, crossed over to Broadway.

The boys pursued their way up Broadway, which on Sunday presents a striking contrast in its quietness to the noise and confusion of ordinary weekdays, as far as Union Square, then turned down Fourteenth Street, which brought them to Fifth Avenue.

"Suppose we dine at Delmonico's," said Fosdick, looking towards that famous restaurant.

"I'd have to sell some of my Erie shares," said Dick.

A short walk now brought them to the church of which mention has already been made. They stood outside, a little abashed, watching the fashionably attired people who were entering, and were feeling a little undecided as to whether they had better enter also, when Dick felt a light touch upon his shoulder.

Turning round, he met the smiling glance of Mr. Greyson.

"So, my young friend, you have kept your promise," he said. "And whom have you brought with you?"

"A friend of mine," said Dick. "His name is Henry Fosdick."

"I am glad you have brought him. Now follow me, and I will give you seats."

CHAPTER XVII

DICK'S FIRST APPEARANCE IN SOCIETY

IT WAS the hour for morning service. The boys followed Mr. Greyson into the handsome church, and were assigned seats in his own pew.

There were two persons already seated in it,—a good-looking lady of middle age, and a pretty little girl of nine. They were Mrs. Greyson and her only daughter Ida. They looked pleasantly at the boys as they entered, smiling a welcome to them.

The morning service commenced. It must be acknowledged that Dick felt rather awkward. It was an unusual place for him, and it need not be wondered at that he felt like a cat in a strange garret. He would not have known when to rise if he had not taken notice of what the rest of the audience did, and followed their example. He was sitting next to Ida, and as it was the first time he had ever been near so well-dressed a young lady, he naturally felt bashful. When the hymns were announced, Ida found the place, and offered a hymn-book to our hero. Dick took it awkwardly, but his studies had not yet been pursued far enough for him to read the words readily. However, he resolved to keep up appearances, and kept his eyes fixed steadily on the hymn-book.

At length the service was over. The people began to file slowly out of church, and among them, of course, Mr. Greyson's family and the two boys. It seemed very strange to Dick to find himself in such different companionship from what he had been accustomed, and he could not help thinking, "Wonder what Johnny Nolan 'ould say if he could see me now!"

But Johnny's business engagements did not often summon him to Fifth Avenue, and Dick was not likely to be seen by any of his friends in the lower part of the city.

"We have our Sunday school in the afternoon," said Mr. Greyson. "I suppose you live at some distance from here?"

"In Mott Street, sir," answered Dick.

"That is too far to go and return. Suppose you and your friend come and dine with us, and then we can come here together in the afternoon."

Dick was as much astonished at this invitation as if he had really been invited by the Mayor to dine with him and the Board of Aldermen. Mr. Greyson was evidently a rich man, and yet he had actually invited two bootblacks to dine with him.

"I guess we'd better go home, sir," said Dick, hesitating.

"I don't think you can have any very pressing engagements to interfere with your accepting my invitation," said Mr. Greyson, good-humoredly, for he understood the reason of Dick's hesitation. "So I take it for granted that you both accept."

Before Dick fairly knew what he intended to do, he was walking down Fifth Avenue with his new friends.

Now, our young hero was not naturally bashful; but he certainly felt so now, especially as Miss Ida Greyson chose to walk by his side, leaving Henry Fosdick to walk with her father and mother.

"What is your name?" asked Ida, pleasantly.

Our hero was about to answer "Ragged Dick," when it occurred to him that in the present company he had better forget his old nickname.

"Dick Hunter," he answered.

"Dick!" repeated Ida. "That means Richard, doesn't it?"

"Everybody calls me Dick."

"I have a cousin Dick," said the young lady, sociably. "His name is Dick Wilson. I suppose you don't know him?"

"No," said Dick.

"I like the name of Dick," said the young lady, with charming frankness.

Without being able to tell why, Dick felt rather glad she did. He plucked up courage to ask her name.

"My name is Ida," answered the young lady. "Do you like it?"

"Yes," said Dick. "It's a bully name."

Dick turned red as soon as he had said it, for he felt that he had not used the right expression.

The little girl broke into a silvery laugh.

"What a funny boy you are!" she said.

"I didn't mean it," said Dick, stammering. "I meant it's a tip-top name."

Here Ida laughed again, and Dick wished himself back in Mott Street.

"How old are you?" inquired Ida, continuing her examination.

"I'm fourteen,—goin' on fifteen," said Dick.

"You're a big boy of your age," said Ida. "My cousin Dick is a year older than you, but he isn't as large."

Dick looked pleased. Boys generally like to be told that they are large of their age.

"How old be you?" asked Dick, beginning to feel more at his ease.

"I'm nine years old," said Ida. "I go to Miss Jarvis's school. I've just begun to learn French. Do you know French?"

"Not enough to hurt me," said Dick.

Ida laughed again, and told him that he was a droll boy.

"Do you like it?" asked Dick.

"I like it pretty well, except the verbs. I can't remember them well. Do you go to school?"

"I'm studying with a private tutor," said Dick.

"Are you? So is my cousin Dick. He's going to college this year. Are you going to college?"

"Not this year."

"Because, if you did, you know you'd be in the same class with my cousin. It would be funny to have two Dicks in one class."

They turned down Twenty-fourth Street, passing the Fifth Avenue Hotel on the left, and stopped before an elegant house with a brown stone front. The bell was rung, and the door being opened, the boys, somewhat abashed, followed Mr. Greyson into a handsome hall. They were told where to hang their hats, and a moment afterwards were ushered into a comfortable dining-room, where a table was spread for dinner.

Dick took his seat on the edge of a sofa, and was tempted to rub his eyes to make sure that he was really awake. He could hardly believe that he was a guest in so fine a mansion.

Ida helped to put the boys at their ease.

"Do you like pictures?" she asked.

"Very much," answered Henry.

The little girl brought a book of handsome engravings, and, seating herself beside Dick, to whom she seemed to have taken a decided fancy, commenced showing them to him.

"There are the Pyramids of Egypt," she said, pointing to one engraving.

"What are they for?" asked Dick, puzzled. "I don't see any winders."

"No," said Ida, "I don't believe anybody lives there. Do they, papa?"

"No, my dear. They were used for the burial of the dead. The largest of them is said to be the loftiest building in the world with one exception. The spire of the Cathedral of Strasburg is twenty-four feet higher, if I remember rightly."

"Is Egypt near here?" asked Dick.

"Oh, no, it's ever so many miles off; about four or five hundred. Didn't you know?"

"No," said Dick. "I never heard."

"You don't appear to be very accurate in your information, Ida," said her mother. "Four or five thousand miles would be considerably nearer the truth."

After a little more conversation they sat down to dinner. Dick seated himself in an embarrassed way. He was very much afraid of doing or saying something which would be considered an impropriety, and had the uncomfortable feeling that everybody was looking at him, and watching his behavior.

"Where do you live, Dick?" asked Ida, familiarly.

"In Mott Street."

"Where is that?"

"More than a mile off."

"Is it a nice street?"

"Not very, " said Dick. "Only poor folks live there."

"Are you poor?"

"Little girls should be seen and not heard," said her mother, gently.

"If you are," said Ida, "I'll give you the five-dollar gold-piece aunt gave me for a birthday present."

"Dick cannot be called poor, my child," said Mrs. Greyson, "since he earns his living by his own exertions."

"Do you earn your living?" asked Ida, who was a very inquisitive young lady, and not easily silenced. "What do you do?"

Dick blushed violently. At such a table, and in presence of the servant who was standing at that moment behind his chair, he did not like to say that he was a shoe-black, although he well knew that there was nothing dishonorable in the occupation.

Mr. Greyson perceived his feelings, and to spare them, said, "You are too inquisitive, Ida. Sometime Dick may tell you, but you know we don't talk of business on Sundays."

Dick in his embarrassment had swallowed a large spoonful of hot soup, which made him turn red in the face. For the second time, in spite of the prospect of the best dinner he had ever eaten, he wished himself back in Mott Street. Henry Fosdick was more easy and unembarrassed than Dick, not having led such a vagabond and neglected life. But it was to Dick that Ida chiefly directed her conversation, having apparently taken a fancy to his frank and handsome face. I believe I have already said that Dick was a very good-looking boy, especially now since he kept his face clean. He had a frank, honest expression, which generally won its way to the favor of those with whom he came in contact.

Dick got along pretty well at the table by dint of noticing how the rest acted, but there was one thing he could not manage, eating with his fork, which, by the way, he thought a very singular arrangement.

At length they arose from the table, somewhat to Dick's relief. Again Ida devoted herself to the boys, and exhibited a profusely illustrated Bible for their entertainment. Dick was interested in looking at the pictures, though he knew very little of their subjects. Henry Fosdick was much better informed, as might have been expected.

When the boys were about to leave the house with Mr. Greyson for the Sunday school, Ida placed her hand on Dick's, and said persuasively, "You'll come again, Dick, won't you?"

"Thank you," said Dick, "I'd like to," and he could not help thinking Ida the nicest girl he had ever seen.

"Yes," said Mrs. Greyson, hospitably, "we shall be glad to see you both here again."

"Thank you very much," said Henry Fosdick, gratefully. "We shall like very much to come."

I will not dwell upon the hour spent in Sunday school, nor upon the remarks of Mr. Greyson to his class. He found Dick's ignorance of religious subjects so great that he was obliged to begin at the beginning with him. Dick was interested in hearing the children sing, and readily promised to come again the next Sunday.

When the service was over Dick and Henry walked homewards. Dick could not help letting his thoughts rest on the sweet little girl who had given him so cordial a welcome, and hoping that he might meet her again.

"Mr. Greyson is a nice man,—isn't he, Dick?" asked Henry, as they were turning into Mott Street, and were already in sight of their lodging-house.

"Ain't he, though?" said Dick. "He treated us just as if we were young gentlemen."

"Ida seemed to take a great fancy to you."

"She's a tip-top girl," said Dick, "but she asked so many questions that I didn't know what to say."

He had scarcely finished speaking, when a stone whizzed by his head, and, turning quickly, he saw Micky Maguire running round the corner of the street which they had just passed.

CHAPTER XVIII

MICKY MAGUIRE

DICK was no coward. Nor was he in the habit of submitting passively to an insult. When, therefore, he recognized Micky Maguire as his assailant, he instantly turned and gave chase. Micky anticipated pursuit, and ran at his utmost speed. It is doubtful if Dick would have overtaken him, but Micky had the ill luck to trip just as he had entered a narrow alley, and, falling with some violence, received a sharp blow from the hard stones, which made him scream with pain.

"Ow!" he whined. "Don't you hit a feller when he's down."

"What made you fire that stone at me?" demanded our hero, looking down at the fallen bully.

"Just for fun," said Micky.

"It would have been a very agreeable s'prise if it had hit me," said Dick. "S'posin' I fire a rock at you jest for fun."

"Don't!" exclaimed Micky, in alarm.

"It seems you don't like agreeable s'prises," said Dick, "any more'n the man did what got hooked by a cow one mornin', before breakfast. It didn't improve his appetite much."

"I've most broke my arm," said Micky, ruefully, rubbing the affected limb.

"If it's broke you can't fire no more stones, which is a very cheerin' reflection," said Dick. "Ef you haven't money enough to buy a wooden one I'll lend you a quarter. There's one good thing about wooden ones, they ain't liable to get cold in winter, which is another cheerin' reflection."

"I don't want none of yer cheerin' reflections," said Micky, sullenly. "Yer company ain't wanted here."

"Thank you for your polite invitation to leave," said Dick, bowing ceremoniously. "I'm willin' to go, but ef you throw any more stones at me, Micky Maguire, I'll hurt you worse than the stones did."

The only answer made to this warning was a scowl from his fallen opponent. It was quite evident that Dick had the best of it, and he thought it prudent to say nothing. . . .

It will not be necessary to chronicle the events of the next few weeks. A new life had commenced for Dick. . . . He spent two hours every evening in study. His progress was astonishingly rapid. He was gifted with a natural quickness; and he was stimulated by the desire to acquire a fair education as a means of "growin' up 'spectable," as he termed it. Much was due also to the patience and perseverance of Henry Fosdick, who made a capital teacher.

"You're improving wonderfully, Dick," said his friend, one evening, when Dick had read an entire paragraph without a mistake.

"Am I?" said Dick, with satisfaction.

"Yes. If you'll buy a writing-book to-morrow, we can begin writing to-morrow evening."

"What else do you know, Henry?" asked Dick.

"Arithmetic, and geography, and grammar."

"What a lot you know!" said Dick, admiringly.

"I don't know any of them," said Fosdick. "I've only studied them. I wish I knew a great deal more."

"I'll be satisfied when I know as much as you," said Dick.

"It seems a great deal to you now, Dick, but in a few months you'll think differently. The more you know, the more you'll want to know."

"Then there ain't any end to learnin'?" said Dick.

"No."

"Well," said Dick, "I guess I'll be as much as sixty before I know everything."

"Yes; as old as that, probably," said Fosdick, laughing.

"Anyway, you know too much to be blackin' boots. Leave that to ignorant chaps like me."

"You won't be ignorant long, Dick."

"You'd ought to get into some office or countin'-room."

"I wish I could," said Fosdick, earnestly. "I don't succeed very well at blacking boots. You make a great deal more than I do."

"That's cause I ain't troubled with bashfulness," said Dick. "Bashfulness ain't as natural to me as it is to you. I'm always on hand, as the cat said to the milk. You'd better give up shines, Fosdick, and give your 'tention to mercantile pursuits."

"I've thought of trying to get a place," said Fosdick; "but no one would take me with these clothes;" and he directed his glance to his well-worn suit, which he kept as neat as he could, but which, in spite of all his care, began to show decided marks of use. There was also here and there a stain of blacking upon it, which, though an advertisement of his profession, scarcely added to its good appearance.

"I almost wanted to stay at home from Sunday school last Sunday," he continued, "because I thought everybody would notice how dirty and worn my clothes had got to be."

"If my clothes wasn't two sizes too big for you," said Dick, generously, "I'd change. You'd look as if you'd got into your great-uncle's suit by mistake."

"You're very kind, Dick, to think of changing," said Fosdick, "for your suit is much better than mine; but I don't think that mine would suit you very well. The pants would show a little more of your ankles than is the fashion, and you couldn't eat a very hearty dinner without bursting the buttons off the vest."

"That wouldn't be very convenient," said Dick. "I ain't fond of lacin' to show my elegant figger. But I say," he added with a sudden thought, "how much money have we got in the savings' bank?"

Fosdick took a key from his pocket, and went to the drawer in which the bank-books were kept, and, opening it, brought them out for inspection. . . .

"How much does that make, the lot of it?" asked Dick. "I ain't much on figgers yet, you know."

"It makes twenty-five dollars and thirty-five cents, Dick," said his companion, who did not understand the thought which suggested the question.

"Take it, and buy some clothes, Henry," said Dick, shortly.

"What, your money too?"

"In course."

"No, Dick, you are too generous. I couldn't think of it. Almost three-quarters of the money is yours. You must spend it on yourself."

"I don't need it," said Dick.

"You may not need it now, but you will some time."

"I shall have some more then."

"That may be; but it wouldn't be fair for me to use your money, Dick. I thank you all the same for your kindness."

"Well, I'll lend it to you, then," persisted Dick, "and you can pay me when you get to be a rich merchant."

"But it isn't likely I ever shall be one."

"How d'you know? I went to a fortun' teller once, and she told me I was born under a lucky star with a hard name, and I should have a rich man for my particular friend, who would make my fortun'. I guess you are going to be the rich man."

Fosdick laughed, and steadily refused for some time to avail himself of Dick's generous proposal; but at length, perceiving that our hero seemed much disappointed, and would be really glad if his offer were accepted, he agreed to use as much as might be needful.

This at once brought back Dick's good-humor, and he entered with great enthusiasm into his friend's plans.

The next day they withdrew the money from the bank, and, when business got a little slack, in the afternoon, set out in search of a clothing store. Dick knew enough of the city to be able to find a place where a good bargain could be obtained. He was determined that Fosdick should have a good serviceable suit, even if it took all the money they had. The result of their search was that for twenty-three dollars Fosdick obtained a very neat outfit, including a couple of shirts, a hat, and a pair of shoes, besides a dark mixed suit, which appeared stout and of good quality.

"Shall I send the bundle home?" asked the salesman, impressed by the off-hand manner in which Dick drew out the money in payment for the clothes.

"Thank you," said Dick, "you're very kind, but I'll take it home myself, and you can allow me something for my trouble."

"All right," said the clerk, laughing; "I'll allow it on your next purchase."

Proceeding to their apartment in Mott Street, Fosdick at once tried on his new suit, and it was found to be an excellent fit. Dick surveyed his new friend with much satisfaction.

"You look like a young gentleman of fortun'," he said, "and do credit to your governor."

"I suppose that means you, Dick," said Fosdick, laughing.

"In course it does."

"You should say of course," said Fosdick, who, in virtue of his position as Dick's tutor, ventured to correct his language from time to time.

"How dare you correct your gov'nor?" said Dick, with comic indignation. "I'll cut you off with a shillin', you young dog,' as the Markis says to his nephew in the play at the Old Bowery."

CHAPTER XIX

FOSDICK CHANGES HIS BUSINESS

FOSDICK did not venture to wear his new clothes while engaged in his business. This he felt would have been wasteful extravagance. About ten o'clock in the morning, when business slackened, he went home, and dressing himself went to a hotel where he could see copies of the "Morning Herald" and "Sun," and, noting down the places where a boy was wanted, went on a round of applications. But he found it no easy thing to obtain a place. Swarms of boys seemed to be out of employment, and it was not unusual to find from fifty to a hundred applicants for a single place.

There was another difficulty. It was generally desired that the boy wanted should reside with his parents. When Fosdick, on being questioned, revealed the fact of his having no parents, and being a boy of the street, this was generally sufficient of itself to insure a refusal. Merchants were afraid to trust one who had led such a vagabond life. Dick, who was always ready for an emergency, suggested borrowing a white wig, and passing himself off for Fosdick's father or grandfather. But Henry thought this might be rather a difficult character for our hero to sustain. After fifty applications and as many failures, Fosdick began to get discouraged. There seemed to be no way out of his present business, for which he felt unfitted.

"I don't know but I shall have to black boots all my life," he said, one day, despondently, to Dick.

"Keep a stiff upper lip," said Dick. "By the time you get to be a gray-headed veteran, you may get a chance to run errands for some big firm on the Bowery, which is a very cheerin' reflection."

So Dick by his drollery and perpetual good spirits kept up Fosdick's courage.

"As for me," said Dick, "I expect by that time to lay up a colossal fortun' out of shines, but live in princely style on the Avenoo."

But one morning, Fosdick, straying into French's Hotel, discovered the following advertisement in the columns of "The Herald,"—

"WANTED—A smart, capable boy to run of errands, and make himself generally useful in a hat and cap store. Salary three dollars a week at first. Inquire at No. — Broadway, after ten o'clock, A.M."

He determined to make application, and, as the City Hall clock just then struck the hour indicated, lost no time in proceeding to the store, which was only a few blocks distant from the Astor House. It was easy to find the store, as from a dozen to twenty boys were already assembled in front of it. They surveyed each other askance, feeling that they were rivals, and mentally calculating each other's chances.

"There isn't much chance for me," said Fosdick to Dick, who had accompanied him. "Look at all these boys. Most of them have good homes, I suppose, and good recommendations, while I have nobody to refer to."

"Go ahead," said Dick. "Your chance is as good as anybody's."

While this was passing between Dick and his companion, one of the boys, a rather supercilious-looking young gentleman, genteelly dressed, and evidently having a very high opinion of his dress and himself turned suddenly to Dick, and remarked,—

"I've seen you before."

"Oh, have you?" said Dick, whirling round; "then p'r'aps you'd like to see me behind."

At this unexpected answer all the boys burst into a laugh with the exception of the questioner, who, evidently considered that Dick had been disrespectful.

"I've seen you somewhere," he said, in a surly tone, correcting himself.

"Most likely you have," said Dick. "That's where I generally keep myself."

There was another laugh at the expense of Roswell Crawford, for that was the name of the young aristocrat. But he had his revenge ready. No boy relishes being an object of ridicule, and it was with a feeling of satisfaction that he retorted,—

"I know you for all your impudence. You're nothing but a boot-black."

This information took the boys who were standing around by surprise, for Dick was well-dressed, and had none of the implements of his profession with him.

"S'pose I be," said Dick. "Have you got any objection?"

"Not at all," said Roswell, curling his lip; "only you'd better stick to blacking boots, and not try to get into a store."

"Thank you for your kind advice," said Dick. "Is it gratooitous, or do you expect to be paid for it?"

"You're an impudent fellow."

"That's a very cheerin' reflection," said Dick, good-naturedly.

"Do you expect to get this place when there's gentlemen's sons applying for it? A boot-black in a store! That would be a good joke."

Boys as well as men are selfish, and, looking upon Dick as a possible rival, the boys who listened seemed disposed to take the same view of the situation.

"That's what I say," said one of them, taking sides with Roswell.

"Don't trouble yourselves," said Dick. "I ain't agoin' to cut you out. I can't afford to give up a independent and loocrative purfession for a salary of three dollars a week."

"Hear him talk!" said Roswell Crawford, with an unpleasant sneer. "If you are not trying to get the place, what are you here for?"

"I came with a friend of mine," said Dick, indicating Fosdick, "who's goin' in for the situation."

"Is he a boot-black, too?" demanded Roswell, superciliously.

"He!" retorted Dick, loftily. "Didn't you know his father was a member of Congress, and intimately acquainted with all the biggest men in the State?"

The boys surveyed Fosdick as if they did not quite know whether to credit this statement, which, for the credit of Dick's veracity, it will be observed he did not assert, but only propounded in the form of a question. There was no time for comment, however, as just then the proprietor of the store came to the door, and, casting his eyes over the waiting group, singled out Roswell Crawford, and asked him to enter.

"Well, my lad, how old are you?"

"Fourteen years old," said Roswell, consequentially.

"Are your parents living?"

"Only my mother. My father is dead. He was a gentleman," he added complacently.

"Oh, was he?" said the shop-keeper. "Do you live in the city?"

"Yes, sir. In Clinton Place."

"Have you ever been in a situation before?"

"Yes, sir," said Roswell, a little reluctantly.

"Where was it?"

"In an office on Dey Street."

"How long were you there?"

"A week."

"It seems to me that was a short time. Why did you not stay longer?"

"Because," said Rosewell, loftily, "the man wanted me to get to the office at eight o'clock, and make the fire. I'm a gentleman's son, and am not used to such dirty work."

"Indeed!" said the shop-keeper. "Well young gentleman, you may step aside a few minutes. I will speak with some of the other boys before making my selection."

Several other boys were called in and questioned. Roswell stood by and listened with an air of complacency. He could not help thinking his chances the best. "The man can see I'm a gentleman, and will do credit to his store," he thought.

At length it came to Fosdick's turn. He entered with no very sanguine anticipations of success. Unlike Roswell, he set a very low estimate upon his qualifications when compared with those of other applicants. But his modest bearing, and quiet, gentlemanly manner, entirely free from pretension, prepossessed the shop-keeper, who was a sensible man, in his favor.

"Do you reside in the city?" he asked.

"Yes, sir," said Henry.

"What is your age?"

"Twelve."

"Have you ever been in any situation?"

"No, sir."

"I should like to see a specimen of your handwriting. Here, take the pen and write your name."

Henry Fosdick had a very handsome handwriting for a boy of his age, while Roswell, who had submitted to the same test, could do little more than scrawl.

"Do you reside with your parents?"

"No, sir, they are dead."

"Where do you live, then?"

"In Mott Street."

Roswell curled his lip when this name was pronounced, for Mott Street, as my New York readers know, is in the immediate neighborhood of the Five-Points, and very far from a fashionable locality.

"Have you any testimonials to present?" asked Mr. Henderson, for that was his name.

Fosdick hesitated. This was the question which he had foreseen would give him trouble.

But at this moment it happened most opportunely that Mr. Greyson entered the shop with the intention of buying a hat.

"Yes," said Fosdick, promptly; "I will refer to this gentleman."

"How do you do, Fosdick?" asked Mr. Greyson, noticing him for the first time. "How do you happen to be here?"

"I am applying for a place, sir," said Fosdick. "May I refer the gentleman to you?"

"Certainly, I shall be glad to speak a good word for you. Mr. Henderson, this is a member of my Sunday-school class, of whose good qualities and good abilities I can speak confidently."

"That will be sufficient," said the shop-keeper, who knew Mr. Greyson's high character and position. "He could have no better recommendation. You may come to the store to-morrow morning at half-past seven o'clock. The pay will be three dollars a week for the first six months. If I am satisfied with you, I shall then raise it to five dollars."

The other boys looked disappointed, but none more so than Roswell Crawford. He would have cared less if any one else had obtained the situation; but for a boy who lived in Mott Street to be preferred to him, a gentleman's son, he considered indeed humiliating. In a spirit of petty spite, he was tempted to say, "He's a boot-black. Ask him if he isn't."

"He's an honest and intelligent lad," said Mr. Greyson. "As for you, young man, I only hope you have one-half his good qualities."

Roswell Crawford left the store in disgust, and the other unsuccessful applicants with him.

"What luck, Fosdick?" asked Dick, eagerly, as his friend came out of the store.

"I've got the place," said Fosdick, in accents of satisfaction; "but it was only because Mr. Greyson spoke up for me."

"He's a trump," said Dick, enthusiastically.

The gentleman, so denominated, came out before the boys went away, and spoke with them kindly.

Both Dick and Henry were highly pleased at the success of the application. The pay would indeed be small, but, expended economically, Fosdick thought he could get along on it, receiving his room rent, as before, in return for his services as Dick's private tutor. Dick determined, as soon as his education would permit, to follow his companion's example.

"I don't know as you'll be willin' to room with a boot-black," he said, to Henry, "now you're goin' into business."

"I couldn't room with a better friend, Dick," said Fosdick, affectionately, throwing his arm round our hero. "When we part, it'll be because you wish it."

So Fosdick entered upon a new career.

CHAPTER XX

NINE MONTHS LATER

THE next morning Fosdick rose early, put on his new suit, and, after getting breakfast, set out for the Broadway store in which he had obtained a position. He left his little blacking-box in the room.

"It'll do to brush my own shoes," he said. "Who knows but I may have to come back to it again?"

"No danger," said Dick; "I'll take care of the feet, and you'll have to look after the heads, now you're in a hat-store."

"I wish you had a place too," said Fosdick.

"I don't know enough yet," said Dick. "Wait till I've gradooated."

"And can put A. B. after your name."

"What's that?"

"It stands for Bachelor of Arts. It's a degree that students get when they graduate from college."

"Oh," said Dick, "I didn't know but it meant A Boot-black. I can put that after my name now. Wouldn't Dick Hunter, A. B., sound tip-top?"

"I must be going," said Fosdick. "It won't do for me to be late the very first morning."

"That's the difference between you and me," said Dick. "I'm my own boss, and there ain't no one to find fault with me if I'm late. But I might as well be goin' too. There's a gent as comes down to his store pretty early that generally wants a shine."

The two boys parted at the Park. Fosdick crossed it, and proceeded to the hat-store, while Dick, hitching up his pants, began to look about him for a customer. It was seldom that Dick had to wait long. He was always on the alert, and if there was any business to do he was always sure to get his share of it. He had now a stronger inducement than ever to attend strictly to business; his little stock of money in the savings bank having been nearly exhausted by his liberality to his room-mate. He determined to be as economical as possible, and moreover to study as hard as he could, that he might be able to follow Fosdick's example, and obtain a place in a store or counting-room. As there were no striking incidents occurring in our hero's history within the next nine months, I propose to pass over that period, and recount the progress he made in that time.

Fosdick was still at the hat-store, having succeeded in giving perfect satisfaction to Mr. Henderson. His wages had just been raised to five dollars a week. He and Dick still kept house together at Mrs. Mooney's lodging-house, and lived very frugally, so that both were able to save up money. Dick had been unusually successful in business. He had several regular patrons, who had been drawn to him by his ready wit, and quick humor, and from two of them he had received presents of clothing, which had saved him any expense on that score. His income had averaged quite seven dollars a week in addition to this. Of this amount he was now obliged to pay one dollar weekly for the room which he and Fosdick occupied, but he was still able to save one half the remainder. At the end of nine months therefore, or thirty-nine weeks, it will be seen that he had accumulated no less a sum than one hundred and seventeen dollars. Dick may be excused for feeling like a capitalist when he looked at the long row of deposits in his little bank-book. There were other boys in the same business who had earned as much money, but they had had little care for the future, and spent as they went along, so that few could boast a bank-account, however small.

"You'll be a rich man some time, Dick," said Henry Fosdick, one evening.

"And live on Fifth Avenoo," said Dick.

"Perhaps so. Stranger things have happened."

"Well," said Dick, "if such a misfortin' should come upon me I should bear it like a man. When you see a Fifth Avenoo manshun for sale for a hundred and seventeen dollars, just let me know and I'll buy it as an investment."

"Two hundred and fifty years ago you might have bought one for that price, probably. Real estate wasn't very high among the Indians."

"Just my luck," said Dick; "I was born too late. I'd orter have been an Indian, and lived in splendor on my present capital."

"I'm afraid you'd have found your present business rather unprofitable at that time."

But Dick had gained something more valuable than money. He had studied regularly every evening, and his improvement had been marvellous. He could now read well, write a fair hand, and had studied arithmetic as far as Interest. Besides this he had obtained some knowledge of grammar and geography. If some of my boy readers, who have been studying for years, and got no farther than this, should think it incredible that Dick, in less than a year, and studying evenings only, should have accomplished it, they must remember that our hero was very much in earnest in his desire to improve. He knew that, in order to grow up respectable, he must be well advanced, and he was willing to work. But then the reader must not forget that Dick was naturally a smart boy. His street education had sharpened his faculties, and taught him to rely upon himself. He knew that it would take him a long time to reach the goal which he had set before him, and he had patience to keep on trying. He knew that he had only himself to depend upon, and he determined to make the most of himself,—a resolution which is the secret of success in nine cases out of ten.

"Dick," said Fosdick, one evening, after they had completed their studies, "I think you'll have to get another teacher soon."

"Why?" asked Dick, in some surprise. "Have you been offered a more loocrative position?"

"No," said Fosdick, "but I find I have taught you all I know myself. You are now as good a scholar as I am."

"Is that true?" said Dick, eagerly, a flush of gratification coloring his brown cheek.

"Yes," said Fosdick. "You've made wonderful progress. I propose, now that evening schools have begun, that we join one, and study together through the winter."

"All right," said Dick. "I'd be willin' to go now; but when I first began to study I was ashamed to have anybody know that I was so ignorant. Do you really mean, Fosdick, that I know as much as you?"

"Yes, Dick, it's true."

"Then I've got you to thank for it," said Dick, earnestly. "You've made me what I am."

"And haven't you paid me, Dick?"

"By payin' the room-rent," said Dick, impulsively. "What's that? It isn't half enough. I wish you'd take half my money; you deserve it."

"Thank you, Dick, but you're too generous. You've more than paid me. Who was it took my part when all the other boys imposed upon me? And who gave me money to buy clothes, and so got me my situation?"

"Oh, that's nothing!" said Dick.

"It's a great deal, Dick. I shall never forget it. But now it seems to me you might try to get a situation yourself."

"Do I know enough?"

"You know as much as I do."

"Then I'll try," said Dick, decidedly.

"I wish there was a place in our store," said Fosdick. "It would be pleasant for us to be together."

"Never mind," said Dick; "there'll be plenty of other chances. P'r'aps A. T. Stewart might like a partner. I wouldn't ask more'n a quarter of the profits."

"Which would be a very liberal proposal on your part," said Fosdick, smiling. "But perhaps Mr. Stewart might object to a partner living on Mott Street."

"I'd just as lieves move to Fifth Avenoo," said Dick. "I ain't got no prejudices in favor of Mott Street."

"Nor I," said Fosdick, "and in fact I have been thinking it might be a good plan for us to move as soon as we could afford. Mrs. Mooney doesn't keep the room quite so neat as she might."

"No," said Dick. "She ain't got no prejudices against dirt. Look at that towel."

Dick held up the article indicated, which had now seen service nearly a week, and hard service at that.—Dick's avocation causing him to be rather hard on towels.

"Yes," said Fosdick, "I've got about tired of it. I guess we can find some better place without having to pay much more. When we move, you must let me pay my share of the rent."

"We'll see about that," said Dick. "Do you propose to move to Fifth Avenoo?"

"Not just at present, but to some more agreeable neighborhood than this. We'll wait till you get a situation, and then we can decide."

A few days later, as Dick was looking about for customers in the neighborhood of the Park, his attention was drawn to a fellow boot-black, a boy about a year younger than himself, who appeared to have been crying.

"What's the matter, Tom?" asked Dick. "Haven't you had luck to-day?"

"Pretty good," said the boy; "but we're havin' hard times at home. Mother fell last week and broke her arm, and to-morrow we've got to pay the rent, and if we don't the landlord says he'll turn us out."

"Haven't you got anything except what you earn?" asked Dick.

"No," said Tom, "not now. Mother used to earn three or four dollars a week; but she can't do nothin' now, and my little sister and brother are too young."

Dick had quick sympathies. He had been so poor himself, and obliged to submit to so many privations that he knew from personal experience how hard it was. Tom Wilkins he knew as an excellent boy who never squandered his money, but faithfully carried it home to his mother. In the days of his own extravagance and shiftlessness he had once or twice asked Tom to accompany him to the Old Bowery or Tony Pastor's, but Tom had always steadily refused.

"I am sorry for you, Tom," he said. "How much do you owe for rent?"

"Two weeks now," said Tom.

"How much is it a week?"

"Two dollars a week—that makes four."

"Have you got anything towards it?"

"No; I've had to spend all my money for food for mother and the rest of us. I've had pretty hard work to do that. I don't know what we'll do. I haven't any place to go to, and I'm afraid mother'll get cold in her arm."

"Can't you borrow the money somewhere?" asked Dick.

Tom shook his head despondingly.

"All the people I know are as poor as I am," said he. "They'd help me if they could, but it's hard work for them to get along themselves."

"I'll tell you what, Tom," said Dick, impulsively, "I'll stand your friend."

"Have you got any money?" asked Tom, doubtfully.

"Got any money!" repeated Dick. "Don't you know that I run a bank on my own account? How much is it you need?"

"Four dollars," said Tom. "If we don't pay that before to-morrow night, out we go. You haven't got as much as that, have you?"

"Here are three dollars," said Dick, drawing out his pocket-book. "I'll let you have the rest to-morrow, and maybe a little more."

"You're a right down good fellow, Dick," said Tom; "but won't you want it yourself?"

"Oh, I've got some more," said Dick.

"Maybe I'll never be able to pay you."

"S'pose you don't," said Dick; "I guess I won't fail."

"I won't forget it, Dick. I hope I'll be able to do somethin' for you sometime."

"All right," said Dick. "I'd ought to help you. I haven't got no mother to look out for. I wish I had."

There was a tinge of sadness in his tone, as he pronounced the last four words; but Dick's temperament was sanguine, and he never gave way to unavailing sadness. Accordingly he began to whistle as he turned away, only adding, "I'll see you to-morrow, Tom." . . .

CHAPTER XXIV

DICK RECEIVES A LETTER

. . . FOSDICK brought home with him in the evening a copy of the "Daily Sun."

"Would you like to see your name in print, Dick?" he asked.

"Yes," said Dick, who was busy at the wash-stand, endeavoring to efface the marks which his day's work had left upon his hands. "They haven't put me up for mayor, have they? 'Cause if they have, I shan't accept. It would interfere too much with my private business."

"No," said Fosdick, "they haven't put you up for office yet, though that may happen sometime. But if you want to see your name in print, here it is."

Dick was rather incredulous, but, having dried his hands on the towel, took the paper, and following the directions of Fosdick's finger, observed in the list of advertised letters the name of "RAGGED DICK."

"By gracious, so it is," said he. "Do you s'pose it means me?"

"I don't know of any other Ragged Dick,—do you?"

"No," said Dick, reflectively; "it must be me. But I don't know of anybody that would be likely to write to me."

"Perhaps it is Frank Whitney," suggested Fosdick, after a little reflection. "Didn't he promise to write to you?"

"Yes," said Dick, "and he wanted me to write to him."

"Where is he now?"

"He was going to a boarding-school in Connecticut, he said. The name of the town was Barnton."

"Very likely the letter is from him."

"I hope it is. Frank was a tip-top boy, and he was the first that made me ashamed of bein' so ignorant and dirty."

"You had better go to the post-office to-morrow morning, and ask for the letter."

"P'r'aps they won't give it to me."

"Suppose you wear the old clothes you used to a year ago, when Frank first saw you? They won't have any doubt of your being Ragged Dick then."

"I guess I will. I'll be sort of ashamed to be seen in 'em though," said Dick, who had considerable more pride in a neat personal appearance than when we were first introduced to him.

"It will be only for one day, or one morning," said Fosdick.

"I'd do more'n that for the sake of gettin' a letter from Frank. I'd like to see him."

The next morning, in accordance with the suggestion of Fosdick, Dick arrayed himself in the long disused Washington coat and Napoleon pants, which he had carefully preserved, for what reason he could hardly explain.

When fairly equipped, Dick surveyed himself in the mirror,—if the little seven-by-nine-inch looking-glass, with which the room was furnished, deserved the name. The result of the survey was not on the whole a pleasing one. To tell the truth, Dick was quite ashamed of his appearance, and, on opening the chamber-door, looked around to see that the coast was clear, not being willing to have any of his fellow-boarders see him in his present attire.

He managed to slip out into the street unobserved, and, after attending to two or three regular customers who came down-town early in the morning, he made his way down Nassau Street to the post-office. He passed along until he came to a compartment on which he read ADVERTISED LETTERS, and, stepping up to the little window, said,—

"There's a letter for me. I saw it advertised in the 'Sun' yesterday."

"What name?" demanded the clerk.

"Ragged Dick," answered our hero.

"That's a queer name," said the clerk, surveying him a little curiously, "Are you Ragged Dick?"

"If you don't believe me, look at my clo'es," said Dick.

"That's pretty good proof, certainly," said the clerk, laughing. "If that isn't your name, it deserves to be."

"I believe in dressin' up to your name," said Dick.

"Do you know any one in Barnton, Connecticut?" asked the clerk, who had by this time found the letter.

"Yes," said Dick. "I know a chap that's at boardin'-school there."

"It appears to be in a boy's hand. I think it must be yours."

The letter was handed to Dick through the window. He received it eagerly, and drawing back so as not to be in the way of the throng who were constantly applying for letters, or slipping them into the boxes provided for them, hastily opened it, and began to read. As the reader may be interested in the contents of the letter as well as Dick, we transcribe it below. It was dated Barnton, Conn., and commenced thus,—

"DEAR DICK,—You must excuse my addressing this letter to 'Ragged Dick'; but the fact is, I don't know what your last name is, nor where you live. I am afraid there is not much chance of your getting this letter; but I hope you will. I have thought of you very often, and wondered how you were getting along, and I should have written to you before if I had known where to direct.

"Let me tell you a little about myself. Barnton is a very pretty country town, only about six miles from Hartford. The boarding-school which I attend is under the charge of Ezekiel Munroe, A.M. He is a man of about fifty, a graduate of Yale College, and has always been a teacher. It is a large two-story house, with an addition containing a good many small bed-chambers for the boys. There are about twenty of us, and there is one assistant teacher who teaches the English branches. Mr. Munroe, or Old Zeke, as we call him behind his back, teaches Latin and Greek. I am studying both these languages, because father wants me to go to college.

"But you won't be interested in hearing about our studies. I will tell you how we amuse ourselves. There are about fifty acres of land belonging to Mr. Munroe; so that we have plenty of room for play. About a quarter of a mile from the house there is a good-sized pond. There is a large, round-bottomed boat, which is stout and strong. Every Wednesday and Saturday afternoon, when the weather is good, we go out rowing on the pond. Mr. Barton, the assistant teacher, goes with us, to look after us. In the summer we are allowed to go in bathing. In the winter there is splendid skating on the pond.

"Besides this, we play ball a good deal, and we have various other plays. So we have a pretty good time, although we study pretty hard too. I am getting on very well in my studies. Father has not decided yet where he will send me to college.

"I wish you were here, Dick. I should enjoy your company, and besides I should like to feel that you were getting an education. I think you are naturally a pretty smart boy; but I suppose, as you have to earn your own living, you don't get much chance to learn. I only wish I had a few hundred dollars of my own. I would have you come up here, and attend school with us. If I ever have a chance to help you in any way, you may be sure that I will.

"I shall have to wind up my letter now, as I have to hand in a composition to-morrow, on the life and character of Washington. I might say that I have a friend who wears a coat that once belonged to the general. But I suppose that coat must be worn out by this time. I don't much like writing compositions. I would a good deal rather write letters.

"I have written a longer letter than I meant to. I hope you will get it, though I am afraid not. If you do, you must be sure to answer it, as soon as possible. You needn't mind if your writing does look like 'hens-tracks,' as you told me once.

"Good-by, Dick. You must always think of me, as your very true friend,
                                        "FRANK WHITNEY."

Dick read this letter with much satisfaction. It is always pleasant to be remembered, and Dick had so few friends that it was more to him than to boys who are better provided. Again, he felt a new sense of importance in having a letter addressed to him. It was the first letter he had ever received. If it had been sent to him a year before, he would not have been able to read it.

But now, thanks to Fosdick's instructions, he could not only read writing, but he could write a very good hand himself.

There was one passage in the letter which pleased Dick. It was where Frank said that if he had the money he would pay for his education himself.

"He's a tip-top feller," said Dick. "I wish I could see him ag'in."

There were two reasons why Dick would like to have seen Frank. One was, the natural pleasure he would have in meeting a friend; but he felt also that he would like to have Frank witness the improvement he had made in his studies and mode of life.

"He'd find me a little more 'spectable than when he first saw me," thought Dick. . . .

CHAPTER XXV

DICK WRITES HIS FIRST LETTER

WHEN Fosdick reached home in the evening, Dick displayed his letter with some pride.

"It's a nice letter," said Fosdick, after reading it. "I should like to know Frank."

"I'll bet you would," said Dick. "He's a trump."

"When are you going to answer it?"

"I don't know," said Dick dubiously. "I never writ a letter."

"There's no reason why you shouldn't. There's always a first time, you know."

"I don't know what to say," said Dick.

"Get some paper and sit down to it, and you'll find enough to say. You can do that this evening instead of studying."

"If you'll look it over afterwards, and shine it up a little."

"Yes, if it needs it; but I rather think Frank would like it best just as you wrote it."

Dick decided to adopt Fosdick's suggestion. He had very serious doubts as to his ability to write a letter. Like a good many other boys, he looked upon it as a very serious job, not reflecting that, after all, letter-writing is nothing but talking upon paper. Still, in spite of his misgivings, he felt that the letter ought to be answered, and he wished Frank to hear from him. After various preparations, he at last got settled down to his task, and, before the evening was over, a letter was written. As the first letter which Dick had ever produced, and because it was characteristic of him, my readers may like to read it. Here it is,—

"DEAR FRANK,—I got your letter this mornin', and was very glad to hear you hadn't forgotten Ragged Dick. I ain't so ragged as I was. Open work coats and trousers has gone out of fashion. I put on the Washington coat and Napoleon pants to go to the post-office, for fear they wouldn't think I was the boy that was meant. On my way back I received the congratulations of my intimate friend, Micky Maguire, on my improved appearance.

"I've give up sleepin' in boxes, and old wagons, findin' it didn't agree with my constitution. I've hired a room in Mott Street, and have got a private tooter, who rooms with me and looks after my studies in the evenin'. Mott Street ain't very fashionable; but my manshun on Fifth Avenoo isn't finished yet, and I'm afraid it won't be till I'm a gray-haired veteran. I've got a hundred dollars towards it, which I've saved up from my earnin's. I haven't forgot what you and your uncle said to me, and I'm tryin' to grow up 'spectable. I haven't been to Tony Pastor's, or the Old Bowery, for ever so long. I'd rather save up my money to support me in my old age. When my hair gets gray, I'm goin' to knock off blackin' boots, and go into some light, genteel employment, such as keepin' an apple-stand, or disseminatin' pea-nuts among the people.

"I've got so as to read pretty well, so my tooter says. I've been studyin' geography and grammar also. I've made such astonishin' progress that I can tell a noun from a conjunction as far away as I can see 'em. Tell Mr. Munroe that if he wants an accomplished teacher in his school, he can send for me, and I'll come on by the very next train. Or, if he wants to sell out for a hundred dollars, I'll buy the whole concern, and agree to teach the scholars all I know myself in less than six months. Is teachin' as good business, generally speakin', as blackin' boots? My private tooter combines both, and is makin' a fortun' with great rapidity. He'll be as rich as Astor some time, *if he only lives long enough.*

"I should think you'd have a bully time at your school. I should like to go out in the boat, or play ball with you. When are you comin' to the city? I wish you'd write and let me know when you do, and I'll call and see you. I'll leave my business in the hands of my numerous clerks, and go round with you. There's lots of things you didn't see when you was here before. They're getting on fast at the Central Park. It looks better than it did a year ago.

"I ain't much used to writin' letters. As this is the first one I ever wrote, I hope you'll excuse the mistakes. I hope you'll write to me again soon. I can't write so good a letter as you; but I'll do my best, as the man said when he was asked if he could swim over to Brooklyn backwards. Good-by, Frank. Thank you for all your kindness. Direct your next letter to No. — Mott Street.

"Your true friend,
"DICK HUNTER."

When Dick had written the last word, he leaned back in his chair, and surveyed the letter with much satisfaction.

"I didn't think I could have wrote such a long letter, Fosdick," said he.

"Written would be more grammatical, Dick," suggested his friend.

"I guess there's plenty of mistakes in it," said Dick. "Just look at it, and see."

Fosdick took the letter, and read it over carefully.

"Yes, there are some mistakes," he said; "but it sounds so much like you that I think it would be better to let it go just as it is. It will be more likely to remind Frank of what you were when he first saw you."

"Is it good enough to send?" asked Dick, anxiously.

"Yes; it seems to me to be quite a good letter. It is written just as you talk. Nobody but you could have written such a letter, Dick. I think Frank will be amused at your proposal to come up there as teacher."

"P'r'aps it would be a good idea for us to open a seleck school here in Mott Street," said Dick, humorously. "We could call it 'Professor Fosdick and Hunter's Mott Street Seminary.' Boot-blackin' taught by Professor Hunter."

The evening was so far advanced that Dick decided to postpone copying his letter till the next evening. By this time he had come to have a very fair handwriting, so that when the letter was complete it really looked quite creditable, and no one would have suspected that it was Dick's first attempt in this line.

Our hero surveyed it with no little complacency. In fact, he felt rather proud of it, since it reminded him of the great progress he had made. He carried it down to the post-office, and deposited it with his own hands in the proper box. Just on the steps of the building, as he was coming out, he met Johnny Nolan, who had been sent on an errand to Wall Street by some gentleman, and was just returning.

"What are you doin' down here, Dick?" asked Johnny.

"I've been mailin' a letter."

"Who sent you?"

"Nobody."

"I mean, who writ the letter?"

"I wrote it myself."

"Can you write letters?" asked Johnny, in amazement.

"Why shouldn't I?"

"I didn't know you could write. I can't."

"Then you ought to learn."

"I went to school once; but it was too hard work, so I give it up."

"You're lazy, Johnny,—that's what's the matter. How'd you ever expect to know anything, if you don't try?"

"I can't learn."

"You can, if you want to."

Johnny Nolan was evidently of a different opinion. He was a good-natured boy, large of his age, with nothing particularly bad about him, but utterly lacking in that energy, ambition, and natural sharpness, for which Dick was distinguished. He was not adapted to succeed in the life which circumstances had forced upon him; for in the street-life of the metropolis a boy needs to be on the alert, and have all his wits about him, or he will find himself wholly distanced by his more enterprising competitors for popular favor. To succeed in his profession, humble as it is, a boot-black must depend upon the same qualities which gain success in higher walks in life. It was easy to see that Johnny, unless very much favored by circumstances, would never rise much above his present level. For Dick, we cannot help hoping much better things.

CHAPTER XXVI

AN EXCITING ADVENTURE

DICK now began to look about for a position in a store or counting-room. Until he should obtain one he determined to devote half the day to blacking boots, not being willing to break in upon his small capital. He found that he could earn enough in half a day to pay all his necessary expenses, including the entire rent of the room. Fosdick desired to pay his half; but Dick steadily refused, insisting upon paying so much as compensation for his friend's services as instructor.

It should be added that Dick's peculiar way of speaking and use of slang terms had been somewhat modified by his education and his intimacy with Henry Fosdick. Still he continued to indulge in them to some extent, especially when he felt like joking, and it was natural to Dick to joke, as my readers have probably found out by this time. Still his manners were considerably improved, so that he was more likely to obtain a situation than when first introduced to our notice.

Just now, however, business was very dull, and merchants, instead of hiring new assistants, were disposed to part with those already in their employ. After making several ineffectual applications, Dick began to think he should be obliged to stick to his profession until the next season. But about this time something occurred which considerably improved his chances of preferment.

This is the way it happened.

As Dick, with a balance of more than a hundred dollars in the savings bank, might fairly consider himself a young man of property, he thought himself justified in occasionally taking a half holiday from business, and going on an excursion. On Wednesday afternoon Henry Fosdick was sent by his employer on an errand to that part of Brooklyn near Greenwood Cemetery. Dick hastily dressed himself in his best, and determined to accompany him.

The two boys walked down to the South Ferry, and, paying their two cents each, entered the ferry boat. They remained at the stern, and stood by the railing, watching the great city, with its crowded wharves, receding from view. Beside them was a gentleman with two children,—a girl of eight and a little boy of six. The children were talking gayly to their father. While he was pointing out some object of interest to the little girl, the boy managed to creep, unobserved, beneath the chain that extends across the boat, for the protection of passengers, and, stepping incautiously to the edge of the boat, fell over into the foaming water.

At the child's scream, the father looked up, and, with a cry of horror, sprang to the edge of the boat. He would have plunged in, but, being unable to swim, would only have endangered his own life, without being able to save his child.

"My child!" he exclaimed in anguish,—"who will save my child? A thousand—ten thousand dollars to any one who will save him!"

There chanced to be but few passengers on board at the time, and nearly all these were either in the cabins or standing forward. Among the few who saw the child fall was our hero.

Now Dick was an expert swimmer. It was an accomplishment which he had possessed for years, and he no sooner saw the boy fall than he resolved to rescue him. His determination was formed before he heard the liberal offer made by the boy's father. Indeed, I must do Dick the justice to say that, in the excitement of the moment, he did not hear it at all, nor would it have stimulated the alacrity with which he sprang to the rescue of the little boy.

Little Johnny had already risen once, and gone under for the second time, when our hero plunged in. He was obliged to strike out for the boy, and this took time. He reached him none too soon. Just as he was sinking for the third and last time, he caught him by the jacket. Dick was stout and strong, but Johnny clung to him so tightly, that it was with great difficulty he was able to sustain himself.

"Put your arms round my neck," said Dick.

The little boy mechanically obeyed, and clung with a grasp strengthened by his terror. In this position Dick could bear his weight better. But the ferryboat was receding fast. It was quite impossible to reach it. The father, his face pale with terror and anguish, and his hands clasped in suspense, saw the brave boy's struggles, and prayed with agonizing fervor that he might be successful. But it is probable, for they were now midway of the river, that both Dick and the little boy whom he had bravely undertaken to rescue would have been drowned, had not a row-boat been fortunately near. The two men who were in it witnessed the accident, and hastened to the rescue of our hero.

"Keep up a little longer," they shouted, bending to their oars, "and we will save you."

Dick heard the shout, and it put fresh strength into him. He battled manfully with the treacherous sea, his eyes fixed longingly upon the approaching boat.

"Hold on tight, little boy," he said. "There's a boat coming."

The little boy did not see the boat. His eyes were closed to shut out the fearful water, but he clung the closer to his young preserver. Six long, steady strokes, and the boat dashed along side. Strong hands seized Dick and his youthful burden, and drew them into the boat, both dripping with water.

"God be thanked!" exclaimed the father, as from the steamer he saw the child's rescue. "That brave boy shall be rewarded, if I sacrifice my whole fortune to compass it."

"You've had a pretty narrow escape, young chap," said one of the boatmen to Dick. "It was a pretty tough job you undertook."

"Yes," said Dick. "That's what I thought when I was in the water. If it hadn't been for you, I don't know what would have 'come of us."

"Anyhow you're a plucky boy, or you wouldn't have dared to jump into the water after this little chap. It was a risky thing to do."

"I'm used to the water," said Dick, modestly. "I didn't stop to think of the danger, but I wasn't going to let that little fellow drown without tryin' to save him."

The boat at once headed for the ferry wharf on the Brooklyn side. The captain of the ferry-boat, seeing the rescue, did not think it necessary to stop his boat, but kept on his way. The whole occurrence took place in less time than I have occupied in telling it.

The father was waiting on the wharf to receive his little boy, with what feelings of gratitude and joy can be easily understood. With a burst of happy tears he clasped him to his arms. Dick was about to withdraw modestly, but the gentleman perceived the movement, and, putting down the child, came forward, and, clasping his hand, said with emotion, "My brave boy, I owe you a debt I can never repay. But for your timely service I should now be plunged into an anguish which I cannot think of without a shudder."

Our hero was ready enough to speak on most occasions, but always felt awkward when he was praised.

"It wasn't any trouble," he said, modestly. "I can swim like a top."

"But not many boys would have risked their lives for a stranger," said the gentleman. "But," he added with a sudden thought, as his glance rested on Dick's dripping garments, "both you and my little boy will take cold in wet clothes. Fortunately I have a friend living close at hand, at whose house you will have an opportunity of taking off your clothes, and having them dried."

Dick protested that he never took cold; but Fosdick, who had now joined them, and who, it is needless to say, had been greatly alarmed at Dick's danger, joined in urging compliance with the gentleman's proposal, and in the end our hero had to yield. His new friend secured a hack, the driver of which agreed for extra recompense to receive the dripping boys into his carriage, and they were whirled rapidly to a pleasant house in a side street, where matters were quickly explained, and both boys were put to bed.

"I ain't used to goin' to bed quite so early," thought Dick. "This is the queerest excursion I ever took."

Like most active boys Dick did not enjoy the prospect of spending half a day in bed; but his confinement did not last as long as he anticipated.

In about an hour the door of his chamber was opened, and a servant appeared, bringing a new and handsome suit of clothes throughout.

"You are to put on these," said the servant to Dick; "but you needn't get up till you feel like it."

"Whose clothes are they?" asked Dick.

"They are yours."

"Mine! Where did they come from?"

"Mr. Rockwell sent out and bought them for you. They are the same size as your wet ones."

"Is he here now?"

"No. He bought another suit for the little boy, and has gone back to New York. Here's a note he asked me to give you."

Dick opened the paper, and read as follows,—

"Please accept this outfit of clothes as the first instalment of a debt which I can never repay. I have asked to have your wet suit dried, when you can reclaim it. Will you oblige me by calling to-morrow at my counting room, No. —, Pearl Street.

"Your friend,
"JAMES ROCKWELL."

CHAPTER XXVII

CONCLUSION

WHEN Dick was dressed in his new suit, he surveyed his figure with pardonable complacency. It was the best he had ever worn, and fitted him as well as if it had been made expressly for him.

"He's done the handsome thing," said Dick to himself; "but there wasn't no 'casion for his givin' me these clothes. My lucky stars are shinin' pretty bright now. Jumpin' into the water pays better than shinin' boots; but I don't think I'd like to try it more'n once a week."

About eleven o'clock the next morning Dick repaired to Mr. Rockwell's counting-room on Pearl Street. He found himself in front of a large and handsome warehouse. The counting-room was on the lower floor. Our hero entered, and found Mr. Rockwell sitting at a desk. No sooner did that gentleman see him than he arose, and, advancing, shook Dick by the hand in the most friendly manner.

"My young friend," he said, "you have done me so great service that I wish to be of some service to you in return. Tell me about yourself, and what plans or wishes you have formed for the future."

Dick frankly related his past history, and told Mr. Rockwell of his desire to get into a store or counting-room, and of the failure of all his applications thus far. The merchant listened attentively to Dick's statement, and, when he had finished, placed a sheet of paper before him, and, handing him a pen, said, "Will you write your name on this piece of paper?"

Dick wrote in a free, bold hand, the name Richard Hunter. He had very much improved in his penmanship, as has already been mentioned, and now had no cause to be ashamed of it.

Mr. Rockwell surveyed it approvingly.

"How would you like to enter my counting-room as clerk, Richard?" he asked.

Dick was about to say "Bully," when he recollected himself, and answered, "Very much."

"I suppose you know something of arithmetic, do you not?"

"Yes, sir."

"Then you may consider yourself engaged at a salary of ten dollars a week. You may come next Monday morning."

"Ten dollars!" repeated Dick, thinking he must have misunderstood.

"Yes; will that be sufficient?"

"It's more than I can earn," said Dick, honestly.

"Perhaps it is at first," said Mr. Rockwell, smiling; "but I am willing to pay you that. I will besides advance you as fast as your progress will justify it."

Dick was so elated that he hardly restrained himself from some demonstration which would have astonished the merchant; but he exercised self-control, and only said, "I'll try to serve you so faithfully, sir, that you won't repent having taken me into your service."

"And I think you will succeed," said Mr. Rockwell, encouragingly. "I will not detain you any longer, for I have some important business to attend to. I shall expect to see you on Monday morning."

Dick left the counting-room, hardly knowing whether he stood on his head or his heels, so overjoyed was he at the sudden change in his fortunes. Ten dollars a week was to him a fortune, and three times as much as he had expected to obtain at first. Indeed he would have been glad, only the day before, to get a place at three dollars a week. He reflected that with the stock of clothes which he had now on hand, he could save up at least half of it, and even then live better than he had been accustomed to do; so that his little fund in the savings bank, instead of being diminished, would be steadily increasing. Then he was to be advanced if he deserved it. It was indeed a bright prospect for a boy who, only a year before, could neither read nor write, and depended for a night's lodging upon the chance hospitality of an alley-way or old wagon. Dick's great ambition to "grow up 'spectable" seemed likely to be accomplished after all.

"I wish Fosdick was as well off as I am," he thought generously. But he determined to help his less fortunate friend, and assist him up the ladder as he advanced himself.

When Dick entered his room on Mott Street, he discovered that some one else had been there before him, and two articles of wearing apparel had disappeared.

"By gracious!" he exclaimed; "somebody's stole my Washington coat and Napoleon pants. Maybe it's an agent of Barnum's, who expects to make a fortun' by exhibitin' the valooable wardrobe of a gentleman of fashion."

Dick did not shed many tears over his loss, as, in his present circumstances, he never expected to have any further use for the well-worn garments. It may be stated that he afterwards saw them adorning the figure of Micky Maguire; but whether that estimable young man stole them himself, he never ascertained. As to the loss, Dick was rather pleased that it had occurred. It seemed to cut him off from the old vagabond life which he hoped never to resume. Henceforward he meant to press onward, and rise as high as possible.

Although it was yet only noon, Dick did not go out again with his brush. He felt that it was time to retire from business. He would leave his share of the public patronage to other boys less fortunate than himself. That evening Dick and Fosdick had a long conversation. Fosdick rejoiced heartily in his friend's success, and on his side had the pleasant news to communicate that his pay had been advanced to six dollars a week.

"I think we can afford to leave Mott Street now," he continued. "This house isn't as neat as it might be, and I should like to live in a nicer quarter of the city."

"All right," said Dick. "We'll hunt up a new room to-morrow. I shall have plenty of time, having retired from business. I'll try to get my reg'lar customers to take Johnny Nolan in my place. That boy hasn't any enterprise. He needs somebody to look out for him."

"You might give him your box and brush, too, Dick."

"No," said Dick; "I'll give him some new ones, but mine I want to keep, to remind me of the hard times I've had, when I was an ignorant boot-black, and never expected to be anything better."

"When, in short, you were 'Ragged Dick.' You must drop that name, and think of yourself now as—"

"Richard Hunter, Esq.," said our hero, smiling.

"A young gentleman on the way to fame and fortune," added Fosdick.

Here ends the story of Ragged Dick. As Fosdick said, he is Ragged Dick no longer. He has taken a step upward, and is determined to mount still higher. . . .

Printed and bound by CPI Group (UK) Ltd, Croydon, CR0 4YY

09/06/2025

14686100-0003